Goodyear Education Series

Theodore W. Hipple, Editor
UNIVERSITY OF FLORIDA

Will the real teacher please stand up?

Library of Congress Catalog Card Number: 75-179002

ISBN: 0-87620-963-0 (paper)
      0-87620-964-9 (cloth)

Y-9630-8 (paper)
Y-9649-8 (cloth)
Current printing (last digit):

10 9 8 7 6 5 4 3 2 1

Printed in the United States of America

Will the real teacher please stand up?

By Mary Greer
& Bonnie Rubinstein

A PRIMER IN HUMANISTIC EDUCATION

GOODYEAR PUBLISHING COMPANY, INC.
Pacific Palisades, California

This book is dedicated to all our real teachers and helpers, some of whom are: our students; our consultants Patsy Garlan and Theodore W. Hipple; Jim Levy, Jack Pritchard, Gene Schwartz, Ann Harris, and the production staff of Goodyear Publishing Company; John Isely—the designer of this book—and Doug Armstrong; Gordon Heasley, Sheila Fay, Ann Timmins, Sonia Blackman, Shelly Lemon, Viola Spolin, George and Judith Brown, Yankee Logan, Dick and Eva Korn, John Argue, Ed Bourg, Bernard Gunther, Joe Shaff, Don Hongisto, Tom Cottingim, Madeline Gleason, Elizabeth, Kathy, and Dave Johnson, Martin, Paul, and Gaby Rubinstein, Irene and Michael Paull, and Leo the Lion. A special note of appreciation to Ed Laureano, Pat Evans, Nancy Ong, Bob Traller, Nathan Rabin, the Sun and Farrallones Design—whose photography contributed so much to this book—and to Dr. H. Van Kerckhove of Hasselt, Belgium, for making available to us "Le prêtre marié" by René Magritte for the cover.

CONTENTS

Will the real teacher please stand up?

TO THE READER

FIRST   there were experiences, happy, sad, yes ones, no ones, maybe ones, discouraging, encouraging experiences.

THEN   there were talks about the experiences, happy, sad, yes talks, no talks, maybe talks, discouraging, encouraging talks.

AFTER   there were pages about the talks about the experiences, happy, sad, yes pages, no pages, maybe pages, discouraging, encouraging pages.

NOW   there is a book with pages about the talks about the experiences, happy, sad, yes book, no book, maybe book, discouraging, encouraging book. . . .

Mary Greer
Bonnie Rubinstein

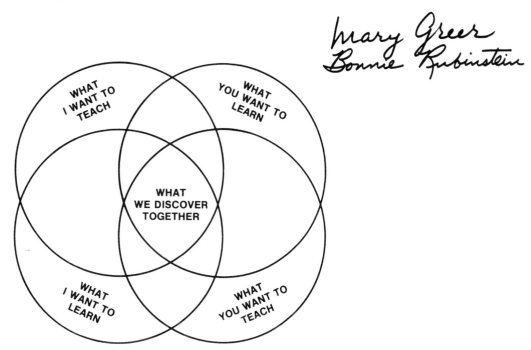

The man in the wilderness asked me,
   How many strawberries grew in the sea?
I answered him as I thought good,
   As many red herrings as grew in the wood.
And I would tell him if I could.
Nursery rhyme

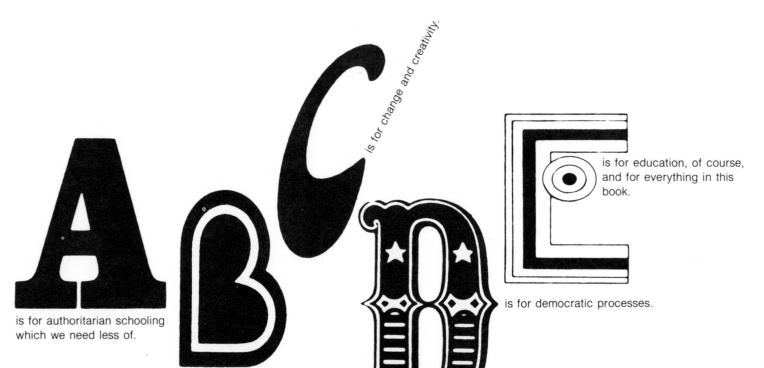

is for change and creativity.

is for education, of course, and for everything in this book.

is for authoritarian schooling which we need less of.

is for democratic processes.

is for beginning to try new ways and for becoming your real self.

H is for humanizing the classroom.

G is for groups and games we play.

f is for freedom, which goes with responsibility, and feeling, which goes with thinking.

I is for individuals who interact and sometimes innovate and ignite.

j is for joy, which belongs in school, and for juicyfruit gum.

K is for kites and kindergarten.

L is for learning, which is part of teaching, and love, which is part of it too.

is for mental health, which schools need more of, and for Mondays, which we need less of.

is for now and new and the name of the person sitting next to you.

is for the open classroom and for oh!, which we hope you will feel like saying.

is for passivity, which limits participation.

is for questions and quandaries.

is for the three of them and for risks you have to take.

U is for up which is where we hope you will stand.

W is for the writings in the book we hope will start you wondering a little.

V is for vibes good and bad.

T is for teaching, which is part of learning, and for teachers, of course.

S is for self and spontaneity and students and survival.

Y is for you and your own teacher, which you can become.

X is for Xanadu, a magic place, and for unknown quantities.

Z is for zap, which spelled backwards is paz, which in Spanish means peace.

INTRO-DUCTION:

THE WARM-UP

Is All Of You Here?

One for the money, two for the show, three to get ready—on your mark, get set—warming up. Children know about it: so do dancers, singers, musicians, and athletes. People in love understand it and so do people who drive cars and people called astronauts. Warming up—a getting ready process, a transition from before to will be, the end of something, the beginning of something else, a bridge.

Everyone needs warm-ups but not everybody knows that. At 8:30 A.M. in Room 3 Mrs. Pinkerton's second graders are showing and telling. Mrs. Reece's class in Room 6 is not. Everybody gets right down to business. Robert's in math but he can't concentrate. He's still in social studies, where he's not supposed to be. It was over at 10 A.M. Mondays are cold and so are 8 o'clocks. Fridays and 11:30 A.M. are pretty warm.

Maybe these words are warming up your page as they go along, and the pages will warm up the book. Try some of the games and exercises. See if they warm you up. See if you feel more like you. This whole book is a warm-up by the way.

As you read, you'll find questions, experiences, and things to do. Keep a journal of what you think and feel about what you do. Invent something of your own. Let yourself be seen.

Introduce yourself.
Throw an object, a
balloon, a ball, an
eraser to someone else
who introduces himself,
and so on.

Close your eyes and picture
the room you are in. Try to remember
how the persons look who are sitting
around you, on your left and right
sides, behind and in front of you.
Open your eyes. Look at the people.
Leave the room and come in again.
Look at the room from every angle;
use all of your senses. Move the
furniture around. Place yourself where
you feel comfortable.

Move about the room.
Look each person in the eye.
Shake left hands with
someone and then with
someone else. Shake right
hands. Don't talk. Take
turns shaking elbows, shoulders,
ear lobes, noses etc. around
the room.

Divide into groups of six or eight
with one person in each center.
If you are the center person, say
your name and place it, as you would
a physical object, into the hands
of each person in the circle. The
receiver repeats your name and then
returns the gift by saying his name
and placing it in your hand. After
everyone has been in the center, break
up the circles and move freely around
the room, giving and receiving names
from hand to hand.

There are other warm-ups in the games section pages 113 and 114.

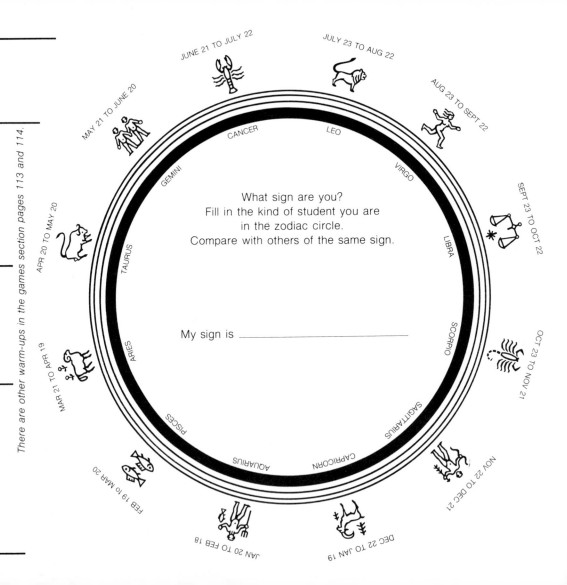

There is a game called education teachers and students play.

A teacher is a tenured revolutionary.

A Teacher Is ....

A Teacher is often lonely...

A teacher is a bore

What is a teacher?

Who are you?

What is a student?

A student is a rebel.

A student is curious.

A student is ...

A teacher is you.

A Student is a listener.

A teacher is a student.

A student is anxious.

A student is a teacher.

A student is lazy.

A TEACHER IS AFRAID.

A teacher is large.

A TEACHER IS HONEST

A teacher is a person

A student is smart.

A student is dumb

A student is a person.

A student is able to think for himself.

A student is a dreamer.

A TEACHER IS MEAN!

A TEACHER IS NOT WHAT YOU THINK HE IS.

A student is me.

A STUDENT IS A PERSON.

A student is a hippie

A teacher is a friend.

A teacher is often larger than his students which causes them to look up to him.

Egomania

I saw it in a book,
In a zoology book—
"Every individual is absolutely unique,
The first and last of its identical kind."

Unique! The first and last!
Never anybody else just like me!
Never!
Never!
I am the only one just like me,
I am a race by myself;
When I die the world will have lost me
Forever.

Spermatogonia, spermatocytes, spermatozoa,
Oogonia, oocytes, ova—
Then oosperm!
And the three hundred thousand billionth chance
Produced me!
Think of it! The three hundred thousand billionth possibility—

Think if it hadn't happened.

But it did—and never can again. Never.
Chromosomes, chromomeres, chromogen, enzymes,
Protoplasm, germ plasm, cytoplasm, somato-plasm,
Permutation, maturation, segregation, differentiation,
Synapsis, mitosis, ontogeny, phylogeny—
All the combinations and changes and chances
That made me
Can never again come together
Exactly the same.

I am a person of distinction.
I am I.
I am that I am.

John Barton

From "What Can Man Become?" by Arthur W. Combs

The kind of openness characteristic of the truly adequate, fully functioning personality the experts are describing for us comes about as a consequence of the individual's own feeling of security in himself. It is a product of his feeling that he is important, that he counts, that he is a part of the situation and the world in which he is moving. This feeling is created by the kind of atmosphere in which he lives and works. It is encouraged by atmospheres we are able to create in the classroom and the halls and laboratories that help young people to develop a feeling of trust in themselves.

What causes a person to feel outside, undermines and destroys his feeling of trust. Differences must be respected and encouraged, not merely tolerated. As Earl Kelley has told us, the goal of education must be the increasing uniqueness of people, not increasing likeness. It is the flowering of individuality we seek, not the production of automatons. This means differences of all kinds must be encouraged, appreciated, valued. Segregation is not only socially undesirable; it is demoralizing and diminishing as well. We need to remind ourselves there is segregation on a thousand other bases than segregation of white and Negro that equally as well get in our way. There is segregation, too, on the basis of age, social status, athletic prowess, dress, language, and religion to name but a few.

This kind of openness we seek in the free personality requires a trust in self and this means to me, we need to change the situation we sometimes find in our teaching where the impression is given the student that all the answers worth having lie "out there." I believe it is necessary for us to recognize that the only important answers are those which the individual has within himself, for these are the only ones that will ever show up in his behavior. . . .

There was a schoolroom

Remember a room in a school
where you wrote your name as a child.
Write your name holding the pencil
or pen in the "wrong" hand and
imagine that room. Draw a floor plan.
Put in the desks and chairs
and everything.
If you can't remember, pretend.
How does it feel to be that pupil again?
Tell somebody else.

There Were Parents

SON, ON THIS YOUR VERY FIRST DAY OF SCHOOL YOUR MOTHER AND I WANT TO REMIND YOU OF A FEW THINGS:

THAT THE BOILED EGGS YOU ATE THIS MORNING WERE COOKED BY **US**.

THAT THE BED YOU SLEPT IN LAST NIGHT WAS MADE BY **US**.

THAT THE CLOTHES YOU WEAR ON YOUR BACK WERE BOUGHT BY **US**.

THAT THE DOCTOR WHO SAVED YOU WHEN YOU HAD APPENDICITIS WAS CALLED BY **US**.

THAT HOWEVER MUCH YOU ARE TAUGHT IN LIFE THE **PRIMARY** LESSON IS THAT **YOU OWE US**.

IS THAT CLEAR, SON?

YES, FATHER.

THEN GO AND BE EDUCATED.

©1967 JULES FEIFFER

9-10

CHAPTER 1

ONCE UPON A TIME THERE WAS A STUDENT...

"The First Day of School"
by William Saroyan

He was a little boy named Jim, the first and only child of Dr. Louis Davy, 717 Mattei Building, and it was his first day at school. His father was French, a small heavy-set man of forty whose boyhood had been full of poverty and unhappiness and ambition. His mother was dead: she died when Jim was born, and the only woman he knew intimately was Amy, the Swedish housekeeper.

It was Amy who dressed him in his Sunday clothes, and took him to school. Jim liked Amy, but he didn't like her for taking him to school. He told her so. All the way to school he told her so.

I don't like you, he said. I don't like you any more.

I like *you*, the housekeeper said.

Then why are you taking me to school? he said.

He had taken walks with Amy before, once all the way to the Court House Park for the Sunday afternoon band concert, but this walk to school was different.

What for? he said.

Everybody must go to school, the housekeeper said.

Did you go to school? he said.

No, said Amy.

Then why do I have to go? he said.

You will like it, said the housekeeper.

He walked on with her in silence, holding her hand. I don't like you, he said. I don't like you any more.

I like you, said Amy.

1

Then why are you taking me to school? he said again.

Why?

The housekeeper knew how frightened a little boy could be about going to school.

You will like it, she said. I think you will sing songs and play games.

I don't want to, he said.

I will come and get you every afternoon, she said.

I don't like you, he told her again.

She felt very unhappy about the little boy going to school, but she knew that he would have to go.

The school building was very ugly to her and to the boy. She didn't like the way it made her feel, and going up the steps with him she wished he didn't have to go to school. The halls and rooms scared her, and him, and the smell of the place too. And he didn't like Mr. Barber, the principal.

Amy despised Mr. Barber.

What is the name of your son? Mr. Barber said.

This is Dr. Louis Davy's son, said Amy. His name is Jim. I am Dr. Davy's housekeeper.

James? said Mr. Barber.

Not James, said Amy, just Jim.

All right, said Mr. Barber. Any middle name?

No, said Amy. He is too small for a middle name. Just Jim Davy.

All right, said Mr. Barber. We'll try him out in the first grade. If he doesn't get along all right we'll try him out in kindergarten.

Dr. Davy said to start him in the first grade, said Amy. Not kindergarten.

All right, said Mr. Barber.

The housekeeper knew how frightened the little boy was, sitting on the chair, and she tried to let him know how much she loved him and how sorry she was about everything. She wanted to say something fine to him about everything, but she couldn't say anything, and she was very proud of the nice way he got down from the chair and stood beside Mr. Barber, waiting to go with him to a classroom.

On the way home she was so proud of him she began to cry.

Miss Binney, the teacher of the first grade, was an old lady who was all dried out. The room was full of little boys and girls. School smelled strange and sad. He sat at a desk and listened carefully.

He heard some of the names: *Charles, Ernest, Alvin, Norman, Betty, Hannah, Juliet, Viola, Polly.*

He listened carefully and heard Miss Binney say, Hannah Winter, what *are* you chewing? And he saw Hannah Winter blush. He liked Hannah Winter right from the beginning.

Gum, said Hannah.

Put it in the waste-basket, said Miss Binney.

He saw the little girl walk to the front of the class, take the gum from her mouth, and drop it into the waste-basket.

And he heard Miss Binney say, Ernest Gaskin, what *you* chewing?

Gum, said Ernest.

And he liked Ernest Gaskin too.

They met in the schoolyard, and Ernest taught him a few jokes.

Amy was in the hall when school ended. She was sullen and angry at everybody until she saw the little boy. She was amazed that he wasn't changed, that he wasn't hurt, or perhaps utterly unalive, murdered. The school and everything about it frightened her very much. She took his hand and walked out of the building with him, feeling angry and proud.

Jim said, What comes after twenty-nine?

Thirty, said Amy.

Your face is dirty, he said.

His father was very quiet at the supper table.

What comes after twenty-nine? the boy said.

Thirty, said his father.

Your face is dirty, he said.

In the morning he asked his father for a nickel.

What do you want a nickel for? his father said.

Gum, he said.

His father gave him a nickel and on the way to school he stopped at Mrs. Riley's store and bought a package of Spearmint.

Do you want a piece? he asked Amy.

Do you want to give me a piece? the housekeeper said.

Jim thought about it a moment, and then he said, Yes.

Do you like me? said the housekeeper.

I like you, said Jim. Do you like me?

Yes, said the housekeeper.

Do you like school?

Jim didn't know for sure, but he knew he liked the part about gum. And Hannah Winter. And Ernest Gaskin.

I don't know, he said.

Do you sing? asked the housekeeper.

No, we don't sing, he said.

Do you play games? she said.

Not in the school, he said. In the yard we do.

He liked the part about gum very much. Miss Binney said, Jim Davy, what are you *chewing*?

Ha ha ha, he thought.

Gum, he said.

He walked to the waste-paper basket and back to his seat, and Hannah Winter saw him, and Ernest Gaskin too. That was the best part of school.

It began to grow too.

Ernest Gaskin, he shouted in the school-yard, *what* are you *chewing*?

Raw elephant meat, said Ernest Gaskin. Jim Davy, what are *you* chewing?

Jim tried to think of something very funny to be chewing, but he couldn't.

Gum, he said, and Ernest Gaskin laughed louder than Jim laughed when Ernest Gaskin said raw elephant meat.

It was funny no matter what you said.

Going back to the classroom Jim saw Hannah Winter in the hall.

Hannah Winter, he said, *what in the world* are you *chewing*?

The little girl was startled. She wanted to say something nice that would honestly show how nice she felt about having Jim say her name and ask her the funny question, making fun of school, but she couldn't think of anything that nice to say because they were almost in the room and there wasn't time enough.

Tutti-frutti, she said with desperate haste.

It seemed to Jim he had never before heard such a glorious word, and he kept repeating the word to himself all day.

Tutti-frutti, he said to Amy on the way home.

Amy Larson, he said, *what, are, you, chewing*?

He told his father all about it at the supper table.

He said, Once there was a hill. On the hill there was a mill. Under the mill there was a walk. Under the walk there was a key. What is it?

I don't know, his father said. What is it?

Milwaukee, said the boy.

The housekeeper was delighted.

Mill. Walk. Key, Jim said.

Tutti-frutti.

What's that? said his father.

Gum, he said. The kind Hannah Winter chews.

Who's Hannah Winter? said his father.

She's in my room, he said.

Oh, said his father.

After supper he sat on the floor with the small red and blue and yellow top that hummed while it spinned. It was all right,

he guessed. It was still very sad, but the gum part of it was very funny and the Hannah Winter part very nice. Raw elephant meat, he thought with great inward delight.

Raw elephant meat, he said aloud to his father who was reading the evening paper. His father folded the paper and sat on the floor beside him. The housekeeper saw them together on the floor and for some reason tears came to her eyes.

3

ABCDEFGHIJKLMNO
PQRSTUVYZŒW
abcdefghijklmno
pqrstuvyz æ œw
.,;.!? .´`^¨
0.1.2.3.4.5.6.7.8.9

ANE

Some of us remember first days. Some of us forget them. Some first days are happy. Some first days are sad. Some are both. Some of the lessons we learned teachers didn't teach us. What did Jim Davy learn? Remember your first day. What did you learn? Act out a first day as it really was. Act out a first day as you'd like it to be.

"The first day of school that I can remember was the first day of the sixth grade. It was a Monday, and I'm sure I was happy because I always got new clothes when school started. I ran all the way to school and tried not to scuff up my new brown oxfords. I wanted to show off my new outfit and find out what everybody had done for the summer. I remember whistling. The Lakeside school had a certain smell. I can't describe it, but I'd know it anywhere. The floors were shiny and polished, because no one had run across them all summer long. The hallways were long and narrow and bare of decorations. I hurried upstairs where the upper grade classes were, and I felt very big, because I was starting sixth grade. But what a shock I had when I opened the door and walked into the classroom! There standing in front of the little rows of desks was a big, tall, hairy man! I had heard all kinds of strange things about men teachers and this was the first one I had ever had. I think I spent the rest of the day in a kind of a trance."

* * *

"Well, when I first came to this school, I was scared. I was left out. I didn't know anybody. To tell you the truth I was scared. I felt nervous. I was jumpy. When I got to know the school a little better, it was all right. I met a few friends and I did not feel left out. I felt like one of the group. I felt good and happy. I felt fine. Now I feel like a man."

* * *

"I honestly can't pull one first day from my memories. There were so many firsts, so many anxieties, so much wanting to succeed, to live up to expectations, mine and mother's, so many sad first days, of wanting to please, of not understanding, of cheating, of being made to sit in the dunce's chair—days of walking out of school and wandering all day."

* * *

"There's a big difference in "first days" when your friends are with you. It's exciting, and you are already "in" before you start. My family always moved a lot. When you're alone, first days are hard."

* * *

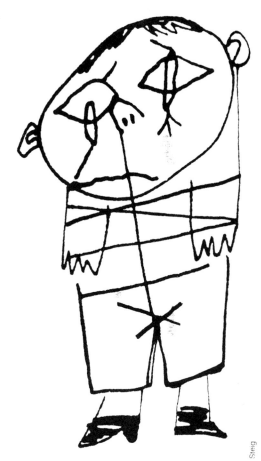

DON'T

From *Agony in the Kindergarten*

"To Die among Strangers"
by Irene Paull

"Dummy!" cried Uncle Lev, his face a grimace of anguish. "You haven't brought in a good load a' cattle in a month! What are you waiting for, the Messiah?"

Papa sat hunched over, silent, blinking his one blue and one brown eye, twisting his powerful head in that perpetual nervous twitch, like a patient horse warding off flies. The dimple in his right cheek where a bull had gored him deepened and looked like a hole in his leathery, sunburnt face.

"Bad market," he muttered, blinking and twisting his head.

"Bad market!" cried Uncle Lev, looking as if he were about to cry. "So I suppose you told Gus Lindquist, 'Hold your cattle, Gus. Don't sell. Hold 'em for a better market.'"

Papa was silent and Uncle Dave hurled him a glance of withering scorn.

"He had lotta trouble," said Papa.

"Lotta trouble!" cried Uncle Lev, springing up and pacing the floor. "You hear that? Lotta trouble, he says. And what about us? All we got is trouble. We'll go bankrupt with a dummy like you buying our cattle. Look, I'm asking you, Moe, what in hell is business? Business is buy cheap and sell high. Get that? Dog eat dog. That's business. It's looking out for number one. You're looking out for Gus, but who in hell is looking out for you?"

"Is that how Pa taught you to buy cattle, you goddam dummy?" growled Uncle Dave.

"Gus was a friend a' Pa's. He liked Pa," said Papa, almost under his breath.

"Don't go tellin' me Pa was a goddam fool like you!" shouted Uncle Dave. "You keep Pa out of it!"

"Shut up, Dave!" snapped Uncle Lev, and then to Papa, wearily, as if he were talking to a child, "Times have changed, Moe. You can't get that in your head but they're changed. When Pa first started buyin' cattle in Dakota, wild horses were still roaming over Montana. It's a tougher world now, Moe. That's what I'm trying to tell you. You can't afford to give the other guy a break or he'll break you. It's him or you. I try to knock this into your head but it's like talkin' sense to a horse."

Papa sensed that Uncle Lev had spent himself and it was safe to change the subject.

"So Debbie's startin' school tomorra, eh? Kinniegarten."

All eyes turned suddenly on me.

I had been watching this familiar scene in mute suffering. The fact that I did not understand it only deepened my depression as I contemplated tomorrow, the first day of school.

"For Chrissake!" cried Uncle Lev, his black eyes darting about like squirrels in his face. "Look at that kid, will you? Hey, everybody! Get a load a' that kid! Who gave her the spittoon haircut?"

"Her Ma must a' put a chamber pot on her head an' cut around it," growled Uncle Dave in dour amusement. "Looks like she just come off the boat."

"Stand up and turn around!" cried Uncle Lev, his laughing eyes almost jumping out of his face.

I did not move. A tear was starting down my cheek.

His quickly changing face became contrite.

"Aw, I didn't mean that, kid. Come on, Debbie, that haircut ain't bad at all, is it Dave, is it bad?" I saw him give Uncle Dave a threatening wink and Uncle Dave conceded grudgingly, "Naw, ain't bad."

"Looks different," clucked Uncle Lev. "Everybody should look a little different. No point everybody looking just like everybody else, eh, Dave? Here, have a stick of gum. Stop worrying. School ain't bad. I'm going to take you there myself tomorrow, take you right to the door, not a thing to worry about."

Papa tried to cheer me up.

"You know, kid, I used to go to that school myself . . . same school . . . bottom of the hill. Had me a little goat called Hymie. Used to follow me to school. Every day. Right through the door. Teacher'd say, 'Get that goat out'a here!' He used to wait for me out in the school yard but one day he got tired waitin' so you know what he done? He went an' butted in the glass door."

"Goat learned more than your Pa did," grimaced Uncle Lev good-naturedly, "only they both quit in the third grade."

Papa fell silent. I could almost hear the twitching of his eyes and the toss and twisting of his face.

Uncle Lev, I thought, torn by my love for him and my compassion for Papa, why do you call my father a dummy when he knows all he needs to know?

For all my five years I had lived "Awf en barg" (on the hill) of this midwestern town, in a section dubbed "Little Jerusalem." It had been transplanted here from the old country and combined some of the spirit of the American frontier with the flavor and custom of a Ukrainian ghetto. We had two barns full of cattle, two horses, and the yard was always alive with matronly hens, arrogant roosters and a brood of little chickens peeping and scratching after them. Sometimes I followed the cows to the pastures high above the town and sat while they grazed, looking out upon Lake Superior, stretching for endless miles to Canada. At other times I waited for the sound of cowbells and Uncle Dave in the summer twilight walking home the cows. There was the synagogue and the familiar chanting and the bearded men going in and out. There was Shlaema's store where you could buy salt herring in barrels, kasha, salt crackers and penny candy. There was Lazar, the shoemaker, who also fixed harnesses for the horses. Everything was loving and safe and familiar, and now they were sending me to school. It was only four blocks from my ghetto . . . at the bottom of the hill, but it was as foreign to me as if it had been located a hundred miles away.

I wanted to say to Papa, don't send me to school. You know all there is to know. You can teach me. I don't need to know any more. Just the clap clap of the horse's hooves on the sunny country road above the town as we ride together in the black and red enameled buggy. The click of crickets in the fields of buttercup and clover and the tiny blue flowers that always grow on the hills. Below us the inland sea with the long boats trailing smoke. And your face not twitching so much . . . peaceful somehow, brown and rocky, part of the earth and hills. You are so big and powerfully strong, yet you hold the reins gently in your sunburned hands. I say, "Papa, let's stop awhile and let the horse rest," and you say, "Okay, kid, let 'im rest." I ask you questions like, "Papa, why do they call pigs 'pigs'?" And you answer, "Because they're piggish, that's why. You ask foolish questions." And then the buggy turning into Chris Westlund's farm, the smell of manure, the lowing of cattle, the chunking sound of pigs feet and the cluck of chickens. And Chris coming out of the barn wiping the milk off his hairy red arms. And Papa and Chris slapping each other on the back. "Well, how are ya, you ole coot, eh? Well, what do'ya know, you old son of a gun! Ain't seen ya in a dog's age. How's the world treatin' ya, eh? Well, ain't that fine. For Chrissake, ain't that fine!"

And gathering violets and wild iris in the swamps to the steady hum of Papa's and Chris Westlund's voices . . . Why did I have to go to school? What more did I need to know?

I was crying bitterly now but Papa had no comfort to offer. He sat, blinking at me, with his one brown eye and one blue.

Baba, my grandmother, tried to come to my rescue.

"Why does she have to go so soon?" she asked. "Let her wait another year. She's only a baby. What is the big rush to send her there among the Gentiles?"

I looked hopefully at my grandmother but intercepted the flash of my mother's eyes. On this issue her mother-in-law was not going to have her way.

"She will go to school when all the others go," said Mama. "I would have given my right arm for the right to go to school. Without education a person can die of thirst on a sea of fresh water." And from Papa's silence and Mama's look I knew that school was inexorable. Nothing in the world could intervene for you. It was like death. When Grandpa died they put him in a box and carried him away and nobody, nothing could ever bring him back. Nobody, nothing could keep me out of school. Tomorrow would come and I would have to go.

And now it was tomorrow. Uncle Lev held me tightly by the hand as I plodded with him down the hills, my heart as heavy as my feet clad in clodhoppers from another era.

"Look, kid, you're gonna get an education. You should be happy. You're even going to college some day. That's what I wanted to do. Get the hell out'a this town. Be an engineer or something. Any goddam thing but cattle. Education is worth more than all the goddam cattle in the St. Paul Stockyards and here you're cryin'." He held my hand so tight I winced.

There it was. The great brick building where I would begin my sentence. There was the school. Named after some man Uncle Lev admired called Benjamin Franklin.

Uncle Lev rushed me quickly up the steps and into the hall and left me there. Then he ran. I tried to run after him but he turned and waved me back.

I stood alone in the big strangely smelling hallway and looked around. There were children everywhere. They were chattering to each other. The mothers were kissing the youngest ones goodbye. But they looked different from me. The girls had pretty curls, most of them blonde. And some had braids tied with bright ribbons. They wore short, stiffly starched dresses above their knees, half socks and patent leather slippers. I looked down at my heavy shoes and the thick black cotton stockings. My dress was of a heavy red and black plain cotton reaching almost to my ankles. And my lank dark hair was bristling about my head in a spittoon haircut! I was different. It made you feel as if you were in the middle of the lake, drowning,

and there was nobody to help because nobody even knew that you were there.

At this point a tall gaunt lady with white hair and thick glasses that made her eyes look like an owl's took me by the wrist and drew me into a big room. There were lots of little red chairs around low red tables. She sat down at the piano and played some kind of marching tune, while a younger lady marched us around the tables until everyone of us had a place. We stood there until the old lady, fixing us with her great owl's eyes, gave us our first orientation.

"Now, if any of you want to go to the toilet," she said, "raise your hand. If you have to go number one, raise one finger. If you have to go number two, raise two fingers. Does everybody understand?"

The children answered, "Yes, teacher." My lips moved, but I knew I wasn't uttering a sound.

"Now, sometimes you only think you have to go , but if you wait long enough you find out you really don't have to go that bad. In fact, if you try hard enough, you can hold it until class is dismissed. I don't like my children jumping up every minute and running in and out. If you have to raise your hand, be pretty sure you really need to go. Understand?"

Again the class replied, "Yes, teacher," and again no word issued out of me.

The young teacher passed out paper and crayons and scissors. I touched them ginger-

ly. I had never even seen colored crayons before. I watched the other children scribbling with them on the paper, but I did not dare touch them. They were not mine. I watched the children cutting little figures out of colored paper. Everybody seemed to know exactly what to do as if they had done it many times before, but I didn't know. I played with chickens and followed the cows to pasture. I played with dolls made out of clothespins. I played hopscotch in front of the synagogue, but I didn't know how to do what all these children seemed to know how to do.

The children were giggling and talking to each other, but nobody talked to me. I sat frozen in the little red chair, gripped in a horrible anxiety. What if I had to go? What if I had to raise my hand?

I pictured myself raising my hand, the eyes of the old teacher fastened on me. I once saw an owl staring at a mouse just before it spread its wings and pounced on it. "If you really want to, you can hold it until class is dismissed," she would say, and everybody would turn around and look at me and giggle. I pictured them giggling to each other, "Spittoon haircut! Her mother must have put a chamber pot on her head and cut around it!" And with everybody tittering behind my back, I pictured myself walking out of the big room and down the hall and then not even knowing where to go!

And as I sat anxiously contemplating this eventuality, I was paralyzed by a slowly dawning realization. . . . I had to go!

What could I do now? I tried to raise my hand but I couldn't lift it. It was like trying to scream in a dream. If I côuld only sit still like this until class was over everything would by okay . . . maybe. I would just sit tight like this and hold on. All around me as if from some great distance were the sounds of children chattering, cutting, scribbling . . . they sounded very far away like the voices of the doctor and nurse when they put a chloroform mask on my face the time I had my tonsils out.

And suddenly the voice of the old teacher struck me like a strap.

"Everybody stand!"

We all stood.

"Push your chair in!"

We pushed our chairs in.

"Oh, God, please help me raise my hand!" something in me was praying, but I couldn't raise it. And how could I hang on now, now that I was standing up. I shifted from one foot to the other. "Hang on! Hang on!" I was alone, all alone out on the vast lake, drowning and there was no one to save me. They had sent me out of Little Jerusalem alone . . . they all loved me but they had sent me out to die of torment and humiliation . . . to die among strangers . . . if only the teacher wouldn't make us move. . . .

But she was teaching us some strange jibberish.

"I pledge allegiance to the flag. . . ."

Now it was too late to raise my hand.

They wouldn't even see my hand with everybody's hand stuck out like that. . . . I couldn't stand it any more . . . no . . . I couldn't hold on. I was going to go down . . . right into the middle of the lake . . . I was sinking. . . .

The old teacher was back at the piano again and she was thundering, "Forward, march!"

My face was feverish and my hands clammy. I moved out of the little puddle by my chair. It was all over. The crime was done and now I must face the punishment, the execution.

The younger teacher ordered us to sit cross-legged in a circle around her, while she prepared to tell us a story.

Perhaps the morning would soon be over. Perhaps I would get away before I was discovered. If only the time would go fast, and nobody would see the little puddle on the floor!

And then it happened!

The owl pounced! With a fierce, stern look the old teacher appeared, whispered something in the young teacher's ear and then took over.

"Children!" she said, fastening us with her huge bird's eyes, "I have something very serious and unpleasant to tell you. You know when you first came to school this morning, I told you about raising your hand if you have to go and one finger for number one? Do you remember?"

Again the chorus, "Yes, teacher." Again my tongue felt cleft to my mouth.

"Did any of you have any questions about it?"

"No, teacher."

"Well, I want you to know that one person in this class did not pay any attention to my instructions. That person piddled on the floor. Now I want that person to get up and come here to the front of the room. I want to know who that person was."

The children exchanged unhappy glances. I did not move a muscle of my face.

"Will that person come up here or will I have to find out for myself?" demanded the teacher.

Nobody moved.

"All right then," she snapped. It took me awhile to realize the horror of what was happening. She was moving from one child to another feeling in each one's underpants. I watched her, fascinated, as she moved ever closer, as if I were watching preparations for my own hanging. And suddenly she was upon me, her claws about to clutch me, her eyes so huge they were ready to devour me.

"No!" I screamed.

Before she could lay her hands on me, I pushed her away with all my strength and tore through the open door. Up the hills I ran . . . away from these terrible strangers . . . back to the warmth of my family, my own people.

"Baba!" I screamed, "Mama!" It was Baba, my grandmother who saw me first.

She clutched me in her arms. Her black

eyes that always smoldered like live coals deep in their sockets caught fire and three thousand years of anger and hatred were blazing in them. "Oh," she cried, "a black year on them! What have they done to my child! Oh, may they roast in hell, the Gentiles and their schools and their teachers and all their works! May their schools burn down! May the cholera seize them! May the earth open and swallow them up and may they suffer a thousand years for all the suffering they have brought upon us!" She rocked me back and forth on her breast. To the music of Baba's curses my hysteria abated, but I saw Mama looking down at me. Her eyes were sorrowful, but unrelenting. From what one must do there is no escape. Tomorrow I would have to go back to school. And nobody could help me. Even Baba could not protect me from this fearful thing that every child must do. Nobody could know my suffering and nobody could share it with me. I was all alone in the world and tomorrow I would have to go . . . far from my ghetto . . . to die among strangers . . . but for this moment, for this precious moment at least, I was safe.

████████████████████████

Could this same story happen today? What was Debbie learning? What is the difference between being unique and being "different"? Are there ways to change one into the other? Have you ever felt unique or different? Why did you feel one way rather than the other?

Write a secret about yourself on a piece of paper. Place it in a box or a hat. Others add their secrets. Each in turn draws a secret, reads it aloud, and says it as if it were his own secret. Speak in the first person.

Finish these sentences. Share your answers with somebody or put the sentences in a hat, draw them out, and take turns answering aloud.

I particularly like people who _____

I'm regarded by most people as _____

Strangers make me feel _____

If you ask me _____

If only _____

I believe that _____

In a new situation I usually _____

When I'm 30, I think I'll be _____

I feel really happy when _____

I feel sad when _____

What makes me furious is . . . .
When I'm in trouble, I turn to . . . .
What I like best about school is . . . .
What makes me anxious is . . . .
If there were no grades, I'd . . . .
If I think a teacher doesn't like me, I . . . .
When there's no right answer, I feel . . . .
What embarrasses me the most is . . . .
I learn best when . . . .

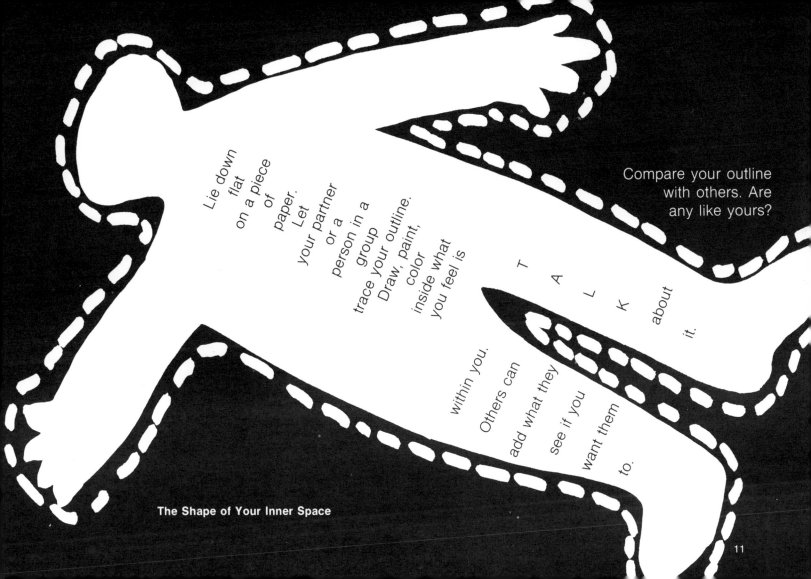

Compare your outline with others. Are any like yours?

Lie down flat on a piece of paper. Let your partner or a person in a group trace your outline. Draw, paint, color inside what you feel is

within you. Others can add what they see if you want them to.

T A L K about it.

The Shape of Your Inner Space

Upon Hearing that My Son Sits All Day under the Table at Nursery School

But I wanted you to be on top,
Skipping!
A harum, scarum, freckled
Ego.
Laughing out of treehouses,
Swinging on the confidence
Of buddies, peanut butter, and skis on square
shoulders.
Instead you sit in shadows.
Tracing the underside with a finger of your
mind.
And to the world of icy droplets, greenish
molds.
And muffled sounds of phantom feet,
Where the familiar wear hoods,
And strangers don terror masks;
To the vantage point of weepers and poets,
Your mother's world,
Welcome!

Joyce A. Richardson

What kind of son did this mother want? What kind of boy is he? Can she accept him?

. . . You see, really and truly, apart from the things anyone can pick up (the dressing and the proper way of speaking, and so on), the difference between a lady and a flower girl is not how she behaves, but how she's treated. I shall always be a flower girl to Professor Higgins, because he always treats me as a flower girl, and always will; but I know I can be a lady to you, because you always treat me as a lady, and always will.

From G. B. Shaw, *Pygmalion*

✦✦✦✦✦✦✦✦✦✦✦✦✦✦✦✦✦✦✦✦✦✦✦✦✦✦✦✦✦✦✦

From *Pygmalion in the Classroom* by Robert Rosenthal and Lenore Jacobson

For those children whose educability is in doubt there is a label. They are the educationally, or culturally, or socioeconomically, deprived children and, as things stand now, they appear not to be able to learn as do those who are more advantaged. The advantaged and the disadvantaged differ in parental income, in parental values, in scores on various tests of achievement and ability, and often in skin color and other phenotypic expressions of genetic heritage. Quite inseparable from these differences between the advantaged and the disadvantaged are the differences in their teachers' expectations for what they can achieve in school. . . .

Nothing was done directly for the disadvantaged child at Oak School. There was no crash program to improve his reading ability, no special lesson plan, no extra time for tutoring, no trips to museums or art galleries. There was only the belief that the children bore watching, that they had intellectual competencies that would in due course be revealed. . . .

As teacher-training institutions begin to teach the possibility that teachers' expectations of their pupils' performance may serve as self-fulfilling prophecies, there may be a new expectancy created. The new expectancy may be that children can learn more than had been believed possible.

How does what we expect affect how we see others? How we treat others? How they learn? What was the "self-fulfilling prophecy" for the children at Oak School?

Johnny

Johnny used to find content
In standing always rather bent,
Like an inverted J.
His angry relatives would say,
"Stand up! Don't slouch! You've got a spine!
Stand like a lamppost, not a vine!"
One day they heard an awful crack—
He'd stood up straight—it broke his back.

From Hugh Mearns, *Creative Power*

From *Woman as Nigger*
by Naomi Weisstein

. . . Our culture and our psychology characterize women as inconsistent, emotionally unstable, lacking in a strong superego, weaker, nurturant rather than productive, intuitive rather than intelligent, and if she knows her place (the home), she is really a quite lovable, loving creature, happy and childlike. In a review of the intellectual differences between little boys and little girls, Eleanor Maccoby has shown that no difference exists until high school, or, if there is a difference, girls are slightly ahead of boys. In high school, girls begin to do worse on a few intellectual tasks, and beyond high school the productivity and accomplishment of women drops off even more rapidly. . . .

In light of the social expectations about women, it is not surprising that women end up where society expects them to; the surprise is that little girls don't get the message that they are supposed to be stupid until they get into high school. It is no use to talk about women being different-but-equal; all the sex-difference tests I can think of have a "good" outcome and a "bad" outcome. Women usually end up with the bad outcome.

Except for their genitals, I don't know what immutable differences exist between men and women. Perhaps there are some other unchangeable differences; probably there are a number of irrelevant differences. But it is clear that until social expectation for men and women are equal, until we provide equal respect for both sexes, answers to this question will simply reflect our prejudices.

The teenage label has . . . assumed the character of a downright prejudicial stereotype. By this I mean that we deprive people of their personalities and individuality, of their roles as "persons" in our lives, and make them into something that just happens to remind us of the undesirable imputed characteristics of a group we really don't like. As in the case with all prejudicial stereotypes, the teenage label also carries with it the implication that the teenager is guilty until proven innocent. The mere fact that we have to reassure ourselves that we are still capable of making exceptions because "some of our best friends are teenagers" only proves how deeply we distrust the group as such.

From Fritz Redl, *When We Deal with Children*

Which one of you does not feel deprived in one way or another?

Were you ever treated as a category, not as a person? Because you were a girl or a boy, black or white, poor or rich, young or old? Because _____

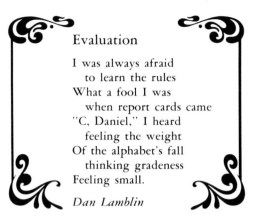

Evaluation

I was always afraid
    to learn the rules
What a fool I was
    when report cards came
"C, Daniel," I heard
    feeling the weight
Of the alphabet's fall
    thinking gradeness
Feeling small.

Dan Lamblin

How can evaluation make one feel "big" rather than "small"? What connections are there between expectations and evaluations?

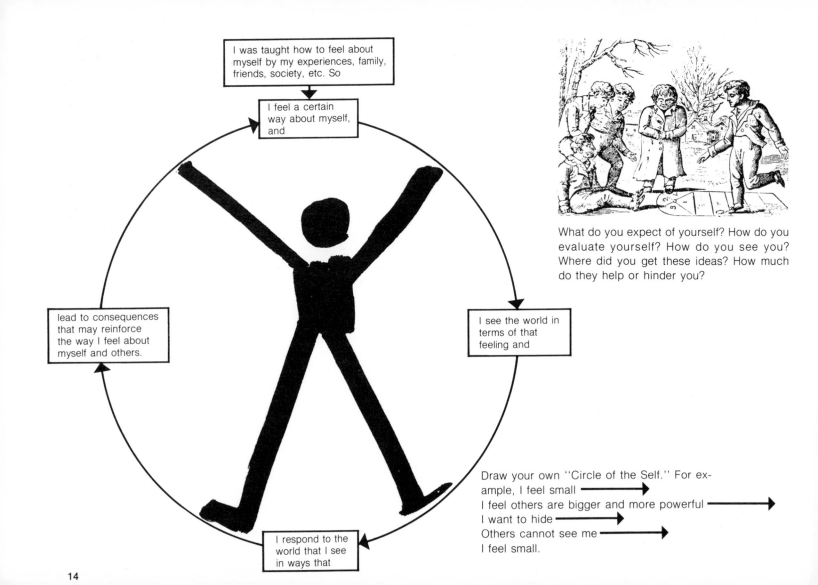

I was taught how to feel about myself by my experiences, family, friends, society, etc. So

I feel a certain way about myself, and

lead to consequences that may reinforce the way I feel about myself and others.

I see the world in terms of that feeling and

I respond to the world that I see in ways that

What do you expect of yourself? How do you evaluate yourself? How do you see you? Where did you get these ideas? How much do they help or hinder you?

Draw your own "Circle of the Self." For example, I feel small ⟶
I feel others are bigger and more powerful ⟶
I want to hide ⟶
Others cannot see me ⟶
I feel small.

14

From *An Experiment in Education*
by Sybil Marshall

We were all a little surprised, at the end of that term, after we had finished our examination in eight subjects for the Oxford School Certificate, to be told that we were to have a school examination in art. Once more I was told to "bring something to draw *or paint.*" The magic lay in the last two words.

I had no paints worthy of the name, for until that time I had never needed them except for map-making: but my brother had. He had always had the urge to draw, and spent a good deal of his time executing caricatures of our neighbors on the walls of the barn when he should have been dressing corn, and on the newly papered walls of his bedroom by the light of his candle in the early hours of the morning when he should have been asleep. His twenty-first birthday was several years behind him, and a family of neighbors had marked the occasion by giving him a box of good paints. They were a greatly valued treasure, and I knew he would not lend them, but that did not prevent me from borrowing them. Then I stole one of my mother's treasures, too—a perfect half-open Madame Butterfly rose-bud.

Into the painting of that rose-bud went the same zest that years before had carried the cats towards Yarmouth; but it was intensified now by a conscious urge to create, and a desire to crystallize the folk-culture, of which I had always been vaguely aware, into some positive existence. What I produced was, in fact, no more than a reasonably good pictorial resemblance of a rose, and I doubt if it had any quality about it that I should now characterize as art; be that as it may, when the results were read out the next morning, my name headed the list. Later that morning the headmaster came to my desk with my painting in his hand. He was a little surprised at my sudden progression, as in a country dance, from the very bottom of the set to the very top. I could not then put into words, as I now have done, the reason for my sudden "success" as an "artist."

"It's a funny thing," he said to me, "but I have always thought you ought to be able to do art. Why have you not produced this sort of thing before?"

There was only one answer, the same answer which so many, many children could still give to their teachers even in these art-conscious days. At the risk of being considered impertinent, I gave it.

"No one ever asked me to," I said.

Have you ever felt invisible or that you just didn't matter? What do you do well? Write, tape record, draw, make a collage, or express in some other way your expectations of school and how it really was. Why is it important to assess your own schooling now?

Sit in a chair in the center of a circle. Each chair represents an important person in your life, and as you sit in each chair, play the part of that person. Talk to these persons about what you are, and what they want of you, and what you want for yourself. If others are warmed-up to the parts, have them play the roles of the important persons.

Focus on a conflict. Use three chairs. Let the adult in you talk to the child in you and the parent in you. Parents tell you what you should do, and children want to do what they want to do. What do your voices say?

Pick out someone you don't know very well. Look at him carefully. Tell him everything you think he is, what he does, and why. Tell his story in your terms. How much of you is him? How much of him is you?

Think of another important person. Does he see the real you? Tell him what you resent and what you appreciate about him. Use the present tense.

Recall one of your teachers. Imagine your parents talking to this teacher at a PTA meeting. Play all the parts.

What are these students saying? Write your own captions. What do *you* expect of them?

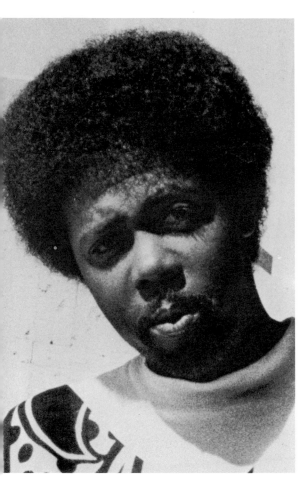

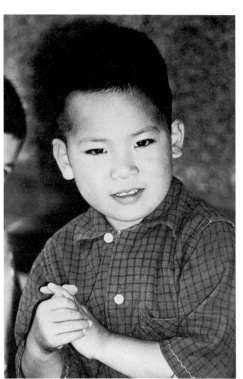

_____

_____
_____

_____

17

There Was the Game of School

We are all experts at the game of school. You'll need markers, dice or a spin wheel, and drawcards. Good luck!

Get a drink of water. Move two spaces.

Perfect attendance. Move five spaces.

Sharpen your pencil. Go ahead one space.

Teacher's pet Advance three spaces

Stomachache. Go to the nurse's office.

Late for school. Lose a turn

Water the plants. Go Ahead two spaces

Be quiet for one turn.

Go to the principal's office.

Feed the fish. Go ahead one space.

Gold star. Take another card.

A smile from the teacher. Take another turn.

Go to the auditorium.

Lead Pledge of Allegiance. Advance one space.

Busywork assignment. Stay where you are.

Hall pass to go to the bathroom.

Suspended for fighting. Lose two turns.

Suspended for smoking. Lose two turns.

Take a field trip. Move three spaces.

Go to the library.

Fold your hands for one turn.

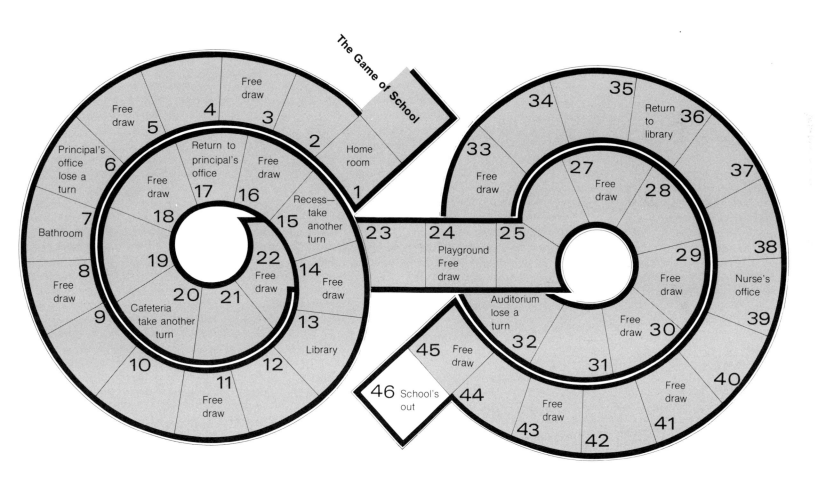

The Game of School

Free draw — 3
4
Free draw — 5
Principal's office lose a turn — 6
Bathroom — 7
Free draw — 8
9
10
11 Free draw
12
13 Library
14 Free draw
Free draw — 22
21
20
19
18 Free draw
17 Return to principal's office
16
Free draw — 15
Recess— take another turn
2
1
Home room
Cafeteria take another turn

23
24 Playground Free draw
25
Auditorium lose a turn
45 Free draw
46 School's out
44

34
35
Return to library — 36
33
27
37
Free draw — 28
38 Nurse's office
29
Free draw — 30
39
40
41 Free draw
42
43 Free draw
32
31
Free draw

21

○○○○○○○○○○○○○○○○○○○○○○○○○○○○○

What do you think of the game of school? Does it fit your own experience? What does it leave out? What doesn't belong? Is the winner still the student who gets out first? Do the rules have to be changed or is the game OK? Make up your own draw cards for the way school could be. What changes would you make on the board? Or don't you want to play at all? Why?

○○○○○○○○○○○○○○○○○○○○○○○○○○○○○

They Say to the Child

They say to the child'
"Do everything well,
Outward precision
Is the sign of inward strength;
Perfect yourself, excel.

"Add to the length
And breadth
Of all you are
The total perfection
Of a star."
The longest day one lives
Is that on which he tries
To grasp, with his imperfect being,
What must, if it be anything,
Be part of Paradise.

What world is this
Those ninnies bid him find,
That never was
Or can be
Fair game for the mind.

After going astray,
And secretly burning
At so many failures,
He takes a new way,
And in his turning
Finds nothing whole,
But everything broken or split;
Nothing perfect there,
Only the hope of it.

Madeline Gleason

"University Days" by James Thurber

I passed all the other courses that I took at my University, but I could never pass botany. This was because all botany students had to spend several hours a week in a laboratory looking through a microscope at plant cells, and I could never see through a microscope. I never once saw a cell through a microscope. This used to enrage my instructor. He would wander around the laboratory pleased with the progress all the students were making in drawing the involved and, so I am told, interesting structure of flower cells, Until he came to me. I would just be standing there. "I can't see anything," I would say. He would begin patiently enough, explaining how anybody can see through a microscope, but he would always end up in a fury, claiming that I could *too* see through a miscroscope but just pretended that I couldn't. "It takes away from the beauty of flowers anyway," I used to tell him. "We are not concerned with beauty in this course," he would say. "We are concerned solely with what I call the *mechanics* of flars." "Well," I'd say, "I can't see anything." "Try it just once again," he'd say, and I would put my eye to the microscope and see nothing at all, except now and again a nebulous milky substance—a phenomenon of maladjustment. We were supposed to see a vivid, restless clockwork of sharply defined plant cells. "I see what looks like a lot of milk," I would tell him. This, he claimed, was the result of my not having adjusted the microscope properly, so he would readjust it for me, or rather, for himself. And I would look again and see milk.

I finally took a deferred pass, as they called it, and waited a year and tried again. (You had to pass one of the biological sciences or you couldn't graduate.) The professor had come back from vacation brown as a berry, bright-eyed, and eager to explain cell structure again to his classes. "Well," he said to me, cheerily, when we met in the first laboratory hour of the semester, "we're going to see cells this time, aren't we?" "Yes, sir,"

I said. Students to right of me and to left of me and in front of me were seeing cells; what's more, they were quietly drawing pictures of them in their notebooks. Of course, I didn't see anything.

"We'll try it," the professor said to me, grimly, "with every adjustment of the microscope known to man. As God is my witness, I'll arrange this glass so that you see cells through it or I'll give up teaching. In twenty-two years of botany, I—" He cut off abruptly for he was beginning to quiver all over, like Lionel Barrymore, and he genuinely wished to hold onto his temper; his scenes with me had taken a great deal out of him.

So we tried it with every adjustment of the microscope known to man. With only one of them did I see anything but blackness or the familiar lacteal opacity, and that time I saw, to my pleasure and amazement, a variegated constellation of flecks, specks, and dots. These I hastily drew. The instructor, noting my activity, came back from an adjoining desk, a smile on his lips and his eyebrows high in hope. He looked at my cell drawing. "What's that?" he demanded, with a hint of a squeal in his voice. "That's what I saw," I said. "You didn't' you didn't, you *did*n't!" he screamed, losing control of his temper instantly, and he bent over and squinted into the microscope. His head snapped up. "That's your eye!" he shouted. "You've fixed the lens so that it reflects! You've drawn your eye!"

Another course that I didn't like, but somehow managed to pass, was economics.

I went to that class straight from the botany class, which didn't help me any in understanding either subject. I used to get them mixed up. But not as mixed up as another student in my economics class who came there direct from a physics laboratory. He was a tackle on the football team, named Bolenciecwcz. At that time Ohio State University had one of the best football teams in the country, and Bolenciecwcz was one of its outstanding stars. In order to be eligible to play it was necessary for him to keep up in his studies, a very difficult matter, for while he was not dumber than an ox he was not any smarter. Most of his professors were lenient and helped him along. None gave him more hints, in answering questions, or asked him simpler ones than the economics professor, a thin timid man named Bassum. One day when we were on the subject of transportation and distribution, it came Bolenciecwcz's turn to answer a question. "Name one means of transportation," the professor said to him. No light came into the big tackle's eyes. "Just any means of transportation," said the professor. Bolenciecwcz sat staring at him. "That is," pursued the professor, "any medium, agency, or method of going from one place to another." Bolenciecwcz had the look of a man who is being led into a trap. "You may choose among steam, horse-drawn, or electrically propelled vehicles," said the instructor. "I might suggest the one which we commonly take in making long journeys across land." There was a profound silence in which

CHOO CHOO CHOO

everybody stirred uneasily, including Bolenciecwcz and Mr. Bassum. Mr. Bassum abruptly broke this silence in an amazing manner. "Choo-choo-choo," he said, in a low voice, and turned instantly scarlet. He glanced appealingly around the room. All of us, of course, shared Mr. Bassum's desire that Bolenciecwcz should stay abreast of the class in economics, for the Illinois game, one of the hardest and most important of the season, was only a week off. "Toot, tooot, too-toooooooot!" some student with a deep voice moaned, and we all looked encouragingly as Bolenciecwcz. Somebody else gave a fine imitation of a locomotive letting off steam. Mr. Bassum himself rounded off the little show. "Ding, dong, ding, dong," he said hopefully. Bolenciecwcz was staring at the floor now, trying to think, his great brow furrowed, his huge hands rubbing together, his face red.

"How did you come to college this year, Mr. Bolenciecwcz?" asked the professor. "*Chuffa*, chuffa, *chuffa*, chuffa."

"M'father sent me," said the football player.

"What on?" asked Bassum.

"I git an 'lowance," said the tackle, in a low, husky voice, obviously embarrassed.

"No, no," said Bassum. "Name a means of transportation. What did you *ride* here on?"

"Train," said Bolenciecwcz.

"Quite right," said the professor. "Now, Mr. Nugent, will you tell us—"

If I went through anguish in botany and

economics—for different reasons—gymnasium work was even worse. I don't even like to think about it. They wouldn't let you play games or join in the exercises with your glasses on and I couldn't see with mine off. I bumped into professors, horizontal bars, agricultural students, and swinging iron rings. Not being able to see, I could take it but I couldn't dish it out. Also, in order to pass gymnasium (and you had to pass it to graduate) you had to learn to swim if you didn't know how. I didn't like the swimming pool, I didn't like swimming, and I didn't like the swimming instructor, and after all these years I still don't.I never swam but I passed my gym work anyway, by having another student give my gymnasium number (978) and swim across the pool in my place. He was a quiet, amiable blonde youth, number 473, and he would have seen through a microscope for me if we could have got away with it, but we couldn't get away with it. Another thing I didn't like about gymnasium work was that they made you strip the day you registered. It is impossible for me to be happy when I am stripped and being asked a lot of questions. Still, I did better than a lanky agricultural student who was cross-examined just before I was. They asked each student which college he was in—that is, whether Arts, Engineering, Commerce, or Agriculture. "What college are you in?" the instructor snapped at the youth in front of me. "Ohio State University," he said promptly.

It wasn't that agricultural student but it was another a whole lot like him who decided to take up journalism, possibly on the ground that when farming went to hell he could fall back on newspaper work. He didn't realize, of course, that that would be very much like falling back full-length on a kit of carpenter's tools. Haskins didn't seem cut out for journalism, being too embarrassed to talk to anybody and unable to use a typewriter, but the editor of the college paper assigned him to the cow barns, the sheep house, the horse pavilion, and the animal husbandry department generally. This was a genuinely big "beat," for it took up five times as much ground and got ten times as great a legislative appropriation as the College of Liberal Arts. The agricultural student knew animals, but nevertheless his stories were dull and colorlessly written. He took all afternoon on each of them, on account of having to hunt for each letter on the typewriter. Once in a while he had to ask somebody to help him hunt. "C" and "L," in particular, were hard letters for him to find. His editor finally got pretty much annoyed at the farmer-journalist because his pieces were so uninteresting. "See here, Haskins," he snapped at him one day, "why is it we never have anything hot from you on the horse pavilion? Here we have two hundred head of horses on this campus—more than any other university in the Western Conference except Purdue—and yet you never get any real low down on them. Now shoot over to the horse barns and dig up something lively." Haskins shambled out and came back in about an hour; he said he had something. "Well, start it off snappily," said the editor. "Something people will read." Haskins set to work and in a couple of hours brought a sheet of typewritten paper to the desk; it was a 200-word story about some disease that had broken out among the horses. Its opening sentence was simple but arresting. It read: "Who has noticed the sores on the tops of the horses in the animal husbandry building?"

Ohio State was a land grant university and therefore two years of military drill was compulsory. We drilled with old Springfield rifles and studied the tactics of the Civil War even though the World War was going on at the time. At 11 o'clock each morning thousands of freshmen and sophomores used to deploy over the campus, moodily creeping up on the old chemistry building. It was good training for the kind of warfare that was waged at Shiloh but it had no connection with what was going on in Europe. Some people used to think there was German money behind it, but they didn't dare say so or they would have been thrown in jail as German spies. It was a period of muddy thought and marked, I believe, the decline of higher education in the Middle West.

As a soldier I was never any good at all. Most of the cadets were glumly indifferent soldiers, but I was no good at all. Once General Littlefield, who was commandant of the cadet corps, popped up in front of me during regimental drill and snapped, "You are the main trouble with this university!" I think he meant that my type was the main trouble with the university but he may have meant me individually. I was mediocre at drill, certainly—that is, until my senior year. By that time I had drilled longer than anybody else in the Western Conference, having failed at military at the end of each preceding year so that I had to do it all over again. I was the only senior still in uniform. The uniform which, when new, had made me look like an interurban railway conductor, now that it had become faded and too tight made me look like Bert Williams in his bellboy act. This had a definitely bad effect on my morale. Even so, I had become by sheer practise little short of wonderful at squad manoeuvres.

One day General Littlefield picked our company out of the whole regiment and tried to get it mixed up by putting it through one movement after another as fast as we could execute them: squads right, squads left, squads on right into line, squads right about, squads left front into line, etc. In about three minutes one hundred and nine men were marching in one direction and I was marching away from them at an angle of 40 degrees, all alone. "Company, halt!" shouted General Littlefield, "That man is the only man who has it right!" I was made a corporal for my achievement.

The next day General Littlefield summoned me to his office. He was swatting flies when I went in. I was silent and he was silent too, for a long time. I don't think he remembered me or why he had sent for

me, but he didn't want to admit it. He swatted some more flies, keeping his eyes on them narrowly before he let go with the swatter. "Button up your coat!" he snapped. Looking back on it now I can see that he meant me although he was looking at a fly, but I just stood there. Another fly came to rest on a paper in front of the general and began rubbing its hind legs together. The general lifted the swatter cautiously. I moved restlessly and the fly flew away. "You startled him" barked General Littlefield, looking at me severely. I said I was sorry. "That won't help the situation!" snapped the general, with cold military logic. I didn't see what I could do except offer to chase some more flies toward his desk, but I didn't say anything. He stared out the window at the faraway figures of coeds crossing the campus toward the library. Finally, he told me I could go. So I went. He either didn't know which cadet I was or else he forgot what he wanted to see me about. It may have been that he wished to apologize for having called me the main trouble with the university; or maybe he had decided to compliment me on my brilliant drilling of the day before and then at the last minute decided not to. I don't know. I don't think about it much any more.

In what ways have university days changed since this essay was written? Remained the same? What lesson did Thurber learn in his botany class? Should we all learn to swim? Can you remember a relevant class? Describe that class.

One hears much about relevance today. How, then, do we know when something is relevant? It is relevant when it is personally meaningful, when we have feelings about it, whatever "it" may be. There has been concern in the educational establishment for motivating learners, but this is usually only fancy wrapping on the package. If the contents of the package are not something the learner can feel about, real learning will not take place. We must attend not only to that which motivates but to that which sustains as well.

From George Isaac Brown, *Human Teaching for Human Learning*

How much of yourself did you bring to school? How much did school bring out of you? What are the contents of your package of relevance?

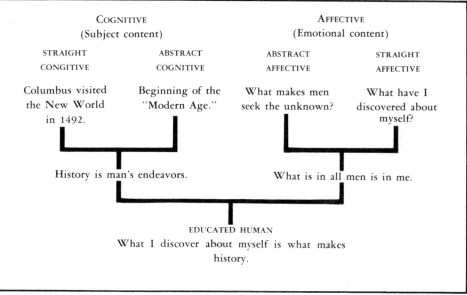

Make up your own examples of cognitive and affective content. Show how they are interrelated.

George Isaac Brown, *Human Teaching for Human Learning*

From "On Achieving the Highest Grade Point Average"
by Brian McGuire

I have been informed that I have the highest grade point average of any graduating senior in the College of Letters and Science. The first thing I would like to say to you is that it was not worth it.

My compulsive effort for a high grade point in my years at Berkeley contributed to an almost total alienation of myself from other people. When I was a freshman here in 1964–65, I noticed that many students were reading Camus's novel *The Stranger.* I read the book and found a part of myself in Meursault. Like him I could not find within myself the power to participate in the values of the societies around me.

The Free Speech Movement totally confused me, for I could not then understand the issues at stake. I withdrew into the chambers of my own mind and developed my own values. These personal standards were brutal, but they were mine. The main thing was to learn and to display that learning as well as possible to my teachers.

I became subject to a paralyzing mental machinery: if I did not study twelve hours a day, I was a failure. If I did not compose at the speed of a thousand words an hour while writing a paper, I was a failure. If I did not go through required reading at thirty-three pages an hour or more, I was a failure. I pushed myself to maintain my quotas until I was more enchained than a Russian factory worker in the 1930s.

Most of the time I acquiesced to my personal autocracy and tried to tell myself that I was doing the only worthwhile thing there was for me to do: learning. Everything else seemed absurd and meaningless. But at times I felt a revolt in myself, a desire for more than printed pages and letter grades. The feeling would come at night as I would be walking home from the library in Berkeley or in St. Andrews, where I spent a year in Education Abroad. I would look at the lights in the windows and think to myself: inside those windows, close to those lights are people. Real, live, human, fleshy, thinking, feeling, loving, despairing people. I am out here and they are in there. They will never come out here to me, and they would never allow me to come inside to them. . . .

Such experiences did not then lead me to the conclusions to which they are now bringing me. I thought I could find happiness by perfecting my mental universe through total immersion in the learning process. Instead of encouraging me to form human bonds with my fellow students, the grade-oriented system of the University of California made it possible and sometimes comfortable for me to become caught up in the prison of my mind.

Have you ever read a book that helped you know who you are? Or won a prize that wasn't worth it? Or been caught "in the prison of your mind"? Have your school experiences given you a feeling of belonging to the family of man? Have they helped you form human bonds with your fellow students?

"My Personal Experience"
by Calvin Ketter

I want to speak from a personal experience I encountered coming from a low income area or a socially deprived background. I was brought up in an all black environment. The elementary school I attended was located in the deepest part of West Oakland. I remember as a child we used to refer to our school as being in the "piney woods."

First off, the environment surrounding the school: Everyone's heard people speak, or maybe some of you have taken care of some business on 7th Street. Well, for those of you who haven't, I'll give you a brief description. When I spoke of business, I meant such business as prostitution, gambling, dope, and stolen goods. The school I attended was located one block from 7th Street, where all these businesses were conducted. All this was a nice healthy learning environment.

Next, a look at the school itself. It was run down. Many of the teachers did just enough for a student to pass him on to the next grade. I can remember that most of the stress of my early education was on sports, drawing, and dancing. Forget about reading, writing, and arithmetic. So I went along with this game from first grade to sixth. Later when I entered junior high school, I found myself unprepared. I went through those years of junior high trying to catch up with what I'd missed in elementary. Upon entering high school, I finally came to the conclu-sion that I had been shortchanged in all my early education.

I went out of my district to go to high school after telling many lies. The high school was in a nice environment, full of rolling green lawns with Japanese gardens about ten blocks from a lake. It was my first time in school ever being around non-black faces. I saw a blonde here and a brunette there with a kind of tight almond eyes, hair down her back. I sort of had to adjust myself to the new environment.

Let me get to the main point of how bad my early education had prepared me for high school. I took all the courses that would prepare me for college. I realized how dumb I was. One of the classes was Humanities. There was no pre-registration for this class. You must came with what you knew. It was then that I found out that I knew NOTHING. The teacher would ask questions about Socrates and Aristotle. I didn't know any answers. Much of the same thing happened in my other classes. I finally came to the conclusion that the reason that these students had such good knowledge was that they had been prepared better in their early educational life. They did not attend schools in poverty areas. The instructor would ask for Wright's theory of function. My hand stayed down. One of my blond friends would say, "Wright's theory was that form follows function." All this was Greek to me. This went on throughout the whole year, me being dumb. It got so bad that I was ready to call it quits for good. The background I had did not prepare me for the rest of society.

Now if the teacher had asked me such questions as: "Can you tell me the difference between a pimp and a hustler?" or "What does the term 'hot' mean'," or "What is a roach?" "What does it taste like?" I could have answered all these questions and got A's throughout the year, because all of these questions were part of my environment. I'd seen a pimp. I'd seen girls on the streets waiting for a trick, and I'd seen a roach or a joint being smoked. I had seen all of this.

It seems to me that the area I had my early education in, and the area these other students, some blacks included, had their early education in, were in two entirely different worlds. My world spoke a different language, had different needs, and now my world is striving to break out of the ghetto that kept us back so long.

Calvin Ketter knows a lot about a lot of things that have nothing to do with school, yet he feels dumb. How could the school have helped? He also feels he has learned nothing helpful. Is this feeling justified or did he learn more than he realizes? What did he have to teach? What did he learn? How could school have been more relevant to him? Have you learned because of the teaching you received or in spite of it?

Are you trying to figure out if school makes any difference to us, because if that's it, I can tell you, man, here in my heart, it don't much. You learn a few tricks with the numbers, and how to speak like someone different, but you forget it pretty fast when you leave the building, and I figure everyone has to put in his time one place or the other until he gets free; but my friend, he says most people get caught, and they are never themselves, just parrots for the teacher or someone else. That's bad, real bad. . . .

From Robert Coles, *Teachers and the Children of Poverty*

The self concept, we know, is learned. People *learn* who they are and what they are from the ways in which they have been treated by those who surround them in the process of their growing up. This is what Sullivan called "learning about self from the mirror of other people." People discover their self concepts from the kinds of experiences they have had with life; not from telling, but from experience. People develop feelings that they are liked, wanted, acceptable and able from *having been* liked, wanted, accepted and from *having been* successful. One learns that he is these things, not from being told so, but only through the experience of *being treated as though he were so.* Here is the key to what must be done to produce more adequate people. To produce a positive self, it is necessary to provide experiences that teach individuals they are positive people.

From Arthur W. Combs, "A Perceptual View of the Adequate Personality"

Observe students in several different schools: city, suburban, integrated, segregated, poor, rich, public, private. Walk around the neighborhoods of these schools. Visit your old school. What are the similarities or differences between these schools? What schools seem to be providing positive experiences for their students? What schools seem to tell students they are liked, wanted, accepted? What do students say about school?

I'd like to sit for a while, because all we ever do is stand in line.

SCHOOL'S OK. NO CHANGES NEEDED.

I never get a chance to finish . . .

There should be more black teachers.

Teachers and students don't communicate at all. the teacher does all of the talking, and the students do all the homework. I need more freedom.

I don't like school because of the rotten system. I think it needs to be changed. This society stinks, especially the school system.

Too much emphasis is placed on attendance.

The kids who eat the fastest have more time to play than the slow eaters.

TEACHERS ARE NOT REALLY CONCERNED ABOUT STUDENTS.

Change the principal. I don't like him.

Interview as many different people as you can: a child, a teenager, a parent, a poet, a fisherman, a friend, a stranger. How do their school experiences compare with yours?

Girl Graduate's Stunning Speech

Liza Hirsch stunned an audience of 4000 persons during her valedictorian address at San Jose High School commencement exercises with a sharp attack on the school system.

Miss Hirsch, 16, is an honor student who has won a scholarship to Reed College, Oregon.

She described the school system as "a 13-year stretch of babysitting."

Principal Pete Mesa of San Jose High School said yesterday that all the reaction he has received to Miss Hirsch's Wednesday night address has been favorable.

PRAISE

"The people have praised her for her insight, courage, articulateness and honesty," Mesa said.

Miss Hirsch declared in her address:

"When we ask questions on how to stop or avoid pregnancy, the teachers are not allowed to tell us much more than 'take a cold shower.' If they do, they are subject to punishment by the hypocrites in the district office who still think that babies come from storks.

". . . when we ask important questions about drugs, for example, do they send us a doctor? No, they send us a cop with a gun and a badge and he implies that one puff on a joint and we're hooked on heroin for life.

"If that were true," she said, as the audience listened raptly, "one half of us here tonight would be junkies."

She concluded:

"We're not ungrateful snobs. We're not criminals. We're not bomb-throwers. We're not insane and we are not your enemies.

"We are your children.

"And when we become angry and when we cry out, it is because we feel pain.

"How can you ignore us . . . ?"

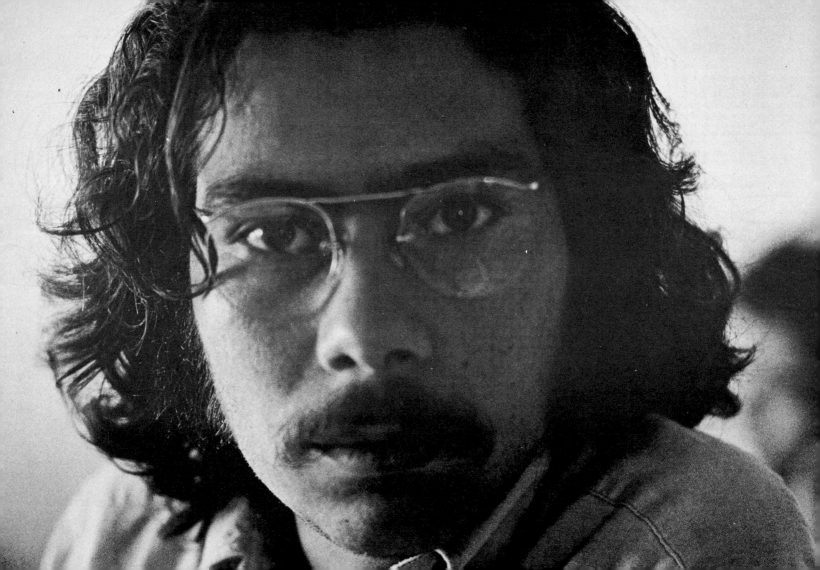

Chapter Two
Let Yourself Be Seen

From "Some Educational Implications of the Humanistic Psychologies" by Abraham H. Maslow

. . . We are now being confronted with a choice between two extremely different, almost mutually exclusive conceptions of learning. What we have in practically all the elementary and advanced textbooks of psychology, and in most of the brands of "learning theory" which all graduate students are required to learn, is what I want to call for the sake of contrast and confrontation, *extrinsic learning*, i.e., learning of the outside, learning of the impersonal, or arbitrary associations of arbitrary conditioning, that is, of arbitrary (or at best, culturally determined) meanings and responses. In this kind of learning, most often it is not the person himself who decides, but rather a teacher or an experimenter who says, "I will use a buzzer," "I will use a bell," "I will use a red light," and most important, "I will reinforce this but not that." In this sense the learning is extrinsic to the learner, extrinsic to the personality, and is extrinsic also in the sense of *collecting* associations, conditionings, habits, or modes of action. It is as if these were *possessions* which the learner accumulates in the same way that he accumulates keys or coins and puts them in his pocket. They have little or nothing to do with the actualization or growth of the peculiar, idiosyncratic kind of person he is.

I believe this is the model of education which we all have tucked away in the back of our heads and which we don't often make explicit. In this model the teacher is the active one who teaches a passive person who gets shaped and taught and who is *given* something which he then accumulates and which he may then lose or retain, depending upon the efficiency of the initial indoctrination process, and of his own accumulation-of-fact process. I would maintain that a good 90% of "learning theory" deals with learnings that have nothing to do with the intrinsic self that I've been talking about, nothing to do with its specieshood and biological idiosyncracy. This kind of learning too easily reflects the goals of the teacher and ignores the values and ends of the learner himself. It is also fair, therefore, to call such learning amoral.

Now I'd like to contrast this with another kind of learning, which is actually going on, but is usually unconscious and unfortunately happens more outside the classroom than inside. It often comes in the great personal learning experiences of our lives.

For instance, if I were to list the most important learning experiences in my life, there come to mind getting married, discovering my life work, having children, getting psychoanalyzed, the death of my best friend, confronting death myself, and the like. I think I would say that these were more important learning experiences for me than my Ph.D. or any 15 or 150 credits or courses that I've ever had. I certainly learned more about *myself* from such experiences. I learned,

if I may put it so, to throw aside many of my "learnings," that is, to push aside the habits and traditions and reinforced associations which had been imposed upon me. Sometimes this was at a very trivial, and yet meaningful, level. I particularly remember when I learned that I really hated lettuce. My father was a "nature boy," and I had lettuce two meals a day for the whole of my early life. But one day in analysis after I had learned that I carried my father inside me, it dawned on me that it was my father, through *my* larynx, who was ordering salad with every meal. I can remember sitting there, realizing that *I* hated lettuce and then saying, "My God, take the damn stuff away!" I was emancipated, becoming in this small way me, rather than my father. I didn't eat any more lettuce for months, until it finally settled back to what my body calls for. I have lettuce two or three times each week, which I now enjoy. But *not* twice a day.

Now observe, this experience which I mentioned occurred just once and I could give many other similar examples. It seems to me that we must call into question the generality of repetition, of learning by drilling. The experiences in which we uncover our intrinsic selves are apt to be unique moments, not slow accumulations of reinforced bits. (How do you repeat the death of your father?) These are the experiences in which we discover identity. These are the experiences in which we learn who we are, what we love, what we hate, what we value, what we are committed to, what makes us

feel anxious, what makes us feel depressed, what makes us feel happy, what makes us feel great joy.

It must be obvious by now that you can generate consequences of this second picture of learning by the hundred. (And again I would stress that these hypotheses can be stated in testable, disconfirmable, confirmable form.) One such implication of the point of view is a change in the whole picture of the teacher. If you are willing to accept this conception of two kinds of learning, with the learning-to-be-a-person being more central and more basic than the impersonal learning of skills or the acquisition of habits; and if you are willing to concede that even the more extrinsic learnings are far more useful, and far more effective if based upon a sound identity, that is, if done by a person who knows what he wants, knows what he is, and where he's going and what his ends are; then you *must* have a different picture of the good teacher and of his functions.

In the first place, unlike the current model of teacher as lecturer, conditioner, reinforcer, and boss, the Taoist helper or teacher is receptive rather than intrusive. I was told once that in the world of boxers, a youngster who feels himself to be good and who wants to be a boxer will go to a gym, look up one of the managers and say, "I'd like to be a pro, and I'd like to be in your stable. I'd like you to manage me." In this world, what is then done characteristically is to try him out. The good manager will select one of his professionals and say, "Take him on in the ring. Stretch him. Strain him. Let's see what he can do. Just let him show his very best. Draw him out." If it turns out that the boxer has promise, if he's a "natural," then what the good manager does is to take that boy and train him to be, if this is Joe Doakes, a *better Joe Doakes*. That is, he takes his style as given and builds upon that. He does not start all over again, and say, "Forget all you've learned, and do it this new way," which is like saying, "Forget what kind of body you have," or "Forget what you are good for." He takes him and builds upon his *own* talents and builds him up into the very best Joe Doakes-type boxer that he possibly can.

It is my strong impression that this is the way in which much of the world of education could function. If we want to be helpers, counselors, teachers, guiders, or psychotherapists, what we must do is to accept the person and help him learn what kind of person he is already. What is his style, what are his aptitudes, what is he good for, not good for, what can we build upon, what are his good raw materials, his good potentialities? We would be nonthreatening and would supply an atmosphere of acceptance of the child's nature which reduces fear, anxiety and defense to the minimum possible. Above all, we would care for the child, that is enjoy him and his growth and self-actualization. So far this sounds much like the Rogerian therapist, his "unconditional positive regard," his congruence, his openness and his caring. And indeed there is evidence by now that this "brings the child out," permits him to express and to act, to experiment, and even to make mistakes; to let himself be seen. Suitable feedback at this point, as in T-groups or basic encounter groups, or nondirective counseling, then helps the child to discover what and who he is.

In closing, I would like to discuss briefly the role that peak experiences can play in the education of the child. We have no systematic data on peak experiences in children but we certainly have enough anecdotes and introspections and memories to be quite confident that young children have them, perhaps more frequently than adults do. However, they seem at least in the beginning to come more from sensory experiences, color, rhythm, or sounds, and perhaps are better characterized by the words wonder, awe, fascination, absorption, and the like.

. . . Using peak experiences or fascination or wonder-experiences as an intrinsic reward or goal at *many* points in education is a very real possibility, and is congruent with the whole philosophy of the humanistic educator. At the very least, this new knowledge can help wean teachers away from their frequent uneasiness with and even disapproval and persecution of these experiences. If they learn to value them as great moments in the learning process, moments in which both cognitive and personal growth take place simultaneously, then this valuing can be transmitted to the child. He in turn is then taught to value rather than to suppress his greatest moments of illumination, moments which can validate and make worthwhile the more usual trudging and slogging and "working through" of education.

There is a very useful parallel here with the newer humanistic paradigm for science in which the more everyday cautious and patient work of checking, validating and replicating is seen, not as *all* there is to science but rather as follow-up work, *subsequent* to the great intuitions, intimations, and illuminations of the creative and daring, innovative, breakthrough scientist. Caution is then seen to *follow* upon boldness and proving comes *after* intuition. The creative scientist then looks more like a gambler than a banker, one who is willing to work hard for seven years because of a dazzling hunch, one who feels certain in the *absence* of evidence, *before* the evidence, and only *then* proceeds to the hard work of proving or disproving his precious revelation. First comes the emotion, the fascination, the falling in love with a possibility, and *then* comes the hard work, the chores, the stubborn persistence in the face of disappointment and failure.

As a supplement to this conception in which a noetic illumination plays such an important role, we can add the harsh patience of the psychotherapist who has learned from many bitter disappointments that the breakthrough insight doesn't do the therapeutic job all by itself, as Freud originally thought. It needs consolidation, repetition, rediscovery, application to one situation after another. It needs patience, time and hard work—what the psychoanalysts call "working through." Not only for science but also for psychotherapy may we say that the process *begins* with an emotional-cognitive flash but *does not end there*! It is this model of science and therapy that I believe we may now fairly consider for the process of education, if not as an exclusive model, at least as an additional one.

We must learn to treasure the "jags" of the child in school, his fascination, absorptions, his persistent wide-eyed wonderings, his Dionysian enthusiasms. At the very least, we can value his more diluted raptures, his "interests" and hobbies, etc. They can lead to much. Especially can they lead to hard work, persistent, absorbed, fruitful, educative.

And conversely I think it is possible to think of the peak-experience, the experience of awe, mystery, wonder, or of perfect completion, as the goal and reward of learning as well, its end as well as its beginning. If this is true for the *great* historians, mathematicians, scientists, musicians, philosophers and all the rest, why should we not try to maximize these studies as sources of peak experiences for the child as well?

What were your most important learning experiences? What were the peaks? How can school promote this kind of learning? What are you unlearning? Did your father like lettuce?

From *The Story of My Life*
by Helen Keller

The most important day I remember in all my life is the one on which my teacher, Anne Mansfield Sullivan, came to me. I am filled with wonder when I consider the immeasurable contrasts between the two lives which it connects. It was the third of March, 1887, three months before I was seven years old.

On the afternoon of that eventful day, I stood on the porch, dumb, expectant. I guessed vaguely from my mothers's signs and from the hurrying to and fro in the house that something unusual was about to happen, so I went to the door and waited on the steps. The afternoon sun penetrated the mass of honeysuckle that covered the porch, and fell on my upturned face. My fingers lingered almost unconsciously on the familiar leaves and blossoms which had just come forth to greet the sweet southern spring. I did not know what the future held of marvel or surprise for me. Anger and bitterness had preyed upon me continually for weeks and a deep languor had succeeded this passionate struggle.

Have you ever been at sea in a dense fog, when it seemed as if a tangible white darkness shut you in, and the great ship, tense and anxious, groped her way toward the shore with plummet and sounding-line, and you waited with beating heart for something to happen? I was like that ship before my education began, only I was without compass or sounding-line, and had no way of knowing how near the harbour was. "Light! give me light!" was the wordless cry of my soul, and the light of love shone on me in that very hour.

I felt approaching footsteps. I stretched out my hand as I supposed to my mother. Some one took it, and I was caught up and held close in the arms of her who had come to reveal all things to me, and, more than all things else, to love me.

The morning after my teacher came she led me into her room and gave me a doll. The little blind children at the Perkins Institution had sent it and Laura Bridgman had dressed it; but I did not know this until afterward. When I had played with it a little while, Miss Sullivan slowly spelled into my hand the word "d-o-l-l." I was at once interested in this finger play and tried to imitate it. When I finally succeeded in making the letters correctly I was flushed with childish pleasure and pride. Running downstairs to my mother I held up my hand and made the letters for doll. I did not know that I was spelling a word or even that words existed; I was simply making my fingers go in monkey-like imitation. In the days that followed I learned to spell in this uncomprehending way a great many words, among them *pin*, *hat*, *cup* and a few verbs like *sit*, *stand* and *walk*. But my teacher had been with me several weeks before I understood that everything has a name.

One day, while I was playing with my new doll, Miss Sullivan put my big rag doll into my lap also, spelled "d-o-l-l" and tried to make me understand that "d-o-l-l" applied to both. Earlier in the day we had had a tussle over the words "m-u-g" and "w-a-t-e-r." Miss Sullivan had tried to impress it upon me that "m-u-g" is *mug* and that "w-a-t-e-r" is *water*, but I persisted in confounding the two. In despair she had dropped the subject for the time, only to renew it at the first opportunity. I became impatient at her repeated attempts and, seizing the new doll, I dashed it upon the floor. I was keenly delighted when I felt the fragments of the broken doll at my feet. Neither sorrow nor regret followed my passionate outburst. I had not loved the doll. In the still, dark world in which I lived there was no strong sentiment or tenderness. I felt my teacher sweep the fragments to one side of the hearth, and I had a sense of satisfaction that the cause of my discomfort was removed. She brought me my hat, and I knew I was going out into the warm sunshine. This thought, if a wordless sensation may be called a thought, made me hop and skip with pleasure.

We walked down the path to the well-house, attracted by the fragrance of the honeysuckle with which it was covered. Someone was drawing water and my teacher placed my hand under the spout. As the cool stream gushed over one hand she spelled into the other the word *water*, first slowly, then rapidly. I stood still, my whole attention fixed upon the motions of her fingers. Suddenly I felt a misty consciousness as of something forgotten—a thrill of returning thought; and somehow the mystery of language was revealed to me. I knew then that "w-a-t-e-r" meant the wonderful cool something that was flowing over my hand. That living word awakened my soul, gave it light, hope, joy, set it free! There were barriers still, it is true, but barriers that could in time be swept away.

I left the well-house eager to learn. Everything had a name, and each name gave birth to a new thought. As we returned to the house every object which I touched seemed to quiver with life. That was because I saw everything with the strange, new sight that had come to me. On entering the door I remembered the doll I had broken. I felt my way to the hearth and picked up the pieces. I tried vainly to put them together. Then my eyes filled with tears; for I realized what I had done, and for the first time I felt repentance and sorrow.

I learned a great many new words that day. I do not remember what they all were; but I do know that mother, father, sister, teacher were among them—words that were to make the world blossom for me, "like Aaron's rod, with flowers." It would have been difficult to find a happier child than I was as I lay in my crib at the close of that eventful day and lived over the joys it had brought me, and for the first time longed for a new day to come.

I had now the key to all language, and

I was eager to learn to use it. Children who hear acquire language without any particular effort; the words that fall from others' lips they catch on the wing, as it were, delightedly, while the little deaf child must trap them by a slow and often painful process. But whatever the process, the result is wonderful. Gradually from naming an object we advance step by step until we have traversed the vast distance between our first stammered syllable and the sweep of thought in a line of Shakespeare.

At first, when my teacher told me about a new thing I asked very few questions. My ideas were vague, and my vocabulary was inadequate; but as my knowledge of things grew, and I learned more and more words, my field of inquiry broadened, and I would return again and again to the same subject, eager for further information. Sometimes a new word revived an image that some earlier experience had engraved on my brain.

I remember the morning that I first asked the meaning of the word *love*. This was before I knew many words. I had found a few early violets in the garden and brought them to my teacher. She tried to kiss me: but at that time I did not like to have anyone kiss me except my mother. Miss Sullivan put her arm gently round me and spelled into my hand, "I love Helen."

"What is love?" I asked.

She drew me closer to her and said, "It is here," pointing to my heart, whose beats I was conscious of for the first time. Her words puzzled me very much because I did not then understand anything unless I touched it.

I smelt the violets in her hand and asked, half in words, half in signs, a question which meant, "Is love the sweetness of flowers?"

"No," said my teacher.

Again I thought. The warm sun was shining on us.

"Is this not love?" I asked, pointing in the direction from which the heat came. "Is this not love?"

It seemed to me that there could be nothing more beautiful than the sun, whose warmth makes all things grow. But Miss Sullivan shook her head, and I was greatly puzzled and disappointed. I thought it strange that my teacher could not show me love.

A day or two afterward I was stringing beads of different sizes in symmetrical groups—two large beads, three small ones, and so on. I had made many mistakes, and Miss Sullivan had pointed them out again and again with gentle patience. Finally I noticed a very obvious error in the sequence and for an instant I concentrated my attention on the lesson and tried to think how I should have arranged the beads. Miss Sullivan touched my forehead and spelled with decided emphasis, "Think."

In a flash I knew that the word was the name of the process that was going on in my head. This was my first conscious perception of an abstract idea.

For a long time I was still—I was not thinking of the beads in my lap, but trying to find a meaning for "love" in the light of this new idea. The sun had been under a cloud all day, and there had been brief showers; but suddenly the sun broke forth in all its southern splendour.

Again I asked my teacher, "Is this not love?"

"Love is something like the clouds that were in the sky before the sun came out," she replied. Then in simpler words than these, which at that time I could not have understood, she explained: "You cannot touch the clouds, you know; but you feel the rain and know how glad the flowers and the thirsty earth are to have it after a hot day. You cannot touch love either; but you feel the sweetness that it pours into everything. Without love you would not be happy or want to play."

The beautiful truth burst upon my mind —I felt that there were invisible lines stretched between my spirit and the spirits of others.

Have you ever learned because you needed and wanted to know? Describe that experience. Who was the real teacher?

Write an advertisement for yourself as student.
Tell how good you are.
Talk about what you can do well.
Write a pledge of allegiance to yourself.

Think of something in your life
you'd like to change.
State all the "I can't becauses."
Think of something in school
you'd like to change.
How many of the barriers are real?
How many are merely excuses?

Take a long piece of butcher paper.
Draw your life like a road map.
Show the good places.
Draw the bumpy spots.
Where are you now?
Draw in the barriers.
Fill in where you want to go.
How are you going to get there?

Make an outline map of the world.
Trace your family's origins
and then mark where you would like to go.

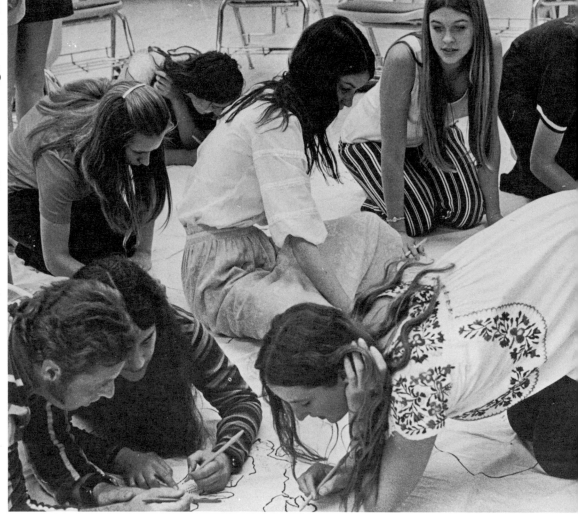

From "Reach, Touch, and Teach"
by Terry Borton

There are two sections to almost every school's statement of educational objectives—one for real, and one for show. The first, the real one, talks about academic excellence, subject mastery, and getting into college or a job. The other discusses the human purpose of school—values, feelings, personal growth, the full and happy life. It is included because everyone knows that it is important, and that it ought to be central to the life of every school. But it is only for show. Everyone knows how little schools have done about it.

In spite of this, the human objectives describe the things all of us cite when we try to remember what "made a difference" in our school careers: the teacher who touched us as persons, or the one who ground out our lives to polish our intellects; the class that moved with the strength and grace of an Olympic team, or the dozens of lessons when each of us slogged separately toward the freedom of 3 o'clock. What we learned, and what we became, depended to a significant degree on how we felt about ourselves, our classmates, and our teachers. The schools were right—the human purposes *were* important. But with the exception of those teachers who were so rare we never forgot them, the schools did little to put their philosophy into practice.

Recently, however, a variety of programs have begun to build curricula and teaching methodology that speak directly to the human objectives. These programs, stemming both from within the schools and from various branches of psychology, point the way to a school practice which not only recognizes the power of feelings, but also combines academic training with an education directly aimed at the student's most important concerns. Schools may soon be explicitly teaching students such things as how to sort out and guide their own psychological growth, or increase their desire to achieve, or handle their aggressive instincts in nonviolent forms.

The new impetus has a variety of names: "psychological education," "affective," "humanistic," "personological," "eupsychian," "synoetic." Some of these names are a bit bizarre, and none has yet gained wide acceptance. But taken together their presence indicates a growing recognition that in the world's present state of social and moral turmoil, the schools' traditional second objective can no longer be for show. Riots, poverty, war, student rebellion, swollen mental hospitals, and soaring crime rates have involved an enormous number of people. They have generated a broadening conviction that society is as responsible for the psychological well-being of each of its members as is each individual. And that conviction has created a receptive audience for new kinds of educational critics.

The new critics do not simply attack the schools for their academic incompetence, as did the Rickovers of a decade ago. They are equally concerned with the schools' basic lack of understanding that students are human beings with feelings as well as intellects. Jonathan Kozol has given a gripping sense of the "destruction of the hearts and minds of Negro children" in his *Death at an Early Age*. In *How Children Fail* John Holt has shown that even in the best "progressive" schools, children live in constant fear which inhibits their learning, and Paul Goodman's *Compulsory Mis-Education* has made a powerful case for his contention that "the present school system is leading straight to 1984." The intuitive warnings of these "romantic critics" have been backed up by statistical evidence from the largest survey of education ever conducted, James Coleman's *Equality of Educational Opportunity*. This survey correlates academic achievement with attitudes such as a student's self concept, sense of control over his fate, and interest in school. The study concludes that these attitudes and feelings are more highly correlated with how well a student achieves academically than a combination of many of the factors which educators have usually thought were crucial, such as class size, salary of teachers, facilities, curriculum.

. . . The project which I codirected with Norman Newberg, the Philadelphia School Board's specialist in "affective education" . . . is being developed from within the schools—in this case by a group of urban teachers trying to find a philosophy and method which would work with the students they were asked to teach. The program is based on the assumption that every person handles massive amounts of information, and needs to be taught both logical and psychological processes for handling it. Two semester-long courses, one in communications, and one in urban affairs, isolate such processes as symbolization, simulation, dreaming, and de-escalating pressure, and teach them in an explicit fashion. At the same time the classes are designed to tie these processes to the amorphous undercurrent of student concerns for self-identity, power, and relationship.

I dropped into a high school communications class one hot day during last summer's field testing, when the teacher was working on "taxonomy of process," or a way of looking at what, why, and how behavior occurs and changes. The purpose of the class was to show the students a simple technique for analyzing their own habitual forms of processing the world around them, and then to show them how they could develop new responses if they wanted to. The class was working in groups of twos, filling in "What Wheels" for each other. One boy in the back was without a partner, so I joined him, and we agreed that I would make a What Wheel for him, and he would make one for me. I drew a circle, filled in the spokes, and wrote down my first impressions of him: "strong, quick, Afro, shy, bright."

The teacher asked us to read each other our What Wheels, select one adjective which interested us most, and ask our partner to draw a "Why Wheel" to explain *why* that adjective was meaningful to him.

Charlie read me his What Wheel—he was perceptive, as students usually are about teachers. Then I read him mine.

"Why'd you write 'shy'? I ain't shy."

"Well, I just met you, so I can't fill out a whole Why Wheel about it. But when I first sat there, I noticed you looked down at your desk instead of up at me. So I just guessed you were shy with strangers—maybe just with strange teachers."

Charlie took his What Wheel from me and looked at it. "You know, that's the truth. I thought nobody, except maybe my mother, knew that about me, but well, it's the truth anyhow."

The murmur of the class's conversation quieted while the teacher told us how to make up "How Wheels" with our partners. We were supposed to write down the range of actions which would either increase or decrease the trait we had been discussing.

"Aw, man, it would be easy to increase being shy," laughed Charlie. "I just wouldn't look at nobody."

"And decreasing it?"

"I'd look at you like I'm looking at you right now," he said, looking me straight in the eye. "And more than that, I'd look at you like that when you first came in here. Teacher, or white man, I wasn't afraid of you; no reason why I should act like I was."

We talked for a while—about my wheels, about the effectiveness of the what, why, how process questions for looking at behavior, and about school. When the bell rang, we shook hands. "See ya around," he said.

"See ya around," I said.

. . . One of the most eclectic approaches in the clinical tradition is the project run by Dr. George Brown of the University of California at Santa Barbara. Brown's project, sponsored by the Ford Foundation through the ebullient Esalen Institute, utilizes many different approaches, but particularly the theories of Gestalt therapy which attempt to get youth in touch with how they are feeling in the "here and now." With such theoretical orientations in their background, the teachers in Brown's project are encouraged to devise their own techniques to integrate academic with affective or emotional learning in order to achieve a more "humanistic education."

I joined the teachers at one of the monthly meetings where they learn about new ideas, and share with each other the techniques they have developed. Gloria Siemons, a pretty first-grade teacher, was describing an exercise that she had first conducted with the entire class, and then used when one child became angry at another. She lined the class up in two rows on the playground, had them find a partner, put their hands up facing each other, and push.

Push they did, laughing all over the field, especially at their teacher, who was being pushed around in a circle by several of the bigger kids.

Later, when two kids got into an argument at recess, Mrs. Siemons simply asked them: "Are you angry now? Would you like to push?"

"Yes, I'm angry. I'm angry at him."

Both agreed to the contest, pushed for a minute as hard as they could, and then collapsed into each other's arms giggling. Their anger was worked out, but without hurting each other.

"What would happen," I asked Mrs. Siemons, "if one kid pushed another hard enough to hurt him?"

"We have a rule about that. 'It's OK to be angry with someone, and it's OK to push, but it's *not* OK to push him into the rosebush.' "

Good teachers, particularly good first-grade teachers such as Mrs. Siemons, have always responded to the emotional side of their students' lives, and it is precisely this intuitive gift which Dr. Brown is capitalizing on. By systematizing such techniques and relating them to a general theoretical framework, he and the teachers of his staff have begun to generate hundreds of ways to integrate the feelings of students with the regular curriculum taught from kindergarten to high school.

The techniques being developed, the dozens of programs, and the various theories differ in many respects, but they have several features in common. First, and most important, all of them deal in a very explicit and direct way with the student's feelings, interpersonal relations, or values. It is the fact that they are so explicit and direct which sets them apart from the vague protestations that schools have usually made about this area. While schools were concentrating on math, science, or English, they often ignored or actively suppressed feelings. The new programs make what was covert behavior the subject of overt discussion; they make the implicit explicit. They legitimize feelings, clarify them for the student, and suggest a variety of behaviors which he can use to express them. They do so on the assumption that these feelings exert a powerful effect on a student's behavior, both in the present and in the future. If schools want to influence behavior, then it makes sense to deal directly with its major sources, not just with the binomial theorem, the gerund, or the Seventeenth Amendment.

A factor in the new field which often causes misunderstanding is that most of the programs use nonverbal experiences, either through physical expression and involvement, or through art, sculpture, or music. For the most part, this involvement with the *non*verbal is not *anti*verbal or *anti*intellectual. Nonverbal educational techniques are based on the obvious but little-utilized fact that a child learns most of his emotional response patterns at a very young age—before he can talk. His knowledge of love, rejection, anger, and need does not come through words, but through his physical senses—touch, a flushed face, a gnawing in his stomach. Even later, when he begins to talk, the words he learns are "Mama," "doggie," "see"—words for things and actions, not feelings. Indeed, many children seem entirely unable to give a name to their current feelings—they have been taught how to say "I am bad," but not "I feel bad." Education that deals with feelings is often facilitated by skipping over the verbal labels which have been learned relatively late in life, regaining the other senses, and then reintegrating them with verbal thought and new behaviors.

Another common technique which causes confusion is the reliance of many of the programs on games, dramatic improvisations, and role playing. Again, though those utilizing the techniques believe in fun and use games, few of them are simply advocating "fun and games." Their interest stems from an insight into the learning process of small children. By playing games—house, fireman, office, war—little children learn what it will be like to be an adult, and begin to develop their own style in that role. But our culture provides few such opportunities for older children or adolescents, even though the society is changing so fast that many of the response patterns they learned as a three year old may be no longer relevant, or even dangerous. Games and improvisation allow a simulation of the self. While they are real and produce real emotions, their tightly defined limits provide a way to try out new behavior without taking the full consequences which might occur if the same action

were performed in ordinary relationships.

There are answers for questions about nonverbal and gaming emphasis, but there are many other questions which the programs raise for which there are no answers. At best, solutions will come slowly, and that is bound to produce tremendous strain in a time when events wait for no one.

. . . The new programs . . . are delicate, and they are moving into an area which is fundamentally new, so they can be expected to suffer from the attention they attract, to make mistakes, and to run into blind alleys. If it takes the big curriculum development corporations a million dollars and three years to build a single course in science or social studies, it will be even more difficult to build a fully developed curriculum in a new field. But the effort should be encouraged. For while it may not be novel to assert that a man's feelings are a crucial determinant of his public behavior and private well-being, there is no question about the novelty and significance of school programs that explicitly educate both the feelings and the intellect. Such programs raise many of society's basic questions about purpose and meaning— tough questions which will not be easy to answer. But they also offer a possibility for building a saner world—a world where people are more open about their feelings, careful in their thinking, and responsible in their actions.

In the selection to follow, students who were part of an experimental program in affective education such as Borton describes talk about their experience. This program, the elementary school teaching project, was initiated by the Fund for the Advancement of Education and The Ford Foundation primarily for poor minority children.

From *Toward Humanistic Education* by Gerald Weinstein and Mario D. Fantini

. . . GW: So, what do you tell yourself now?

STUDENT: I say to myself that if I have an opinion and everybody else don't agree with it, there's no need to give it up or drop it or anything. I say, "It can't be no good. Start over again. You can always have a second chance."

MELANIE: Mine wasn't exactly like theirs. Before, I listened to what the teachers said, and I said, "Yes, Sister, I agree with you." I was a little rebellious because I'd get fed up with it, and I would say what I had to say. And, I could stand on my own two feet, for a while. But, it was always as though I was giving in to them in the end. But, after the program, I think a lot of it helped me to know myself and to realize that there were different parts of me, that I had feelings inside of me that could be respected by other people, and that things I had to say were good, just for the simple fact that they were my own. Now I'll go to school, and I'll tell them, "I don't agree with you." I don't argue. I just get up and say, "I don't agree." I think that's good.

CATHY: Before the program, I thought I was different. It was like a secret. I thought I was a different type of girl. I was unique, you might say. But I didn't tell anyone. I thought, "Oh well, I'll grow old and die, and this is a secret that nobody will find out that Cathy was different." But if I were to give my opinion to my friends, they wouldn't agree with me. They'd look at me like I was strange or something, and then I'd say, "Oh well, never mind. Forget it." And that would be the end of it, but I'd keep it up inside of me. And I used to think, the nuns kind of drummed it into me. They said, "You won't have an opinion before you're 21. Then you can have opinions. Then you can be right. Before then, just keep your mouth closed because nothing you're going to say is going to be intelligent. Just wait till you're 21." And I thought that you had to go to college, you had to do all that stuff, you know, and I think that if I hadn't gone to the summer program I would have fit into my academy very well. I'd be just like the rest of the girls, but I don't fit in there at all, I don't think.

GW: Isn't that harder for you?

CATHY: Well, in a way I feel that I've reached a point that these girls haven't reached yet. I feel that I know something that these girls don't know. They just haven't reached the point I've reached. I feel that I'm more mature than they are because I know myself a little better.

GW: What do you know?

CATHY: Well, I know more about the way I feel and why I feel the way I do, and these girls aren't even going to *wonder.* They don't want to find themselves, because the nuns want them to come out all alike. You're all going to be alike when you graduate.

HAROLD: I think one main problem is educators. You are educated. You're going to decide what the kids of tomorrow are going to have to learn. I just say this, "Don't stigmatize!" Just don't, because you're going to kill them. (I don't mean literally that you're going to shoot them down.)

GW: I don't know what the word "stigmatize" means.

HAROLD: All right, what I mean is drumming in their heads humdrum A plus B plus C. In other words, let them find out for themselves.

GW: Even though it may be a longer and harder process?

HAROLD: It'll be a harder process, but the kids will benefit more. And they'll learn more.

MRS. PLATTOR: What makes you so sure of that?

HAROLD: What makes me so sure of that? Because I've been through it.

MRS. PLATTOR: That doesn't tell me anything.

JANET: I know why I'm sure of that, because, for instance, I learned certain things at school that the teacher would say, "Now here's what we're going to learn. You'll learn it, and then you'll tell what you've learned." Then I'll get out, and I'll be arguing with somebody about this point I've learned in history, and I realize I know the facts but I don't have the foggiest idea of what I'm talking about. I can tell you all the dates, but I don't know why it's in my head. I don't know why I think it, or how I ever reached those conclusions because they really don't go with my ideas at all. And then I went to the summer program, and now anything that happened there I could argue with anyone, because I know why I thought it, because I thought it out in the first place by myself and I *felt* it. At the beginning of that program the whole faculty could have said, "You are going to learn this, this, and this." And we would have learned it. But, the way it happened, we learned the exact same things, but we learned them through a longer process all by ourselves and we knew why we'd learned them. And we came to the exact same conclusions we would have if they'd told us, but we did it by ourselves.

Hey, Teacher

Hey, teacher.
I'm late, see.
Hey teacher, I'm late. See . . . seeeeee.
IIII'mm late. See. Me.

Hey, teacher.
I'm here. I'm here.
See. Here. I'm here.
Presented. All accounted for.
See. Over here. See me!
See? See. See. Me.

Hey, teacher.
I know. I know, teacher.
Yes, I know. Yes. Yes.
Yes, I know. I know! I know.
Yes, teacher, I know. I know. I know. I
know!

Hey, teacher.
Johnny called me a bastard.
Johnny. Called *me* a bastard.
Hey, teacher, he did.
Yes he did.
Yes . . . he did.

Yes.

Hey, teacher.
Jerry's got a girl . . . . friend.
Hhmmmmmmm.
Yes, he has.

A girl . . . friend.
Yes, Jerry's got a girlfriend.
And guess what!
She's my girl . . . friend too.
Yes.
Well.
She was my girl . . . friend, before Jerry's.
Jerry's got a girlfriend.

Hey, teacher.
It was Columbus. Yes. Columbus.
He did it. It was Columbus. Christopher
Columbus. Christopher. Columbus.
Christopher. Chris. Over there.
Yes. Chris. He did it. He did it.
He pinched me. He pinched me.
Here. Right here. Hmmm. Yes.
Yes, he did too. Right here.
Hmmm.   Hmmm.
hmmmhmmmhmmmhmmm.
Yes he did. Rightttttt hereeee.
Yess, it was Chris all right.
Christopher Columbus.

Hey teacher.
Shit. Yea, shit.
Shit. Shiiiiit. Shhhhit.
Yea.
Shit.
No. Shit.
Yea shit.
Shit.
Shit, teacher. Shit, shit, shit, shit, shit.
Teacher . . . . shit.
Yea, shit.

Hey, teacher.
Look at me. Look at me.
Look, teacher. Look here.
Teacher, look here. Look here.
Look, teacher.
Look . . . . teacher.
Teacher. Look. Look. Look. Look. Look.

Hey, teacher.
Wowie zowie!
Hey, teach. Wowie Zowie!
Hey, uptight. Wowie Zowie.
Dig, teach. Wowie Zowie.
Wowie Zowie, teach.
Dig?
Dig, teach. Dig teach.
Wowie Zowies.

Hey, teacher!
See.
Here.
I know.
Bastard
Girl . . . . friend
Christopher Columbus
Shit
Look
Wowie Zowie
Dig.
Hey teacher.

Dan Lamblin

Write your own "Hey Teacher." Make the
teacher see you!

Every child, every person can delight in learning. Every educator can share in that delight. The methods are available. The needs for reform are clear. The chief obstacles are simply inertia and low expectations. Actually, a new education is already here, thrusting up in spite of every barrier built against it. Why not help it happen?

From George Leonard, *Education and Ecstasy*

**A TEACHER
IS A STUDENT**

**A STUDENT
IS A TEACHER**

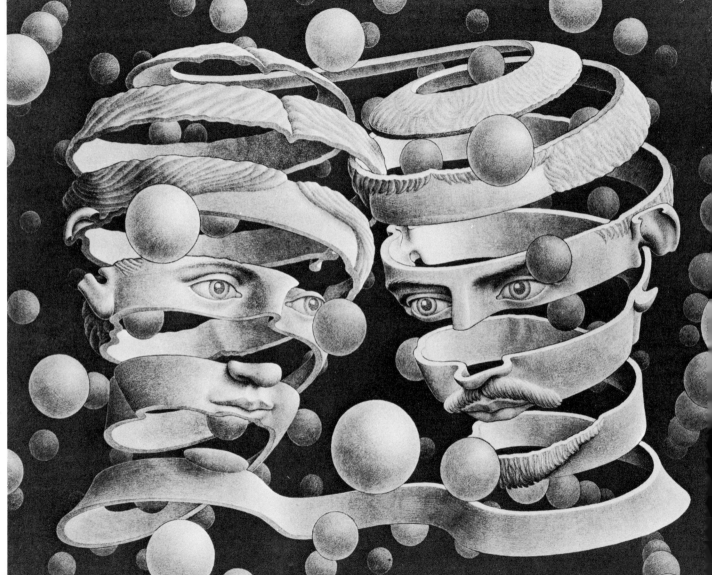

Bond of Union, M. C. Escher, Courtesy of the Vorpal Gallery, San Francisco

CHAPTER THREE

AND NOW THERE IS A TEACHER

How would you like to have a student just like you?

✦✦✦✦✦✦✦✦✦✦✦✦✦✦✦✦✦✦✦✦✦✦✦✦✦✦✦✦✦

Imagine you are walking
along a long hallway.
In the distance you see a
small figure approaching.
As you walk slowly forward, you
recognize the child you were.
What would you as the teacher say to him?
Close your eyes. Play both parts,
the student self and the teacher self.
Carry on a dialogue.
Slowly open your eyes when you have finished.

✦✦✦✦✦✦✦✦✦✦✦✦✦✦✦✦✦✦✦✦✦✦✦✦✦✦✦✦✦

Who is the real teacher? Is there anyone you listen to for advice? Is he as old as Bob Dylan?

There Is a Teaching Vacancy
Write an advertisement for a teacher you want to hire. What kind of person are you looking for? What do you want him to do?

TEACHER WANTED:

Interview the following applicant, whose teacher evaluation is on your desk. What questions would you ask him? ➤➤➤➤

Teacher Evaluation by John Gauss

TEACHER: **Mr. X**

A. PERSONAL QUALIFICATIONS RATING

(high to low)

	1	2	3	4	5	
Personal appearance	—	—	—	—	X	Dresses in an old sheet draped about his body
Self-confidence	—	—	—	X	—	Not sure of himself – always asking questions
Use of English	—	—	—	X	—	Speaks with a heavy Greek accent
Adaptability	—	—	—	—	X	prone to suicide by poison when under duress

B. CLASS MANAGEMENT

	1	2	3	4	5	
Organization	—	—	—	—	X	Does not keep a seating chart
Room appearance	—	—	—	X	—	Does not have eye-catching bulletin boards
Utilization of supplies	X	—	—	—	—	Does not use supplies

C. TEACHER-PUPIL RELATIONSHIPS

	1	2	3	4	5	
Tact and consideration	—	—	—	—	X	places students in embarrassing situation by asking questions
Attitude of class	—	X	—	—	—	class is friendly

50

D. TECHNIQUES OF TEACHING

Daily preparations	___ X ___ ___ ___	*Does not keep daily lesson plans*
Attention to course of study	___ ___ X ___ ___	*Quite flexible—allows students to wander to different topics*
Knowledge of subject matter	___ ___ ___ ___ X	*Does not know material— has to question pupils to gain knowledge*

E. PROFESSIONAL ATTITUDE

Professional ethics	X ___ ___ ___ ___	*Does not belong to professional association or PTA*
In-Service training	___ X ___ ___ ___	*Complete failure here— has not even bothered to attend college*
Parent Relationships	___ ___ X ___ ___	*Needs to improve in this area—parents are trying to get rid of him.*

Who is this teacher? (See answer at the bottom of p. 223.) Would you hire him? Is there a place for teachers who are different in our schools? Do all teachers have to march to the same tune? Have you ever had a "different" teacher?

Be the candidate, with
other students as
the interviewers.
Answer their questions.
Get the job!

What teaching vacancies are there in your school district? Ask the personnel officer at the Board of Education for further information. What does he look for in a candidate? Look at a teacher application form. What does the school district think are important teacher qualifications? Put your teacher on the "hot seat." How did he get his job?

M'Choakumchild's Schoolroom
by Charles Dickens

"Now, what I want is, Facts. Teach these boys and girls nothing but Facts. Facts alone are wanted in life. Plant nothing else, and root out everything else. You can only form the minds of reasoning animals upon Facts: nothing else will ever be of any service to them. This is the principle on which I bring up my own children, and this is the principle on which I bring up these children. Stick to Facts, sir!"

The scene was a plain, bare, monotonous vault of a schoolroom, and the speaker's square forefinger emphasized his observations by underscoring every sentence with a line on the schoolmaster's sleeve. The emphasis was helped by the speaker's square wall of a forehead, which had his eyebrows for its base, while his eyes found commodious cellarage in two dark caves, overshadowed by the wall. The emphasis was helped by the speaker's mouth, which was wide, thin, and hard set. The emphasis was helped by the speaker's voice, which was inflexible, dry, and dictatorial. The emphasis was helped by the speaker's hair, which bristled on the skirts of his bald head, a plantation of firs to keep the wind from its shining surface, all covered with knobs, like the crust of a plum pie, as if the head had scarcely warehouseroom for the hard facts stored inside. The speaker's obstinate carriage, square coat, square legs, square shoulders,—nay, his very neckcloth, trained to take him by the throat with an unaccommodating grasp, like a stubborn fact, as it was,—all helped the emphasis.

"In this life, we want nothing but Facts, sir; nothing but Facts!"

The speaker, and the schoolmaster, and the third grown person present, all backed a little, and swept with their eyes the inclined plane of little vessels then and there arranged in order, ready to have imperial gallons of facts poured into them until they were full to the brim. Thomas Gradgrind, sir. A man of realities. A man of facts and calculations. A man who proceeds upon the principle that two and two are four, and nothing over, and who is not to be talked into allowing for anything over. Thomas Gradgrind, sir—peremptorily Thomas—Thomas Gradgrind. With a rule and a pair of scales, and the multiplication table always in his pocket, sir, ready to weigh and measure any parcel of human nature, and tell you exactly what it comes to. It is a mere question of figures, a case of simple arithmetic. You might hope to get some other nonsensical belief into the head of George Gradgrind, or Augustus Gradgrind, or John Gradgrind, or Joseph Gradgrind (all suppositious, nonexistent persons), but into the head of Thomas Gradgrind—no, sir!

In such terms Mr. Gradgrind always mentally introduced himself, whether to his private circle of acquaintance, or to the public in general. In such terms, no doubt, substituting the words "boys and girls," for "sir," Thomas Gradgrind now presented Thomas

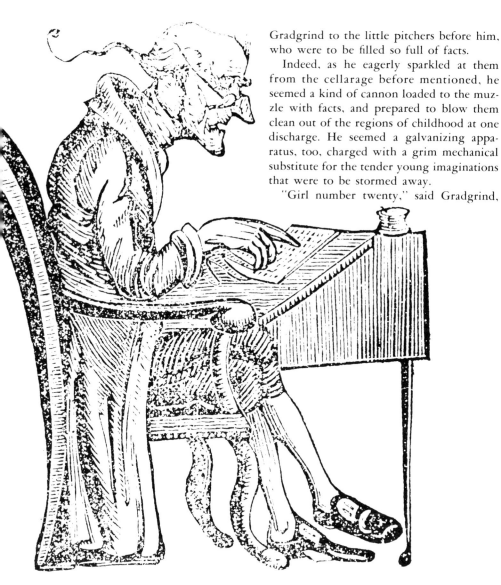

Gradgrind to the little pitchers before him, who were to be filled so full of facts.

Indeed, as he eagerly sparkled at them from the cellarage before mentioned, he seemed a kind of cannon loaded to the muzzle with facts, and prepared to blow them clean out of the regions of childhood at one discharge. He seemed a galvanizing apparatus, too, charged with a grim mechanical substitute for the tender young imaginations that were to be stormed away.

"Girl number twenty," said Gradgrind, squarely pointing with his square forefinger, "I don't know that girl. Who is that girl?"

"Sissy Jupe, sir," explained number twenty, blushing, standing up, and curtseying.

"Sissy is not a name," said Mr. Gradgrind. "Don't call yourself Sissy. Call yourself Cecilia."

"It's father as calls me Sissy, sir," returned the young girl in a trembling voice, and with another curtsey.

"Then he has no business to do it," said Mr. Gradgrind. "Tell him he mustn't. Cecilia Jupe. Let me see. What is your father?"

"He belongs to the horse-riding, if you please, sir."

Mr. Gradgrind frowned, and waved off the objectionable calling with his hand.

"We don't want to know anything about that, here. You mustn't tell us about that, here. Your father breaks horses, don't he?"

"If you please, sir, when they can get any to break, they do break horses in the ring, sir."

"You mustn't tell us about the ring, here. Very well, then. Describe your father as a horsebreaker. He doctors sick horses, I dare say?

"Oh yes, sir."

"Very well, then. He is a veterinary surgeon, a farrier, and horsebreaker. Give me your definition of a horse."

(Sissy Jupe thrown into the greatest alarm by this demand.)

"Girl number twenty unable to define a

horse!" said Mr. Gradgrind, for the general behoof of all the little pitchers. "Girl number twenty possessed of no facts, in reference to one of the commonest of animals! Some boy's definition of a horse. Bitzer, yours."

The square finger, moving here and there, lighted suddenly on Bitzer, perhaps because he chanced to sit in the same ray of sunlight which, darting in at one of the bare windows of the intensely whitewashed room, irradiated Sissy. For, the boys and girls sat on the face of the inclined plane in two compact bodies, divided up the centre by a narrow interval; and Sissy, being at the corner of a row on the sunny side, came in for the beginning of a sunbeam, of which Bitzer, being at the corner of a row on the other side, a few rows in advance, caught the end. But, whereas the girl was so dark-eyed and dark-haired, that she seemed to receive a deeper and more lustrous color from the sun, when it shone upon her, the boy was so light-eyed and light-haired that the self-same rays appeared to draw out of him what little color he ever possessed. His cold eyes would hardly have been eyes, but for the short ends of lashes which, by bringing them into immediate contrast with something paler than themselves, expressed their form. His short-cropped hair might have been a mere continuation of the sandy freckles on his forehead and face. His skin was so unwholesomely deficient in the natural tinge, that he looked as though, if he were cut, he would bleed white.

"Bitzer," said Thomas Gradgrind. "Your definition of a horse."

"Quadruped. Graminivorous. Forty teeth, namely twenty-four grinders, four eyeteeth, and twelve incisive. Sheds coat in the spring; in marshy countries, sheds hoofs, too. Hoofs hard, but requiring to be shod with iron. Age known by marks in mouth." Thus (and much more) Bitzer.

"Now girl number twenty," said Mr. Gradgrind. "You know what a horse is."

She curtseyed again, and would have blushed deeper, if she could have blushed deeper than she had blushed all this time. Bitzer, after rapidly blinking at Thomas Gradgrind with both eyes at once, and so catching the light upon his quivering ends of lashing that they looked like the antennae of busy insects, put his knuckles to his freckled forehead, and sat down again.

The third gentleman now stepped forth. A mighty man at cutting and drying, he was; a government officer; in his way (and in most other people's too), a professed pugilist; always in training, always with a system to force down the general throat like a bolus, always to be heard of at the bar of his little public-office, ready to fight all England. To continue in fistic phraseology, he had a genius for coming up to the scratch, wherever and whatever it was, and proving himself an ugly customer. He would go in and damage any subject whatever with his right, follow up with his left, stop, exchange, counter, bore his opponent (he always fought All England) to the ropes, and fall upon him neatly. He was certain to knock the wind out of common sense, and render that unlucky adversary deaf to the call of time. And he had it in charge from high authority to bring about the great public-office Millennium, when commissioners should reign upon earth.

"Very well," said this gentleman, briskly smiling, and folding his arms. "That's a horse. Now, let me ask you girls and boys, Would you paper a room with representations of horses?"

After a pause, one half of the children cried in chorus, "Yes, sir!" Upon which the other half, seeing in the gentleman's face that Yes was wrong, cried out in chorus, "No, sir!"—as the custom is, in these examinations.

"Of course, No. Why wouldn't you?"

A pause. One corpulent slow boy, with a wheezy manner of breathing, ventured the answer, Because he wouldn't paper a room at all, but would paint it.

"You *must* paper it," said the gentleman, rather warmly.

"You must paper it," said Thomas Gradgrind, "whether you like it or not. Don't tell *us* you wouldn't paper it. What do you mean, boy?"

"I'll explain to you, then," said the gentleman, after another and a dismal pause, "why you wouldn't paper a room with representations of horses. Do you ever see horses walking up and down the sides of rooms in reality—in fact? Do you?"

"Yes, sir!" from one half. "No, sir!" from the other.

"Of course, No," said the gentleman, with an indignant look at the wrong half. "Why, then, you are not to see anywhere, what you don't see in fact; you are not to have anywhere, what you don't have in fact. What is called Taste, is only another name for Fact."

Thomas Gradgrind nodded his approbation.

"This is a new principle, a discovery, a great discovery," said the gentleman. "Now, I'll try you again. Suppose you were going to carpet a room. Would you use a carpet having a representation of flowers upon it?"

There being a general conviction by this time that "No, sir!" was always the right answer to this gentleman, the chorus of No was very strong. Only a few feeble stragglers said Yes: among them Sissy Jupe.

"Girl number twenty," said the gentleman, smiling in the calm strength of knowledge.

Sissy blushed, and stood up.

"So you would carpet your room—or your husband's room, if you were a grown woman, and had a husband—with representations of flowers, would you?" said the gentleman. "Why would you?"

"If you please, sir, I am very fond of flowers," returned the girl.

"And is that why you would put tables and chairs upon them, and have people walking over them with heavy boots?"

"It wouldn't hurt them, sir. They wouldn't crush and wither, if you please, sir. They would be the pictures of what was very pretty and pleasant, and I would fancy—"

"Ay, ay, ay! But you mustn't fancy," cried the gentleman, quite elated by coming so happily to his point. "That's it! You are never to fancy."

"You are not, Cecilia Jupe," Thomas Gradgrind solemnly repeated, "to do anything of that kind."

"Fact, fact, fact!" said the gentleman. And "Fact, fact, fact!" repeated Thomas Gradgrind.

"You are to be in all things regulated and governed," said the gentleman, "by fact. We hope to have, before long, a board of fact, composed of commissioners of fact, who will force the people to be a people of fact, and of nothing but fact. You must discard the word fancy altogether. You have nothing to do with it. You are not to have, in any object of use or ornament, what would be a contradiction in fact. You don't walk upon flowers in fact; you cannot be allowed to walk upon flowers in carpets. You don't find that foreign birds and butterflies come and perch upon your crockery; you cannot be permitted to paint foreign birds and butterflies upon your crockery. You never meet with quadrupeds going up and down walls; you must not have quadrupeds represented upon walls. You must use," said the gentleman, "for all these purposes, combinations and modifications (in primary colors) of mathematical figures which are susceptible of proof and demonstration. This is the new discovery. This is fact. This is taste."

The girl cutseyed, and sat down. She was very young, and she looked as if she were frightened by the matter of fact prospect the world afforded.

"Now, if Mr. M'Choakumchild," said the gentleman, "will proceed to give his first lesson here, Mr. Gradgrind, I shall be happy, at your request, to observe his mode of procedure."

Mr. Gradgrind was much obliged. "Mr. M'Choakumchild, we only wait for you."

So, Mr. M'Choakumchild began in his best manner. He and some one hundred and forty other schoolmasters had been lately turned at the same time, in the same factory, on the same principles, like so many pianoforte legs. He had been put through an immense variety of paces, and had answered volumes of head-breaking questions. Orthography, etymology, syntax, and prosody, biography, astronomy, geography, and general cosmography, the sciences of compound proportion, algebra, land-surveying and levelling, vocal music, and drawing from models, were all at the ends of his ten chilled fingers. He had worked his stony way into Her Majesty's most Honourable Privy Council's Schedule B, and had taken the bloom off the higher branches of mathematics and physical science, French, German, Latin, and Greek.

He knew all about all the Water Sheds of all the world (whatever they are), and all the histories of all the peoples, and all the names of all the rivers and mountains, and all the productions, manners, and customs of all the countries, and all their boundaries and bearings on the two and thirty points of the compass. Ah, rather overdone, M'Choakumchild. If he had only learnt a little less, how infinitely better he might have taught much more!

He went to work in this preparatory lesson, not unlike Morgiana in the Forty Thieves: looking into all the vessels ranged before him, one after another, to see what they contained. Say, good M'Choakumchild. When from thy boiling store, thou shalt fill each jar brim full by-and-by, dost thou think that thou wilt always kill outright the robber Fancy lurking within—or sometimes only maim him and distort him!

Do you recognize this appraoch to teaching? Give examples from your own experience with Gradgrinds or M'Choakumchilds. What attitudes do the teachers hold toward children? What words would we use today for fancy? Do you see fact and fancy as enemies?

From *Beneath the Wheel*
by Hermann Hesse

It is wrong to say that schoolmasters lack heart and are dried-up soulless pedants! No, by no means. When a child's talent which he has sought to kindle suddenly bursts forth, when the boy puts aside his wooden sword, slingshot, bow-and-arrow and other childish games, when he begins to forge ahead, when the seriousness of the work begins to transform the roughneck into a delicate, serious and an almost ascetic creature, when his face takes on an intelligent, deeper and more purposeful expression—then a teacher's heart laughs with happiness and pride. It is his duty and responsibility to control the raw energies and desires of his charges and replace them with calmer, more moderate ideals. What would many happy citizens and trustworthy officials have become but unruly, stormy innovators and dreamers of useless dreams, if not for the effort of their schools? In young beings there is something wild, ungovernable, uncultured which first has to be tamed. It is like a dangerous flame that has to be controlled or it will destroy. Natural man is unpredictable, opaque, dangerous, like a torrent cascading out of uncharted mountains. At the start, his soul is a jungle without paths or order. And, like a jungle, it must first be cleared and its growth thwarted. Thus it is the school's task to subdue and control man with force

and make him a useful member of society, to kindle those qualities in him whose development will bring him to triumphant completion.

How a person views education and a teacher's role depends on how he answers certain questions such as: ''What is the nature of man?'' and ''What is the good life?'' What does Hesse imply as answers? Is he speaking seriously or with tongue-in-cheek? How are the student and teacher seen? How do you like to learn? Will you teach students the way you would like to learn yourself? Will you draw a line between child and adult?

☆☆ THIS ☆☆
is an
English Test

DO <u>NOT</u> CHEAT

You are to ingest all of the facts
on the reverse side of this recept-
acle. You have 30 minutes in which
to do so. At the conclusion of 30
minutes, your instructer will shout:

"Regurgitate the facts!"

This should all go into this bag.

DO NOT BE SLOPPY !

ooooooooooooooooooooo

↓ THE FACTS ↓

1. Hester's Scarlet Letter was
   12 inches high, and weighed
   42 ounces.

2. Silas Marner was a Capricorn
   and had trouble as a child
   with toilet training.

3. Charles Dickens bought his
   quill pens and foolscap from
   a discount office supply shop
   run by E. Scrooge.

4. William Shakespeare's father
   was a butcher and predicted
   that his son would never amount
   to anything.

5. The bridge referred to in the
   poem, "Horatio at the Bridge"
   contained 7,142 board feet of
   douglas fir, and was secured by
   2,131 linear feet of hemp
   lashing.

6. Edgar Allan Poe was a lush.

7. Make a sentence diagram of T.S.
   Eliot's "The Wasteland." (Use
   key below.)

8. Dorothy in "The Wizard of Oz" was
   a junkie. The Tin Woodsman was a
   Narco.

9. "Stuart Little" by E.B. White and
   "Winnie-the-Pooh" are germinal
   works of the pseudo sexual animal
   genre, and contain the key to
   understanding the child's poem,
   "Wichita Vortex Sutra." (A Kansas
   Wheat-Futures epic.)

There Are Fancies

What is a teacher supposed to be? Do you think a teacher should be an entertainer, a computer, a guru, an authority, a friend, a facilitator?

ANSWER TRUE OR FALSE:

If I don't know a teacher, I expect him to be mean

.untrustworthy
a robot
distant
boring

Sir is kind and sir is gentle,
.SIr is strong and sir is mental.

Miss Buss and Miss Beale
Cupid's darts do not feel
How different from us
Miss Beale and Miss Buss.

Mr. MacDonald is a good man,
He goes to church on Sunday.
He prays to God to give him strength
To whip the boys on Monday.

Oh dear, what can the matter be?
Old Miss Proctor's locked in the laboratory
She'll be there from Monday to Saturday.
Nobody cares that she's there.

Pounds, shillings, pence,
Teacher has no sense,
She came to school
To act the fool,
Pounds, shillings, pence.

ANSWER TRUE OR FALSE:

If I don't know a teacher, I expect him to be insecure
absent-minded
an irrelevant intellectual
an effete snob

The "Kid Pinger" by Kris Sagen

Miss Shnossle teaches second grade. She has a secret weapon that a famous scientist invented just for her.

It's called a kid pinger. Whenever a child is bad, all she has to do is push the orange and green button on her nose and a beam comes zooming out.

When the pinger was installed there was a strange reaction in Miss Shnossle's body. She started turning blue. A week later she had purple stripes. Then, her nose grew to be about six inches long.

She had a platform installed in her room so she could pinch the kids better. Pretty soon all the teachers in the world will have a kid pinger. Then the children will start obeying their teachers.

"Instructors' Rebellion"
by William Stimson

Cheney, Wash. (OBS)—Fourteen dissident teachers have barricaded themselves in a science building classroom and transmitted a list of demands to the student body president demanding, among other things, that "intellectualism be given official recognition as an integral part of college life."

The teachers, all members of the English department, are holding an entire English 101 class captive. One of the disruptive teachers said they are prepared to remain in the building "until Dante's Inferno freezes over, lunch notwithstanding."

Among other things, the teachers have demanded that the students they are holding agree to learn something—anything.

In a list of grievances sent to ASB President Mike Murphy, the teachers said the 101 class would be held until each member learned to write a declarative sentence and spell "connoisseur."

Murphy immediately rejected the demand, saying it was unreasonable. He said the other demands are being studied.

Other demands made by the teachers included the setting up of a "meaningful" department of English studies, opening the campus to nonpolitical writers and poets, and elimination of immature freshmen from the campus.

Murphy pointed out to newsmen that the last demand, concerning "immature freshmen," was both redundant and impossible, since there could be no Sweetheart dance without the freshman class.

Murphy sent a letter to the dissidents asking for a meeting to discuss the demands. The teachers graded the letter "C minus" and sent it back.

The student body president told newsmen that the rioting teachers represent only a small minority of the school's teachers.

"The vast majority of our teachers are interested in giving an education. There are only a few, less than 2 percent, who believe they can take academic standards into their own hands," Murphy said.

Meanwhile, the defiant teachers appeared at windows in the building chanting, "Unity! Clarity! Coherence!"

Other teachers gathered outside the science building in support of the English teachers.

Geology instructors threw rocks in the windows to be used as weapons, and political science teachers added copies of Rousseau and Marx. A member of the physical education faculty tossed in a javelin.

One teacher inside the building appeared at the window saying, "Quit helping us and send up some medical supplies!"

When the takeover began the entire campus police force was alerted. He collapsed of exhaustion after trying to form a cordon around the building singlehandedly.

In Olympia, Sen. Marvin Metcow said he will ask for an investigation of the National Literary Guild. He said it is known that all teachers involved in the insurgency are either members of the Literary Guild or sympathetic to its cause.

"This is not an isolated incident. Many of these teachers are known to be intellectuals, and have expressed this anti-American attitude in many ways. J. Edgar Hoover has pointed out it is more than coincidence that they all make regular use of red pencils," Metcow said.

Murphy disputed Metcow's charges. "Only a few of these teachers are hard-core grammarians. The others are excitable adults suffering from an identity trauma," Murphy said.

An undergraduate psychology student who is a recognized authority on teacher unrest gave a similar explanation for the rebellion.

"What is really surprising is that there haven't been more riots among teachers. These clashes will develop whenever communications break down, and it has been clear for decades that teachers cannot communicate with students," he said.

"However," he continued, "this may be changing. Now these teachers are speaking a language any student can understand."

ANSWER TRUE OR FALSE:

I believe that teachers should always be calm and
          moderate
          should always like all stu-
          dents
          should treat all students
          equally
          should have no prejudices
          should put students' feelings
          above his own
          should know all the answers
          should regard learning as
          orderly
          should keep the room quiet
          should be able to help all
          students who need help

What games have you played with teachers
because you expect them to act a certain
way? What games have they played with you
because they expect you to act in a certain
way?

The ideal of the teacher as a flawless moral
exemplar is a devilish trap for the teacher
as well as a burden for the child. I once
had a pupil, Narciso, who was overburdened
by the perfection of adults, and especially,
of teachers. His father demanded he believe
in this perfection as he demanded Narciso
believe in and acquiesce to absolute authority. It was impossible to approach the boy
for his fear and deference. I had terrified
him. He wouldn't work or disobey. He existed frozen in silence. One day he happened to pass by a bar where some other teachers
and I were sitting having beers. He was
crushed; *teachers don't do that.* He believed
so much in what his father and some teachers
wanted him to believe that his world collapsed. He stayed away from school for a
while, then returned. He smiled and I returned the smile. After a while he was at
ease in class and could be himself, delightful
and defiant, sometimes brilliant, often lazy,
an individual reacting in his unique way to
what happened in the classroom.

It is only in the world of Dick and Jane,
Tom and Sally, that the *always* right and
righteous people exist. In a way, most textbooks, and certainly the ones I had to use
in the sixth grade, protect the pure image
of the teacher by showing the child that
somewhere in the ideal world that inspires
books all people are as "good" as the teacher
is supposed to be! It is not insignificant that
it is teachers and not students who select
school readers, nor that, according to a friend
of mine who edits school texts, the books
were written for the teachers and not for
children for this very reason.

From Herbert Kohl, *36 Children*

You are teacher. Stand in the middle of a circle
of chairs.
The chairs represent a student,
another teacher, a parent, a principal,
a member of the community, a board
member.
Play all the parts. Tell the others
what you expect of them. Have them tell
you what they expect of you.
Or have other students play the parts.

Who do you want to be like? Who do you
not want to be like? How many of the men
students are considering teaching kindergarten or primary? How many of the women are
considering teaching college? Why or why
not?

What appears to be operative is a process we cavalierly call identification. The fact of identification is more easily described than explained. It refers to the human tendency to model one's *self* and one's aspirations upon some other person. When we feel we have succeeded in *being like* an identification figure, we derive pleasure from the achievement and, conversely, we suffer when we have *let him down*. Insofar as the identification figure is also *a certain kind of person*—belongs to some category—we extend our loyalties from an individual to a reference group.

In effect, then, identification relates one not only to individuals, but to one's society.

From Jerome S. Bruner, *Toward a Theory of Instruction*

One difference between a student and a teacher is the side of the desk he is on. How different from you are Miss Buss, Miss Beale, Mr. Chips, Our Miss Brooks, Mr. Novak, or the teachers in *Room 222*? Teachers spend most of their time with students rather than with their peers. Is teaching a lonely profession? Are teachers different because of the roles they think they must play? Play The Teacher Game. Should these roles be changed?

THE TEACHER GAME

FILL IN THE BLANKS

A teacher stands in front of the class. A teacher takes attendance. A teacher _____ . A teacher speaks more than students do. A teacher uses a teacher's lounge. A teacher _____ . A teacher grades students. A teacher gets paid for teaching. A teacher sends students to the principal's office. A teacher makes assignments. A teacher _____ . A teacher has yard duty, lunch duty, bus duty, and hall duty. A teacher _____ . A teacher uses the blackboard more than students do. A teacher is called Miss, Mrs., Mr., Dr., or Professor. A teacher dismisses the class. A teacher _____ .

Who sets the rules? Do the rules say anything about what a teacher can do in school? How do schools operate? Who decides what students are in a class or how many, or what books are read or examinations taken, or how students spend their time in school? Have you ever known a teacher who broke the rules? Interview some teachers. What roles do they have to play?

Of Course the Teacher is a moral exemplar —an example of all the confusion, hypocrisy, and indecision, of all the mistakes, as well as the triumphs, of moral man. The children see all this, whatever they pretend to see. Therefore, to be more than an example, to be an educator—someone capable of helping lead the child through the labyrinth of life—the teacher must be honest to the children about his mistakes and weaknesses; he must be able to say that he is wrong or sorry, that he hadn't anticipated the results of his remarks and regretted them, or hadn't understood what a child meant. It is the teacher's struggle to be moral that excites his pupils; it is honesty, not rightness, that moves children.

From Herbert Kohl, *36 Children*

Commencement

I stand alone here
   Stand alone
Hand on the brown oak desk
   And wait.

I stand alone and wait
   Wait alone
Wait for the bell to ring
   Them here.

I stand alone and watch
   Watch them come
in twos and threes and ones
   And sit.

I sit alone and call
   Call their names
And hope someone will hear
   Me call.

I sit alone and feel
   Feel the start
The kick and thrust and pain
   Of us.

Bonnie Rubinstein

There Are Problems

"The First Year" by Sonny Decker
from *The Empty Spoon*

Life is not a bold of cherries
It's a bold of love and
hate and misunderstanding

My sixth-period class was weird. Five months of living with them had provided lots of time to get to know the kids, since there were only thirty-five on roll, with about twenty showing up. But they were a strange bunch, and they lacked that feeling of group-ness that classes usually develop. These eleventh graders had somehow remained isolated from one another. There was no class personality.

Haughty Mae Hall was a toughy. She was tall and lean, and was the only girl in school who wore slacks. Sometime during the year, she'd had her front teeth knocked out, and she didn't even care. She was mean once in a while, but not often, and she did beautiful work. So we got along OK.

Algy Brown was the closest thing I ever had to a discipline problem. It figures, with a name like Algy. He never shut his mouth, and took great pride in his ability to disrupt a class in twenty seconds flat. He had a great sense of humor, and I always enjoyed him —except when he hurt my feelings with a nasty crack. He never did any work. He just sat next to Bernice and made noise. And Bernice went along with him, except when we did dictionary work or some other dull, rote thing. She liked that kind of stuff. Ber-nice was mysterious. Her words and expressions were guarded, and she kept everyone at a distance. She was unusually bright. But she kept failing, because the only stuff she'd turn in was dictionary work.

The fat, ugly kid in the back of the room was Diana Ricks. All she did was suck her thumb. And all Robert Jones ever did was intimidate me, with his quiet, searching eyes.

Elvira Jackman was really beautiful, when she did something with her hair. She wore the same clothes every day, all year. She used to hang around my desk before class and tell me secrets—like Mary Ward likes girls. But since I liked Mary Ward, I didn't care. She was the only A student in the class. And the only thing about her that bothered me was her stray eye. It sure was ugly.

One day before class, I heard a commotion in the hall outside my room, and went out to see what was going on. Mary and Elvira had squared off and were obviously ready to tear each other apart. When boys fight, there's little commotion. They just cut each other and go away. But the girls are vicious. I was glad I knew both these girls. All I had to do was get them into class, and we'd talk about it. I walked over to them and suggested they come into the room. They never took their eyes off each other. But they both began to talk at once—accusing each other and telling me to move away. I wasn't scared—after all, they were my girls. But I was awed at the strength and hatred they generated. A crowd began to gather. Once they had an audience, they had to perform. The girls came to watch because they love a good fight. The boys came in the hope that clothes would be ripped off and they'd get a good look at some bare body. The hall was packed.

I spotted someone I knew in the crowd and told her to get some teachers to clear the corridor. I couldn't understand why they hadn't come already—the noise was more than enough to attract attention. After an endless wait, the girl returned, saying none of the teachers on the hall would help—they'd closed their doors. My God, how can a bunch of adults be afraid of kids? And how can they find it in themselves to ignore what's obviously an emergency situation?

"Come on, Mrs. Decker," Mary was saying. "I don't want to hurt you. You better get away."

"Please come with me," I begged. "You're only going to get yourself in trouble."

"I'm gonna kill that bitch," Elvira was wailing. Her eyes were full of tears and fury. I thought I saw the point of a can opener in her hand.

The crowd was pressing in on us. I couldn't just stand there forever, holding things in limbo. The mob in the hall was as dangerous as the girls they encircled. So I backed out and ran to the phone in my room. That was when the fight started. Before too long, there were police and male teachers breaking up the mob. I couldn't see what was happening inside the circle. I could

only try to get kids on the periphery to go to class. That in itself was a difficult task. I felt I had to be superpolite. It would have been stupid to play authoritarian—I didn't have one shred of authority, and we all knew it.

By the time I got to the girls, they were different people. Their hair stuck out from their heads in ugly clumps. Mary's blouse was torn to shreds. Elvira was bleeding from somewhere on her face. And she was hysterical. Each girl was being held against a wall by two men. Their eyes were wild. The hall was quiet now, and I spoke to each of them, trying to calm them. They quieted a little. The fight was over.

It was then that Morris started. Morris Feldman is fat and dumb. He teaches science, I think, and people talk about his tendency to "mishandle" situations. He was one of the men holding Elvira. It seemed that he felt personally threatened in some way by what had happened. Or maybe he just hates kids. Or blacks. He glared at her with his bulgy eyes, and his puffy mouth called her an animal. He terrified me. The biggest trouble with people is that they're people. Few of us ever deal with trying situations without expressing our own feelings. It's hard to be a professional. But Morris never even tried. Before I knew it, he'd grabbed Elvira by the hair and dragged her down a flight of steps. She was mad with fury, screaming and

flailing her arms and legs. He just pulled her down, hair first. I chased them.

"For God's sake," I was screaming, "will you let her stand still for a minute—will you treat her like a human being!"

"Well Goddamn it—" he was all purpley—"if you're so damn smart, you take her!" He grabbed the girl by the shoulders and threw her at me. I nearly fell. When he'd stormed off, Elvira and I sat down on the step and shook. The girl's hysteria had vanished when she saw me threatened. She just kept crying and saying, "It's all right—don't worry—it's all right."

A teaching aide took Elvira to wash her face before she went to the discipline office. My department head found me on the steps and told me to make a report of the fight to the vice principal. Someone would cover my class.

I wanted to cry, but I was too embarrassed. I'd all but forgotten the fight by then. I just kept seeing that hideous, fat bully brutalizing my kid. As I approached the vice principal's office another science teacher stopped me. He acted quiet and a little strange.

"I don't know what you're going to say in there," he began. "But if you're smart, you won't mention what happened after the fight. Unless you want to press charges, of course. And things could get unpleasant if you did that." He walked away. I didn't know what the hell was going on. I was shaking like mad.

I never got to the vice principal's office.

The Disciplinarian called me into her office to report on the girls. Mary and Elvira were sitting on opposite sides of the room. The woman said there was some question about weapons, and had I seen a can opener in Elvira's possession. She explained that both girls would be suspended for fighting, but that if there were weapons, they would be sent to jail.

I said I couldn't be sure I'd seen anything. She didn't believe me, but that was all right. Again, I wanted to cry. It was nerves. I can cope during a crisis, but I fall apart afterward. The girls said they were sorry I had to be involved, and that they wouldn't make any more trouble. I said I didn't expect them to, and went back to class.

Algy Brown was absent, so there was no comic relief at all. The kids are very sensitive to my moods, and I just couldn't talk. I sat at my desk, while the kids squirmed. I'd never behaved that way, and they didn't know what to do with me.

Haughty played with the cuff on her pants, and the others watched one another and me. Diana just sucked her thumb. Bernice read a dictionary. The bell finally rang.

From then on, I felt the class was more of a unit. Lovida Barr began to talk to Diana, and perhaps Diana sucked her thumb a little less. Haughty was pleasant to Elvira and Mary, because they'd proved they could really fight. But Robert Jones was as stern and pensive as ever, and Raymond Tibbs still sat next to the window alone. I had never been able to get him to speak. He'd never smiled.

His work, what little he did, was awful. He spelled his name differently every time he wrote it. He seemed like the loneliest guy in the whole world.

Later in the term, he began to sleep in class. I thought it was a rude way of telling me what a bore I was. Then I found out that he slept in subways at night, because he couldn't face going home. There were thirteen hungry kids there. His father was an alcoholic. He hadn't seen his mother in two years. He spent his afternoons stealing food at supermarkets, but they were getting wise to him. If he went home empty-handed, his father would beat him. So he slept in subways.

What impression do you get of Sunny Decker as a person? What style of teacher does she seem to be? "My God, how can a bunch of adults be afraid of kids?" What's your experience? "It would have been stupid to play authoritarian—I didn't have one shred of authority and we all knew it." What does she mean? How "real" is she? How ideal? What happened to bring this class together? Ask some teachers to recall incidents from their first teaching year

"A Teacher's Problem"
by Mary Greer

One year I applied for a teaching position in San Francisco. I was assigned a sixth grade in a ghetto area. Concerned with keeping the classroom orderly and quiet, I kept the students busy. I found out what textbooks I would have, took a copy of each book home, set up a daily schedule, and kept one page ahead of the students. I watched teachers in nearby rooms, asked questions, got ideas for "seatwork," which is a word for dittoed material that keeps students busy, while the teacher runs from group to group. There weren't enough books to go around and most of the students had difficulty reading them. We marched through the weeks page after page, exercise after exercise, book after book. We worked hard with time out now and then for a classroom game. "Simon Says" was a favorite. I wasn't mean but I kept control, and I taught the class as a unit, rather than in groups or individually, whenever possible. The fast workers always had more free time than the others. I shuffled books, shuffled papers, shuffled students. We enjoyed very little together. Most of the day seemed to be spent lining students up, waiting for quiet, escorting the double line down two flights of stairs to the playground, where the students could run and scream for ten minutes. Then the bell would ring for lineup, and we'd wait for the quietest class to enter the building first. As I look back, I wonder why the children returned to their classes at all. There seemed to be so little for them there. I remember dreading going to school in the mornings. I felt tense and harassed, and I yelled a lot.

At the teachers' meetings the principal handed down the orders, and we went back to our classes and passed the orders down to the students. The students fought back, and the classrooms became daily battlegrounds. I finally realized it was a losing battle for both students and teachers, so I quit. I broke my teaching contract, which is like breaking a marriage vow. I was really depressed and defeated by this experience.

What could have made a difference for this teacher and students? Some of our most embarrassing experiences happen in school. How could these teachers have made their classrooms less threatening for their students? More rewarding?

1. One of the situations that happened to me during my early school days was reading aloud in class and not being able to pronounce some of the words correctly. I was criticized so terribly for it by the teacher and my classmates, that I haven't liked reading since, unless I'm interested in it. This incident has caused me to be slower in some of my classes, because I am not able to comprehend and retain much of my reading.

2. Back in the fifth grade I had to make an oral report, but I really didn't want to get up in front of the class. I was very scared. I remember staying home and finishing the report, hoping that I would miss my turn to give the report. But to my surprise the next day when I returned, I found I still had to give my presentation. I wished at that very moment I could have suddenly disappeared from the class. I think I remember this situation, because it was the first time that I really felt scared in class. Elementary school up to that point was really a lot of fun. I still feel uneasy about speaking in front of large groups of people. I think this is a handicap for me, but I can't bring myself to speak out.

3. In the third grade we learned times tables. The teacher called on students to come to the board and write answers to the problems. She called on just about everyone around me. I was so excited that when she called on me, I got up to do the problem and forgot the answer. I was so ashamed. After a while I sat back down.

4. I remember using crib notes on a chemistry test. As we passed in our papers, the redhaired boy next to me told the teacher I had cheated on the test. I wanted to sink through the floor. I really had liked that boy.

Have your teachers treated you the way they'd like to be treated themselves? How can the teacher establish a cooperative classroom atmosphere in a competitive school system? What can students do to change things? Are you part of the problem or the solution?

The Problem Of "Luther"
by Jay Neugeboren

Luther arrived at Booker T. Washington Junior High School (Columbus Avenue and 107th Street, Manhattan) in September of 1955, six months before I did. I met him at the end of February, the third week I taught there, when one of the assistant principals asked me to cover the cafeteria during fifth period for a teacher who had to be at a conference. "Good luck with the animals," I remember him saying.

I was on my guard when I entered the cafeteria; perhaps even a trifle scared. The stories I had been hearing in the teachers' lounge had prepared me to expect anything. During the winter months the students were not allowed to leave the lunchroom and the results of keeping them penned in—the fights, the food-throwing, the high-pitched incessant chattering in Spanish, the way the Negro and Puerto Rican boys and girls chased each other around the tables—such things did, I had to admit, give the room a zoo-like quality.

The day I was assigned, however, was a Catholic holy day and many of the students were absent. Those who remained filled a little less than half of the large room and though they were noisy, it was relatively easy to keep them in order. Luther sat at a table by himself, near the exit to the food-line. Occasionally, I noticed, a few boys would come and sit next to him. The third time I patrolled his area, however, his table was empty and he stopped me.

"Hey, man," he said, poking me in the arm to get my attention, "you new here?"

He had a stack of about ten cookies in his other hand and he put one into his mouth as he waited for an answer. When I told him that I was not new, he nodded and looked at me. "You have any trouble yet?"

"No," I said, as sternly as possible. Despite my feelings of sympathy for the students, I knew that if I ever hoped to get anywhere with them, I had to appear tough and confident. "No," I repeated, almost, I recall, as if I were challenging him. "I haven't."

Luther cocked his head to one side then and smiled slowly. "You will," he said, and went back to his cookies.

In the teachers' lounge, the first time I told the story, somebody asked if the boy who had stopped me was a little Negro kid, very black, with a slight hunchback. I said he was. The teachers laughed. "That's Luther," one of them said.

"He's batty," said another. "Just leave him be."

I repeated the story endlessly. It was the first anecdote of my teaching experience that excited admiration and some sort of reaction from those I told it to, and this was important to me then. I had no more direct encounters with Luther that term, though I did see him in the halls, between classes. I always smiled at him and he would smile back—or at least I thought he did. I could never be sure. This bothered me, especially the first time it happened. Through my retelling of the story, I realized, he had become so real to me, so much a part of my life that I think I took it for granted that our encounter had assumed equal significance in his life. The possibility that he had not even repeated the story to a single one of his friends disturbed me.

Once or twice during the term I spotted him wandering around the halls while classes were in session, slouching down the corridor, his body pressed against the tile walls. When I asked the other teachers if he was known for cutting classes, they told me again to just leave him be—that the guidance counselor had suggested that the teachers let him do what he wanted to. He was harmless, they said, *if* you left him alone. Those teachers who had him in their classes agreed with the guidance counselor. Left alone, he didn't annoy them. When he wanted to, he worked feverishly—and did competent work; but when he did not want to work he would either sit and stare, or just get up, walk out of the room, and wander around the building. He was, they concluded, a mental case.

I returned to Booker T. Washington Junior High School the following September, and Luther turned up in one of my English classes. He had changed. He was no longer small, having grown a good five inches over the summer, and he was no longer quiet. When classwork bored him now he would stand up, and instead of leaving the room, would begin telling stories. Just like that. He had a favorite topic, too—his cousin Henry who had epilepsy, Willie Mays, what was on sale at the supermarket, the football team he played on, the stories in the latest *Blackhawk* comic book. When he ran out of stories, he would pull *The National Enquirer* out of his back pocket and begin reading from it, always starting with an item in the "Personals" columns that had caught his eye. I never knew what to do. When I would yell at him to sit down and be quiet, he would wave his hand at me, impatiently, and continue. Moreover, no expression on his face, nothing he ever said, indicated that he thought he was doing anything wrong. An hour after disrupting a class, if I would see him in the corridor, he would give me a big smile and a hello. After a while, of course, I gave up even trying to interrupt him. I listened with the other students—laughing, fascinated, amazed.

I tried to remember some of his stories, but when I retold them they never seemed interesting, and so I purposely gave Luther's class a lot of composition work, trying to make the topics as imaginative as possible—with the hope, of course, that he would use one of them to let loose. But all of the topics,

he declared, were "stupid" and he refused to write on any of them. Then, when I least expected it, when I assigned the class a "How To—" composition, he handed one in. It was typewritten on a piece of lined notebook paper, single-spaced, beginning at the very top of the page and ending just at the first ruled line. It was titled: "How To Steal Some Fruits":

How To Steal Some Fruits, by Luther
Go to a fruit store and when the fruitman isn't looking take some fruits. Then run. When the fruitman yells "Hey you stop taking those fruits" run harder. That is how to steal some fruits.

The next day he sat quietly in class. When I looked at him, he looked down at his desk. When I called on him to answer a question, he shrugged and looked away. At three o'clock, however, no more than five seconds after I had returned from escorting my official class downstairs, he bounded into my room, full of life, and propped himself up on the edge of my desk.
"Hey man," he said. "How'd you like my composition? It was deep, wasn't it?"
"Deep?"
"Deep, swift, *cool*—you know."
"I liked it fine," I said, laughing.
"Ah, don't put me on, man—how *was* it?"
"I liked it," I repeated, my hands clasped in front of me. "I mean it."
His face lit up. "You mean it? I worked

hard on it, Mister Carter. I swear to God I did." It was the first time, I remember, that he had ever addressed me by my name. He stopped and wiped his mouth. "How'd you like the typing? Pretty good, huh?"
"It was fine."
"Christ, man," he said, stepping down from my desk and moving to the blackboard. He picked up a piece of chalk and wrote his name, printing it in capital letters. "How come you so tight? Why don't you loosen up? I ain't gonna do nothing. I just want to know about my composition. That's all."
I felt I could reach him, talk to him. I wanted to—had wanted to for some time, I realized, but he was right. I was tight, uncomfortable, embarrassed. "Where'd you get a typewriter?" I offered.
He smiled. "Where I get fruits," he replied, then laughed and clapped his hands. I must have appeared shocked, for before I could say anything, he was shaking his head back and forth. "Oh, man," he said. "You are really deep. I swear. You really are." He climbed onto my desk again. "You mind talking?"
"No," I said.
"Good. Let me ask you something—you married?"
"No," I said. "Do you think I should be married?"
"It beats stealing fruits," he said, and

laughed again. His laugh was loud and harsh and at first it annoyed me, but then his body began rocking back and forth as if his comment had set off a chain of jokes that he was telling himself silently, and before I knew it I was laughing with him.

"I really liked the composition," I said. "In fact, I hope you don't mind, but I've already read it to some of the other teachers."

"No shit."

"They thought it was superb."

"It's superb," he said, shaking his head in agreement. "Oh, it's superb, man," he said, getting up again and walking away. His arms and legs moved in different directions and he seemed so loose that when he turned his back to me and I noticed the way his dirty flannel shirt was stretched tightly over his misshapen back, I was surprised—as if I'd noticed it for the first time. He walked around the room, muttering to himself, tapping on desks with his fingertips, and then he headed for the door. "I'm superb," he said. "So I be rolling on my superb way home—."

"Stay," I said.

He threw his arms apart. "You win!" he declared. "I'll stay." He came back to my desk, looked at me directly, then rolled his eyes and smiled. "People been telling stories to you about me?"

"No."

"None?" he questioned, coming closer.

"All right," I said. "Some—."

"That's all right," he said, shrugging it

off. He played with the binding of a book that was on my desk. Then he reached across and took my grade book. I snatched it away from him and he laughed again, "Oh man," he exclaimed. "I am just so restless!—You know what I mean?"

He didn't wait for an answer, but started around the room again. The pockets of his pants were stuffed and bulging, the cuffs frayed. The corner of a red and white workman's handkerchief hung out of a back pocket. He stopped in the back of the room, gazed into the glass bookcase, and then turned to me and leaned back. "You said to stay—what you got to say?"

The question was in my mind, and impulsively I asked it: "Just curious—do you remember me from last year?"

"Sure," he said, and turned his back to me again. He looked in the bookcase, whirled around and walked to the side of the room, opening a window. He leaned out and just as I was about to say something to him about it, he closed it and came back to the front of the room. "Man," he exclaimed, sitting on my desk again. "Were you ever scared that day! If I'd set off a cherry bomb you'd have gone through the fan." He put his face closer to mine. "Man, you were scared green!"

Was I scared of you, Luther?" I asked, looking straight into his eyes.

"Me? Nah. Nothing to be scared of." He

hopped off the desk and wiped his name off the blackboard with the palm of his hand; then he started laughing to himself. He looked at me, over his shoulder. "Bet I know what you're thinking now," he said.

"Go ahead—."

"You're thinking you'd like to *help* a boy like me. Right? You're getting this big speech ready in your head about—."

"No," I interrupted. "I wasn't."

He eyed me suspiciously. "You sure?"

"I'm sure."

"Not even with compositions? Oh man, if you'd help me with compositions, before we'd be through with me, I'd be typing like a whiz." He banged on a desk with his palms, and then his fingers danced furiously on the wood as he made clicking noises inside his mouth. "Ding!" he said, swinging the carriage across. "Ain't it fun to type!"

"Okay," I said. "Okay. Maybe I was thinking that I would like to help you."

"I knew it, man," he said, to himself. "I just knew it."

"You have a good mind, Luther—much better than you let on."

"I do, I do," he muttered, chuckling. I stood up and went to the closet to get my coat. "Okay. What do I get if I work for you?" he asked.

I shrugged. "Nothing, maybe. I can't promise anything."

"I *like* that, man," he said.

"Could you call me Mister Carter?" I asked, somewhat irritably. "I don't call you, 'hey, you'—."

"Okay, Mister Carter," he said. He took my coat sleeve. "Let me help you on with your coat, Mister Carter."

We walked out of the room and I locked the door. "You ain't a *real* social worker like the others," he commented as we started down the stairs. He held the door open for me. "I do like that." I nodded.

"Playing it close to the vest again, huh? Tight-mouthed."

"Just thinking," I said.

When we were outside he asked me what he had to do.

"For what?" I asked.

"To get you to help me to be somebody, to educate myself—all that stuff."

"Do what you want to do." I said. "Though you might start by doing your homework. Then we'll see—."

"I know," he said, cocking his head to one side again. "If I play ball with you you'll play ball with me. Right? Okay, okay. I know."

Then he was gone, running down the street, his arms spread wide as if he were an airplane, a loud siren-like noise rising and falling from him as he disappeared from view.

The next few months were without doubt the most satisfying to me of any during the eight years I've been a teacher. Luther worked like a fiend. He was bright, learned quickly, and was not really that far behind. He did his homework, he paid attention in class, he studied for tests, and he read books.

That was most important. On every book he read I asked him to write a book report: setting, plot, theme, characters, and his opinion of the book—and once a week, on Thursday afternoons, we would get together in my room for a discussion. During the remainder of the term he must have gone through at least forty to fifty books. Most of them had to do with sports, airplanes, and insects. All the reports came to me typed, and on some he drew pictures—"illustrations" he called them, which, he claimed, would be a help to me in case I had not read the book.

When we would finish talking about books, I would help him with his other subjects, and his improvement was spectacular. I looked forward to my sessions with him, to his reports, to just seeing him—yet from day to day, from moment to moment, I always expected him to bolt from me, and this pleased me. Every time he came to me for a talk I was truly surprised.

When the term ended he asked if I would continue to help him. I said I would. He was not programmed for any of my English classes during the spring term, but we kept up our weekly discussions. As the weather improved, however, he read less and less; I didn't want him to feel as if he *had* to come see me every Thursday, and so, about a week before the opening of the baseball season, I told him that I thought he had reached the point where he could go it alone. "When you feel like talking, just come knocking—" I said. "We don't need a schedule." He seemed relieved, I thought, and I was proud that I had had the sense to release him from any obligation he might have felt.

Then, suddenly, I didn't see him anywhere for three weeks. I asked his home-room teacher about him and she said she hadn't seen him either; she had sent him a few postcards, but had received no reply. That very night—it was almost as if he had been there listening, I thought—he telephoned me at home.

"Is this Mister Carter? This is Luther here."

"Hi, Luther," I said.

"I looked you up in the telephone book. You mind me calling you at home?"

"No, no. I don't mind."

"Okay," he said, breathing hard. "I just wanted to let you know not to worry about me because I'm not in school. Okay?"

"Sure." I said. "Sure."

"I had some things to take care of—you know?"

"Sure," I said.

"Man, you *know* you're itching to ask me *what?*" He laughed. "You are deep. I'll be back Monday."

That was all. On Monday, as he had promised, he returned to school and came to visit me in my room at three o'clock. We talked for a while about the way the pennant race was going, and then he said, "Okay, let's cut the jazz, man. I got something to say to you." He seemed very intense about it and I told him that I was listening carefully. He pointed a finger at me. "Now, we stopped our sessions, right?"

"Right," I said.

"And the day after we stopped, I began to play the hook for three straight weeks, right?"

"Right."

"Okay. Now you can tell me it ain't so, but I'll bet you'll be thinking it was your fault. It ain't. If you want the truth, I ain't done a stick of work all term for *any* teacher—so don't go thinking that I stopped being a good student cause we stopped our meetings."

He let out a long breath. "I'm glad you told me," I said.

"Shit, man," he said, getting up and going to the door. "Don't *say* anything, huh? Why you got to *say* something all the time?" He came toward me. "*Why?*" He was almost screaming and I slid my chair back from the desk. He shook his head frantically. "Why, man?" he said. He reached into his side-pocket and I started to stand up. Abruptly, he broke into laughter. "Oh man, you are deep! You are just so deep!" He clapped his hands and laughed at me some

more. "Ra-ta-tat-tat!" he said as he banged on a desk. "You're real sweet, man! Just so sweet! Ra-ta-tat-tat! Comin' down the street!" He sat down in one of the seats. "But don't worry none. I got seven liberry cards now and books growing out the ceiling. I got a liberry card for Luther King and one for Luther Queen and one for Luther Prince and one for Luther Jones and one for Luther Smith and one for Luther Mays and one for Luther B. Carter." He banged on the top of the desk with his fist, then drummed with his fingers again. "But don't you worry none —ra-ta-tat-tat—just don't you worry—."

"I'm not," I said.

"That's all," he said, and dashed out of the room.

He attended classes regularly for about two weeks and then disappeared again for a week. He returned for a few days, stayed away, returned. The pattern continued. In the halls when we saw each other he would always smile and ask if I was worrying and I would tell him I wasn't. Once or twice, when he was absent, he telephoned me at home and asked me what was new at school. He got a big charge out of this. Then another time, I remember, he came riding through the schoolyard on a bicycle during sixth period, when I was on patrol. "Don't report me, man!" he yelled and rode right back out, waving and shouting something in Spanish that made everybody laugh.

Near the end of May, the assistant principal in charge of the eighth grade called

me into his office. He knew I was friendly with Luther, he said, and he thought that I might talk to the boy. For the past six or seven months, he told me, Luther had been in and out of juvenile court. "Petty thefts," the assistant principal explained. I wasn't surprised; Luther had hinted at this many times. I had never pressed him about it, however, not wanting to destroy our relationship by lecturing him. The assistant principal said he didn't care whether I said anything to Luther or not. In fact, he added, he would have been just as happy to get rid of him—but that before he was shipped off to a 600-school or put away somewhere else, he wanted to give me an opportunity to do what I could. More for me, he said, than for Luther.

About a week after this, on a Friday, Luther telephoned me.

"How've you been?" I asked.

"Superb, man," he said. "Hey listen—we ain't been seeing much of each other lately, have we?"

"No—."

"No. Okay. Listen—I got two tickets to see the Giants play tomorrow. You want to come?" I didn't answer immediately. "Come on—yes or no—tickets are going fast—."

"I'd like to," I said. "Yes. Only—only I was wondering where you got the money for the tickets?" I breathed out, glad I had said it.

Luther just laughed. "Oh man, you're not gonna be like that, are you? You been listening to too many stories again. That judge from the court must of been gassing with you. Tell you what—you come to the game and I'll tell you where I got the tickets. A deal?"

"A deal."

"Meet you in front of the school at 11 o'clock—I like to get there early to see Willie go through batting practice. Batting practice—that's more fun than the game, sometimes. You know?"

He was waiting for me when I got there a few minutes before 11 the following day. "Let's go," he said, flourishing the tickets. "But don't ask me now, man—let's enjoy the game first. Okay?"

I did enjoy the game. The Giants were playing the Cardinals and to Luther's delight, Willie Mays had one of his better days, going three-for-four at bat, and making several brilliant plays in the field. For most of the game, I was truly relaxed. Along about the eighth inning, however, I began to think about the question again—to wonder when would be the best time to ask it. Luther, it seemed, had forgotten all about it. The Giants were winning 5–2.

"Oh man," he said. "If only that Musial don't do something, we're home free. Look at Willie!" he exclaimed. "Ain't he the greatest that ever lived. He is just so graceful! You know? How you like to see a team of Willie Mayses out there? Wow!" Wes Westrum, the Giant catcher, grounded out, short to first, and the eighth inning was over. "One to go, one to go," Luther said. Then he jabbed me in the arm with his finger. "Hey, listen—I been thinking. Instead of an All-Star game every year between the leagues, what they ought to do one year is have the white guys against our guys. What you think?"

I shrugged. "I don't know," I said.

"Sure," he said. "Listen—we got Willie in center. Then we put Aaron in right and Doby in left. He's got the raw power. Some outfield, huh? Then we got Campy catching and Newcombe pitching. You can't beat that. That Newcombe—he's a mean son of a bitch, but he throws. Okay. I been thinking about this a long time—." He used his fingers to enumerate. He was excited, happy. "At first base we put Luke Easter, at second—Junior Gilliam, at short—Ernie Banks, and at third base we bring in old Jackie Robinson just to give the team a little class—you know what I mean? Man, what a line-up! Who could you match it with?"

When I said I didn't know, Luther eyed me suspiciously. "C'mon—Musial, Mantle, Williams, Spahn—you name 'em and I'll match 'em, man for man, your guys against ours." He stopped and cheered as a Cardinal popped out to Whitey Lockman at first. "What's the matter—don't you like the idea? Ha! Face it, man, we'd wipe up the field with you. Swish! Swish!" He laughed and slapped me on the knee. "Hey, I know what's bugging you, I bet—." He leaned toward me, cupping his hand over his mouth, and whispered in my ear. "Tell the truth now, would you have ever offered to help me if I wasn't colored?"

"Would I—?" I stopped. "Sure," I said. "Of course I would. Of course—."

Luther smiled; triumphantly, dubiously. "Look," I said. "As long as we're asking questions, let me ask you something."

"About the tickets, right?"

"No," I said. "Forget the tickets. No long lectures, either. Just a question. Just one: how come you steal?"

"Oh man," he said, laughing. "That's an easy one!—Because I'm not getting what I want and when you don't get what you want, man, you got to take. Don't you know that?"

I stared at him, not sure I had heard right. He winked at me. "Enjoy the ballgame, man! Say hey, Willie!" he shouted, as Mays caught a fly ball, bread-basket style, for the second out. "Ain't he the sweetest!"

A minute later the game was over and the players were racing across the field toward the clubhouse in center field, trying to escape the fans who scrambled after them.

"They won't get Willie," Luther said. "He's too swift, too swift."

When we were outside I thanked Luther and told him how much I had enjoyed the game. "How about a Coke or something?" I offered.

"Nah," he said. "I got things to do." He extended his hand quickly and I shook it, the first time we had ever done that. "Okay. You go get spiffed up and get a wife. Time you were married." He tossed his head back and laughed. "Ain't you married yet? No, no. *Smile*, man—how you gonna get a wife, never smiling." He started away, through the crowd. "Stay loose," he called back. "Don't steal no fruits."

I never questioned him again about stealing, but even if I had wanted to, I wouldn't have had much opportunity. He did not come to see me very often the rest of that year. When he returned to school in September of 1958 for his last year of junior high school, he had grown again. But not up. He never did go higher than the five-five or five-six he had reached by that time. He had taken up weightlifting over the summer, however, and his chest, his neck, his arms—they had all broadened incredibly. Instead of the dirty cotton and flannel shirts he had worn the two previous years, he now walked through the halls in laundry-white T-shirts, the sleeves rolled up to the shoulder, his powerful muscles exposed. There were always a half-dozen Negro boys following him around now also and they all dressed the way he did—white T-shirts, black chino pants, leather wrist straps, and—hanging from their necks on pieces of string—miniature black skulls.

The guidance counselor for the ninth grade came to me one day early in the term and asked me if I could give him any evidence against Luther. He claimed that Luther and his gang were going around the school, beating and torturing those students who refused to "loan" them money. All of the students, he said, were afraid to name Luther. "The kid's a born sadist," he added. I told him I didn't know anything.

The term progressed and the stories and rumors increased. I was told that the police in Luther's neighborhood were convinced that he and his gang were responsible for a series of muggings that had occurred. I tried not to believe it, but Luther all but gave me conclusive proof one afternoon, right before Christmas. He came into my room at three o'clock, alone, and said he had something for me. He said he trusted me not to tell anybody about it or show it to anyone. I said I wouldn't.

"Okay, man—here it is—." His eyes leapt around the room, frenzied, delirious. He took a little card from his wallet. "You might need this sometime—but don't ask me no questions. Ha! And don't you worry none.

I'm doing okay. Expanding all the time. Don't you worry." I took the card from him. "See you now, Mister Carter. See you, see you."

He left and I looked at the card. Across the top was printed: THE BLACK AVENGERS, and below it was written: "Don't touch this white man. He's okay." It was signed by Luther and under his name he had drawn a skull and crossbones. I put the card in my wallet.

In January, to no one's great surprise, Luther was sent away to reform school in upstate New York. I was never exactly clear about the precise event that had led to it—the policeman assigned to our school said it had to do with brutally beating an old man; Luther's friends said it had to do with getting caught in a gang war. They claimed the fight was clean but that the cops had framed Luther. There was nothing in the papers, Luther had not contacted me, and I did not find out about it all until he had already been shipped off.

I received a postcard from him that summer. It was brief.

I hate it here. I can't say anymore or they'll beat shit out of me. I hate it. I'm reading some. I'll visit you when I get out and we'll have a session.

I answered the card with a letter. I told him I was sorry about where he was and that I'd be glad to talk to him whenever he wanted. I gave him some news of the school and included some current baseball clippings. I asked him if there was anything he needed and if there was anybody in his family he wanted me to get in touch with. I told him that in return for the time he'd taken me to the baseball game I had ordered a subscription to *Sport* magazine for him.

He replied with another postcard.

Visiting day this summer is August 21. I'd like for you to come.

When I arrived, he seemed glad to see me, but I remember that he was more polite than he had ever been before, and more subdued. I wondered, at the time, if they were giving him tranquilizers. I was only allowed an hour with him and we spent most of that time just walking around the grounds—the school was a work-farm reformatory—not saying anything.

The visit, I could tell, was a disappointment to him. I don't know what he expected of me, but whatever it was, I didn't provide it. I wrote him a letter when I got home, telling him I had enjoyed seeing him and that I'd be glad to come again if he wanted

me to. He didn't answer it, and I heard no more from him for a year and a half.

Then one day in the spring of 1961, just about the time of the Bay of Pigs invasion of Cuba, I remember, he popped into my room at school. He looked horrible. His face was unshaven, his clothes were filthy and ragged, his eyes were glazed. Underneath his clothes, his body had become flabby and he bent over noticeably when he walked. At first I didn't recognize him.

When I did, I was so glad to see him, I didn't know what to do. "Luther—for crying out loud!" I said, standing up and shaking his hand. "How the hell are you?"

He smiled at me. "I'm superb, man—can't you tell from looking at me?" He laughed then, and I laughed with him.

"You've gotten older," I said.

"Past sixteen," he said. "That means I don't got to go to school no more—"

He waited, but I didn't offer an opinion. "How about going down with me and having a cup of coffee? I'm finished here for the day—just getting through with midterms."

"Nah," he said, looking down and playing with his hands. "I gotta meet somebody. I'm late already. But I was in the neighborhood so I thought I'd come let you know I was still alive." He came to my desk and looked down. He shook his head as if something were wrong.

"What's the matter?" I asked.

"Don't see no wedding ring on your finger yet." He looked straight into my face.

"Hey, man—you ain't a fag, are you?"

"No," I said, laughing. "Not that I know of—."

He laughed, his mouth opening wide. "Okay. That's all the gas for today. I'll see you, man."

During the next few months he visited me several times. Sometimes he looked good, sometimes bad—but I never could find out what he was doing with his days. He never gave a straight answer to my questions. More and more, I felt that he was asking me for some kind of help, but when I would touch on anything personal or even hint that I wanted to do something for him, with him, he would become defensive.

I didn't see him over the summer, but the following fall he came by periodically. He seemed to be getting a hold on himself, and sometimes he would talk about going to night school. Nothing came of the talk, though. In November he was arrested and sent to Riker's Island—to P.S. 616, the combination prison-school for boys between the ages of sixteen and twenty. His sentence was for eighteen months and during the first three months I visited him twice. Both times all he wanted to do was to talk about the English class we had had, and the stories and compositions he had made up. He said he was trying to remember some of them for the English teacher he had there, but couldn't do it all the time. He seemed to be in terrible shape, and I didn't have much hope for him.

So I was surprised when I began getting postcards from him again. "I am studying hard," the first one said. "There is a Negro who comes here to help me. I like him. I will be a new man when I come out. Yours sincerely, Luther." It was neatly and carefully written. The ones that followed were the same and they came at regular intervals of about five weeks. He told me about books he was reading, most of them having to do with Negro history, and about how he was changing. "Improving" was the word he used most.

I answered his cards as best I could, and offered to come see him again, but he never took up any of my offers. When his eighteen months were up, I expected a visit from him. He never came. Sometimes I wondered what had become of him, but after the first few months passed and I didn't hear from him, I thought about him less and less. A year passed—two since we had last seen each other at Riker's Island—and then we met again.

I spotted him first. It was a beautiful summer night and I had gone up to Lewisohn Stadium for a concert. It had been good, I was relaxed and happy as I walked out of the stadium. Luther was standing at the corner of Amsterdam Avenue and 138th Street. He was wearing a dark blue suit, a white shirt and a tie. He was clean shaven, his hair was cut short and he looked healthy and bright. He was stopping people and trying to sell them newspapers.

"How are you, Mister Carter?" he asked, when I walked up to him. His eyes were clear and he seemed very happy to see me. "Interested in buying a newspaper to help the colored people? Only a dime."

"No thanks," I said. The paper he was selling, as I had expected, was *Muhammad Speaks*, the newspaper of the Black Muslims. "You look fine," I added.

"Thanks—excuse me a second." He turned and sold a copy to somebody. People snubbed him but this didn't stop him from smiling or trying. I waited. When the crowd had gone, he asked me where I was going. "Home," I said. "Cup of coffee first?"

"No thanks," he said. "Thanks, but no thanks."

"When did all this start?" I asked, motioning to the newspapers.

"At Riker's Island," he said. He put up a hand, as if to stop my thoughts from becoming words. "I know what you're thinking, what you hear on TV and read in the newspapers about us—but don't believe everything. We're essentially a religious organization, as you may or may not know."

"I know," I said.

"And it's meant a lot to me—I couldn't have made it without their help. They—they taught me to *believe* in myself." His eyes glowed as he twisted his body toward me. "Can you understand that?" It seemed very important to him that I believe him. "*Can* you?" He relaxed momentarily and shrugged. "I don't believe everything they teach, of course, but I follow their precepts: I don't smoke, I don't drink, I don't curse, I don't go out with women who aren't Muslims—I feel good *inside*, Mister Carter. Things are straightening themselves out." He paused. "It hasn't been easy."

"I know," I said, and smiled.

He nodded, embarrassed, I thought. "I'm going back to school also—."

"I'm glad."

"Even my body feels good! I'm lifting weights again, too," he said. Then he laughed and the sound tore through the warm night. His eyes were flashing with delight. "Oh man—someday I'll be the head of a whole damned army! Me and my old hunchback." He laughed again, pleased with himself. Then his laughter subsided and he patted me on the shoulder. "Oh man, you are still so deep, so deep. Don't worry none, Mister Carter. I don't go around advocating no violence." He chuckled. "I've got to go," he said, extending a hand. "It's been good seeing you again. Sure you don't want to buy a copy?"

"I'm sure," I said, shaking his hand. "Good luck to you, Luther. I'm glad to see you the way you are now—."

"Thanks." We looked at each other for a minute and he smiled warmly at me. Then

I started toward the subway station. When I had crossed the street he called to me.

"Hey—Mister Carter—!"

I turned.

"Let me ask you something—do you still have that card I gave you?" He howled at this remark. "Oh man, I'd save that card if I were you! I'd do that. You never know when you might need it. You never know—."

I started back across the street, toward him. He tossed his head back and roared with laughter. "You never know, you never know," he repeated, and hurried away from me, laughing wildly. I stared at him until he disappeared in the darkness. Then I just stood there, dazed, unable to move—I don't know for how long. Finally I made myself turn around, and as I walked slowly toward the lights of Broadway all I could feel was the presence of his muscular body, powerful, gleaming, waiting under his white shirt, his clean suit.

With whom do you identify Carter or Luther? Do you believe Carter would have offered to help Luther if he hadn't been black? What did Luther mean when he said that Carter was not a social worker like the others? What does Luther expect or want from his teacher? What does Luther get? What kind of school curriculum might have appealed to Luther or to Calvin Ketter? Are there gaps in your own education or background which will have to be filled before you can expect some success as a teacher of "Luthers"? Do you think a middle-class white teacher can ever reach or teach a poor black student? Do you think a middle-class black teacher can reach a poor white student? How can you teach someone who is not you?

From *To Make a Difference* by Larry Cuban

Although I criticize how-to-do-it lists because they frame a classroom in terms of a prison or a military campaign and subvert the goals of instruction and curriculum, many of the specific techniques—once learned and used with judgment—are, paradoxically, essential for initial survival in inner-city classrooms. In authoritarian schools, where beliefs that students have enormous intellectual, emotional, and cultural shortcomings merge with an intrinsic lack of faith in youth, such devices are necessary if a teacher intends to last beyond Thanksgiving, mainly because children come to share those beliefs and that faith.

The techniques of managing a large class of youngsters are of critical importance to the new teacher for one reason: students (as early as the second grade) have strong expectations about how teachers should teach, how classrooms should be organized, and what learning is.

These expectations, regardless of how conservative they are, should be accommodated to and eventually changed. Ignore them and the chances of building firm relationships with children and teaching effectively are reduced.

A word on student expectations.[1] Often overlooked, student views have a powerful effect upon behavior, as assuredly as teacher expectations. Students as well as teachers have a mind-set on student types, classroom organization, and the like, and carry around perceptions about them. Regardless of how naive or short-sighted they may appear to be, student feelings in these matters must be recognized, accepted, accommodated to initially, and changed.

Students, for example, expect a teacher to lay down rules, hand out texts, demand silence, and assign homework—in short, to run a tight ship. These expectations don't preclude students testing the limits of the teacher's ability to enforce the rules; it is part of the early trading off that marks the struggle between teacher and class. If the teacher uses the techniques of control satisfactorily while simultaneously proving to children that he can teach, the class will settle into a routine comfortable to them. But if the teacher cannot conform to their expectations or has strong doubts about his use of authority, then clever minds click, strategies change, and tactics shift: another teacher, regardless of his goodwill, exits crying, cursing, and totally exhausted

Veteran teachers and principals recognize the difficulties new teachers face in taking hold with a class and invariably inform newcomers what to do the first few weeks. . . . What often happens, sadly, is that many teachers, not fully knowing themselves, get trapped by such advice: get trapped by the devices they use and get trapped by student expectations.

So often temporary measures harden into permanence. A teacher-dominated, one-way communication system in the fall often sputters to an incoherent end in June. James Herndon's *The Way It Spozed To Be* describes how students burst out in the spring from those classes whose teachers pride themselves on rules, routines, and discipline.

The balance of power in a classroom is so fragile; teachers seldom wish to jeopardize an uneasy truce by changing tactics between September and June. Thus, the trap. What teachers must learn is to adapt the shopping lists of rules to their personality and use them as tools to gain the respect of youngsters; then, still preserving the relationship, refashion with those very same tools and additional ones, the old forms to redefine limits, learning, and teacher-student interactions.[2]

A few examples are in order. Most teachers and educators emphasize the "disadvantaged's" need for structure, a framework of rules and routines for kids to operate within. In most cases this "need" for structure is linked to the concept of a culture of poverty or the general instability of poor families. Inflated to critical importance, rules and routines become ends in themselves, leading some school officials in Washington, D.C., a few years ago, but since rescinded, to order compulsory attendance for all male students in the cadet corps because most of the students who were black and poor needed the stability of military procedures. How's that for a bastardized sociology?

Yet among the many by-products of Head Start, Upward Bound, and the Job Corps was the plain fact that poor youths could operate in both structured and unstructured settings. More to the point, go into the plushest suburban elementary schools and ask teachers about structure for their children. In most instances, they will tell you of the child's need for rules and the importance of order to children being socialized as responsible citizens. No social science excuses about the instability of the family, although the father may be just as absent albeit for different reasons.

Stripping away the excuses, structure is important not because of poverty or affluence, absent fathers or working mothers, intrinsic or extrinsic needs; it is important in

---

[1] The Coleman Report and *Racial Isolation in the Public Schools*, published by the U.S. Commission on Civil Rights, underscored the collective influences of attitudes and behavior when ethnic low-income youngsters form the majority of students. The cumulative influence of peer attitudes and behavior, according to the reports, is the single most important variable influencing achievement. Another strong influence on achievement was the caliber of the teacher. There is some evidence that teachers make a difference.

[2] Some may question this strategy and prefer to start from scratch with a new order of things in September, that is, disregarding student expectations. I've seen this work with well-integrated, strong teachers who had a high tolerance for initial disorder and student resistance. Ignoring the influence of student perceptions increases the risk of failure in the conventional school setting, but gambles for sweet possibility of a real success in terms of student growth which, in my opinion, can go further than the strategy of meeting student expectations from the onset. I recommend what is essentially a conservative approach because it requires the least change from students initially and maximizes the chances of new teachers gaining that degree of confidence in themselves necessary to make eventual changes.

so far as it meets students' expectations and establishes the ground rules for communication between teacher and class and among students.

There are many structures. Some inhibit, others encourage interaction. One form, for example, is the tight-ship framework. Rules are clearly explained and firmly but fairly enforced. Established routines permit tasks to be performed with speed and efficiency. Each student knows precisely what is expected of him at any given point. If the teacher is capable, students are comfortable with this form since it requires of them little more than passive acquiescence; teachers are comfortable with this form since all authority, decision making, and wisdom flow from them. Communication is usually one way with a minimum of feedback from the children.

Unless changes to maximize interaction are introduced by the teacher, this form hardens into rigidity, inhibiting the child's growth in independence and thinking skills. Furthermore, communication reduces itself to a one-way trickle of orders, "suggestions," and reprimands. It does not have to be so.

If the teacher understands the utility of different structures, then diverse learning situations can be gradually introductd. For competitive purposes the class can be broken into groups, for example, to seek answers to problems deriving from the content studied, to search out information, or for any number of reasons. More individualized work can be planned around an assortment of instructional materials where student choices count. Such learning situations often have to be introduced by the teacher since youngsters have had either very little experience with diverse settings or only some slight exposure to them, and these usually have been teacher-dominated and involved no real training. Once children gain skills in working together and once they realize the teacher is sincere in pursuing it seriously as an alternative for them to choose among, multiple-learning situations become commonplace experiences for low-income youngsters.

Just as necessary are mechanisms that permit youngsters to voice disagreement, suggest changes, and make decisions so that by the end of the school year what began as a "tight ship" has been transformed into a more flexible framework of learning in which students play an active role in shaping what happens in the classroom.

All of this is to say that a structure is another tool, not an end product; that to be effective a teacher should establish a form that meets the students' expectations, gains their respect, and then transcends those expectations by creating different ones which open up a real interaction between and among teacher and students. Like all suggested teaching strategies, meeting student perceptions and going beyond them is easy to recommend; but implementation—the real payoff—depends upon individual judgment, personal qualities of the teacher, and first-hand experiences with veteran practitioners who are successful at it.

Do you agree with the author's "gradualism" or are you more revolutionary? Do you have to compromise in order to survive? If so, how can you still provide for student growth? Read *The Open Classroom* by Herbert Kohl for survival techniques for teachers. Make up a teacher's survival kit "to last beyond Thanksgiving." How can a teacher who is creative and unhypocritical survive in the public school system if his methods, and perhaps goals, conflict with those of the students, the administration, or the parents? Give examples of the kind of resistance to change you might expect to meet as a teacher in an urban or suburban school. What alternatives are possible within the public schools?

Beyond Survival

You really learn something when you have to teach it. Imagine yourself the teacher. Draw stick figures to illustrate your location, as teacher, in the classroom in relation to the students in a traditional class. What different arrangements can you make? Which picture do you feel most comfortable in? Is this picture a familiar one to you as student? Would you like to change the arrangement?

Circle the letter of the statement that represents your feelings at the present moment:
1. I think teachers should determine
   A. the entire curriculum for a course.
   B. some of the curriculum.
   C. none of the curriculum.
2. I think students need
   A. more freedom than they are given in schools.
   B. about the same amount of freedom as they're now given in schools.
   C. less freedom.
3. If I become a teacher, I intend to
   A. change things as much as I can.
   B. find a middle ground between the old methods and the new.
   C. teach pretty much as I've been taught.
4. I prefer to learn from
   A. myself.
   B. my friends (peers).
   C. older people.

CHAPTER FOUR

Will the real teacher please stand up?

From *Teaching as a Subversive Activity* by Neil Postman and Charles Weingartner

. . . [W]e will now put before you a list of proposals that attempt to change radically the nature of the existing school environment. Most of them will strike you as thoroughly impractical but only because you will have forgotten for the moment that the present system is among the most impractical imaginable, if the facilitation of learning is your aim. There is yet another reaction you might have to our proposals. You might concede that they are "impractical" and yet feel that each one contains an idea or two that might be translated into "practical" form. If you do, we will be delighted. But as for us, none of our proposals seems impractical or bizarre. They seem, in fact, quite conservative, given the enormity of the problem they are intended to resolve. As you read them, imagine that you are a member of a board of education, or a principal, or supervisor, or some such person who might have the wish and power to lay the groundwork for a new education.

1. Declare a five-year moratorium on the use of all textbooks.

Since with two or three exceptions all texts are not only boring but based on the assumption that knowledge exists prior to, independent of, and altogether outside of the learner, they are either worthless or harmful. If it is impossible to function without textbooks, provide every student with a notebook filled with blank pages, and have him compose his own text.

2. Have "English" teachers "teach" math, math teachers English, social studies teachers science, science teachers art, and so on.

One of the largest obstacles to the establishment of a sound learning environment is the desire of teachers to get something they think they know into the heads of people who don't know it. An English teacher teaching math would hardly be in a position to fulfill this desire. Even more important, he would be forced to perceive the "subject" as a learner, not a teacher. If this suggestion is too impractical, try numbers 3 and 4.

3. Transfer all the elementary-school teachers to high school and vice versa.

4. Require every teacher who thinks he knows his "subject" well to write a book on it.

In this way, he will be relieved of the necessity of inflicting *his* knowledge on other people, particularly his students.

5. Dissolve all "subjects," "courses," and especially "course requirements."

This proposal, all by itself, would wreck every existing educational bureaucracy. The result would be to deprive teachers of the excuses presently given for their failures and to free them to concentrate on their learners.

6. Limit each teacher to three declarative sentences per class, and 15 interrogatives.

Every sentence above the limit would be subject to a 25-cent fine. The students can do the counting and the collecting.

7. Prohibit teachers from asking any questions they already know the answers to.

This proposal would not only force teachers to perceive learning from the learner's perspective, it would help them to learn how to ask questions that produce knowledge.

8. Declare a moratorium on all tests and grades.

This would remove from the hands of teachers their major weapons of coercion and would eliminate two of the major obstacles to their students' learning anything significant.

9. Require all teachers to undergo some form of psychotherapy as part of their in-service training.

This need not be psychoanalysis; some form of group therapy or psychological counseling will do. Its purpose: to give teachers an opportunity to gain insight into themselves, particularly into the reasons they are teachers.

10. Classify teachers according to their ability and make the lists public.

There would be a "smart" group (the Bluebirds), an "average" group (the Robins), and a "dumb" group (the Sandpipers). The lists would be published each year in the community paper. The I.Q. and reading scores of teachers would also be published, as well as the list of those who are "advantaged" and "disadvantaged" by virtue of what they know in relation to what their students know.

11. Require all teachers to take a test prepared by students on what the students know.

Only if a teacher passes this test should he be permitted to "teach." This test could be used for "grouping" the teachers as in number 10 above.

12. Make every class an elective and withhold a teacher's monthly check if his students do not show any interest in going to next month's classes.

This proposal would simply put the teacher on a par with other professionals, e.g., doctors, dentists, lawyers, etc. No one forces you to go to a particular doctor unless you are a "clinic case." In that instance, you must take what you are given. Our present system makes a "clinic case" of every student. Bureaucrats decide who shall govern your education. In this proposal, we are restoring the American philosophy: no clients, no money; lots of clients, lots of money.

13. Require every teacher to take a one-year leave of absence every fourth year to work in some "field" other than education.

Such an experience can be taken as evidence, albeit shaky, that the teacher has been in contact with reality at some point in his life. Recommended occupations: bartender, cab driver, garment worker, waiter. One of the common sources of difficulty with teachers can be found in the fact that most of them simply move from one side of the desk (as students) to the other side (as "teachers") and they have not had much contact with the way things are outside of school rooms.

14. *Require each teacher to provide some sort of evidence that he or she has had a loving relationship with at least one other human being.*

If the teacher can get someone to say, "I love her (or him)," she should be retained. If she can get two people to say it, she should get a raise. Spouses need not be excluded from testifying.

15. *Require that all the graffiti accumulated in the school toilets be reproduced on large paper and be hung in the school halls.*

Graffiti that concern teachers and administrators should be chiseled into the stone at the front entrance of the school.

16. *There should be a general prohibition against the use of the following words and phrases:* teach, syllabus, covering ground, I.Q., makeup, test, disadvantaged, gifted, accelerated, enhancement, course, grade, score, human nature, dumb, college material, and administrative necessity.

Before proceeding to our next series of recommendations, we want to say a further word about the seriousness of the foregoing proposals. Consider, for example, proposals 14 and 15, which some people might regard as facetious, if not flippant. Proposal 14 would require a teacher to present evidence of his having had a loving relationship with another person. Silly, isn't it? What kinds of evidence must teachers presently offer to qualify for their jobs? A list of "courses." Which of these requirements strikes you as more bizarre? From the student's point of view, which requirement would seem more

practical? Bear in mind that it is a very difficult thing for one person to learn anything significant from another. Bear in mind, too, that it is probably not possible for such learning to occur unless there is something resembling a loving relationship between "teacher" and learner. Then ask yourself if you can think of anything sillier than asking an applicant for a teaching job if he has taken a course in Victorian literature?

Proposal 15 concerns making the school's graffiti public in the manner in which various slogans and mottos now adorn school halls and facades.

. . . It is astonishing that so many people do not recognize the extent to which hypocrisy and drivel poison the whole atmosphere of school. And where will you find more concentrated hypocrisy and drivel than on the walls of classrooms, and in the halls, and on the facades of school buildings? To replace these with intimately felt observations would be neither tasteless nor eccentric. Unless, of course, your sense of propriety includes attempting to deceive the young.

Finally, we want to say that, in spite of our belief that it is unreasonable to expect the current crop of teachers to change sufficiently to permit an educational revolution to occur, it is sometimes surprising to discover how wrong we can be. There *are* teachers—some of whom have been at it for ten or 15 years—who know how desperately change is needed, and who are more than

willing to be agents of such change. Such people cannot be dismissed, and, in fact, we spend a considerable amount of our time trying to locate them and lend them support. But the teachers of the future must bring this revolution off or it will not happen.

◆◆◆◆◆◆◆

Are you willing to be an agent of change? Devise a teacher-training curriculum of your own.

◆◆◆◆◆◆◆

Imagine yourself an innovative teacher, or play the "I want to be different but I can't because" game.

◆◆◆◆◆◆◆

Times change, and change—in education, industry, government, anywhere—demands great storehouses of information and men who need to know. Information is the least expensive commodity in the world today. We can get more facts, more concepts, and more information of every kind for less money than anything else, including clean water and clear air.

Our problem and our task is to find a way to bring people and information together into a dynamic, evolving relationship which will honor the integrity of man, the concerns of society, and the nature of knowledge itself. The primary focus, though, must always be on man. Man is the end. Subject matter is the means. Society is the result.

Knowledge is power. Man needs to know.

From Jack R. Frymier, "Stimulation and the Need to Know"

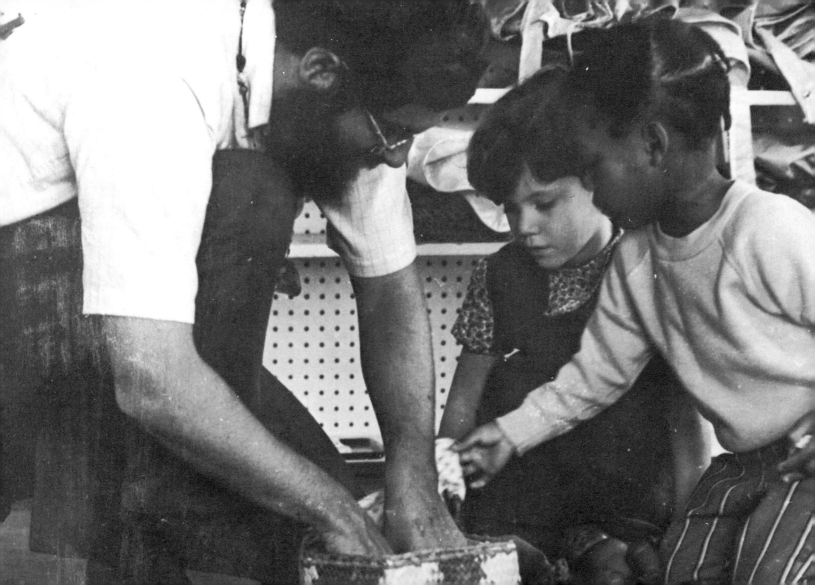

Here are some new developments.

British Infant Schools—American Style
by Beatrice and Ronald Gross

"British infant school," "Leicestershire method," "integrated day," "the open classroom"—these names are heard increasingly among theorists and practitioners of early childhood education. The terms all refer to a new approach to teaching that discards the familiar elementary classroom setup and the traditional, stylized roles of teacher and pupil, for a far freer, highly individualized, child-centered learning experience that may hold the key to a radical reformation of primary education.

This approach—for which the open classroom seems the most useful label—is based on a body of new theory and research on how children do and don't learn, but its attractiveness for educators is even more directly attributable to the fact that it is highly effective under a variety of circumstances for children between the ages of five and twelve. It has spread widely throughout the British school system since World War II, and in the past five years it has been introduced in a variety of American schools, ranging from rural Vermont and North Dakota to innercity classrooms in Philadelphia, Washington, Boston, and New York.

This year the Office of Economic Opportunity sponsored twelve open classroom training centers in nine cities as part of Follow Through, its program for continuing the social and intellectual growth of "de-prived" children graduating from Head Start programs. The open classroom movement has also won the support of the Ford Foundation, which is funding several efforts to encourage its dissemination in public schools.

There are four operating principles of the open classroom. First, the room itself is decentralized: an open, flexible space divided into functional areas, rather than one fixed, homogeneous unit. Second, the children are free for much of the time to explore this room, individually or in groups, and to choose their own activities. Third, the environment is rich in learning resources, including plenty of concrete materials, as well as books and other media. Fourth, the teacher and her aides work most of the time with individual children or two or three, hardly ever presenting the same material to the class as a whole.

The teachers begin with the assumption that the children want to learn and will learn in their fashion; learning is rooted in first-hand experience so that teaching becomes the encouragement and enhancement of each child's own thrust toward mastery and understanding. Respect for and trust in the child are perhaps the most basic principles underlying the open classroom.

From the application of these principles derive the most notable characteristics of learning in such a classroom: a general atmosphere of excitement; virtually complete flexibility in the curriculum; interpenetration of the various subjects and skills; emphasis on learning rather than teaching; focus on each child's thinking and problem-solving processes, and on his ability to communicate with others; and freedom and responsibility for the children.

From the moment you walk in the door of such a classroom, the difference from the conventional procedures is striking. In most classrooms rows of desks or tables and chairs face the front of the room, where the teacher is simultaneously presenting material and controlling the class; the children are either quietly engaged by what the teacher is doing, surreptitiously communicating, daydreaming, or fooling. Even in classrooms using innovative materials, such as the individually prescribed instruction, in which each student works on a math sheet prescribed for his particular level of achievement, the basic pattern is one in which all the children do the same thing at the same time, sitting at their desks with the teacher watching from up front.

But in an open classroom, there is none of this. There is no up front, and one doesn't know where to look to find the teacher or her desk. She is usually to be found working intensively with one or two children, or, if things are going as they should, often standing unobtrusively aside but observing each child's activities with great diligence. There are no desks and few chairs—fewer than the number of children. And the children are everywhere: sprawled on the floor, in groups in the corners, alone on chairs or pillows, out in the hall, or outside in the playground if it's good weather.

"The children are working on fractions." This kind of description of what's going on in a class, which comes so easily in a conventional situation, can never be applied to an open classroom. Each child uses the room differently, according to his own interests, concerns, and feelings on a particular day.

How does the day proceed? As they arrive, the students check the chore chart to see what their housekeeping responsibility is for the day. They take turns doing such chores as bringing up the milk, watering the plants, cleaning the animal cage, mixing new paints, sharpening pencils, taking attendance.

Many open classroom teachers call a general meeting after the children arrive, focusing on some interesting experiment several children did the day before, something brought from home, an unusual item in the newspaper, or a sentence she has written on the board to be corrected by the class. The children squat on their haunches or sit cross-legged in whatever area most comfortably holds the whole group.

After the meeting, children choose the areas in which they would like to begin their day. Some prefer to start quietly reading, curled up in the overstuffed chairs. Some like to get their assigned work out of the way first, but others may not have a choice if the teacher has noticed, for instance, that they have been neglecting math or need work in punctuation, and she tells them that they should start the day working with her. Soon the room is full of action, used as it will be for the remainder of the day, unless some special visitor or specialist focuses the group's attention for a special activity.

The layout of the room supports the program. An aerial view of a typical second-grade class in the middle of a morning would show that the room is divided into six sections, defined by open bookshelves that hold appropriate equipment, all of which is easily accessible to the children.

The child is free to choose, but whatever choice he makes he will be confronted with a wealth of opportunities for exploration and discovery. In the math section is everything he can use to measure and figure, including the Cuisenaire rods, balance scales, rulers and a stop watch, workbooks, and counting games such as Sorry and Pokerino. Similar riches await him in the language arts section, where he can read, make a tape recording or type, write, and play word games and puzzles; or in the arts area with its paints, clay, dyes, and sand. Other corners are devoted to science, music, and blocks.

The child's freedom, autonomy, and independence—as well as his responsibility—are epitomized by the largest and most elaborate of the many charts and pictures around the room. It is the "activity chart," and it lists by word and appropriate picture all the possible activities in the room: from reading, typing, playground, painting, right through to visiting and gerbils. Next to each are several hooks, on which the child hangs his name tag to indicate what he's doing. A simple device, but it says much about the respect for the child and the relationship between the child, the teacher, and the room. The equivalent in the conventional classroom is the notorious Delaney book, still widely used, which represents each student by a little card tucked in a slot corresponding to his desk position, fixing the child in a constrained position, with the teacher clearly in charge.

In the open classroom, each child's day is distinctive and different from every other day. To give him a sense of his progress, each child may keep a diary, which is also used to communicate to the teacher. Some typical entries indicate the flow of activity, and the frustrations and concerns of the children:

Today I read *Horton the Elephant.* I began the green series in SRA. Ollie helped me with the words in the *Horton* book. I helped John and Sara make a staircase with the Cuisenaire rods.

I played in the Block Corner most of the day. We were making a suspension bridge. We talked a lot about our water tower and how it got flooded by Jimmy and what we should charge for a toll. I'll do my math tomorrow. Okay?

We had a turtle race today. Mrs. White taught me how to break words down. I can read words, but I can't break them down. We timed the turtles with the stop watch. They tried to climb over the side of the box.

We're making a book of fables like "How the Snake Lost His Legs"; "How the Elephant Got His Trunk"; "How José Got to Be a Genius"; "How I Got to Be Invisible."

The variety of the activities mentioned in the diaries suggests the highlights of each child's day, but many educators and most parents find it difficult to define clearly what is being learned at any one moment and are usually resistant to the idea that a relaxed and unpressured atmosphere can stimulate serious work.

The evidence that this approach does work and the reasons why were first presented to a wide public in *Children and Their Primary Schools*, a 1967 report of Great Britain's Central Advisory Council for Education. Popularly known as the Plowden Report, after

Lady Bridget Plowden, chairman of the council, these fat volumes were handsomely responsive to the council's mandate to "consider primary education in all its aspects." The Plowden Report is one of those classic official documents that only the British seem capable of producing: generous-spirited, concrete, progressive, and written with charm and spirit.

The report is comprehensive in scope: some half-million words covering topics as diverse as the rate of growth in height for boys and girls, religious instruction, salaries, school building costs, sex education, the handicapped, and team teaching. But the aspect of it that has had the most impact on American educators is its portrayal and analysis of the new mode of teaching.

The Plowden Report does not just discuss the theory and marshal the evidence from various fields and disciplines. It goes the further step of showing that it can be *done*, that in fact it already *is* being done. And it is being done not just in the small private schools that have harbored such education for decades, but in the mainstream of Britain's state-supported, mass education system.

In surveying the state of British primary schooling, the Plowden Report discovered that one-third of the primary schools had already dispensed with a fixed curriculum, a teacher-dominated unified classroom, and narrowly focused one-way teaching measured by tests, and replaced them with open classroom techniques and practices.

To make its preference for this approach

perfectly clear, the Plowden Report gives negative criteria as well as positive ones. In the schools that were found to be damaging children, administrative and teaching practices hadn't changed significantly in the past decade, creative work in the arts was considered a frill, much classroom time was spent in the teacher's teaching in ways that generated few questions from the children (and those narrowly circumscribed by the teacher), and there were too many exercises and rules, resulting in frequent punishments and many tests.

Against this paradigm of educational stultification, the report poses the ideal: emphasis on each child's interests and style, lots of gabble among the kids, an abundance of fascinating concrete materials, and a teacher who stimulates and sometimes steps back.

All of this came to the attention of American educators through a series of articles by Joseph Featherstone in *New Republic* in the autumn of 1967. Featherstone was the perfect publicist for the Plowden Report. His down-to-earth style and modesty matched the report's manner perfectly. By speaking in a low voice, Featherstone raised a storm of interest and triggered a hegira of American educators to England. Lillian Weber, who is now the open classroom expert for New York City's schools, and who was virtually alone in the schools in England in 1965, could hardly elbow her way past the study teams from twenty American cities when she returned in 1969.

The theoretical basis of the open classroom is found in the work of the Swiss child psychologist Jean Piaget. His work began to influence many other experimental psychologists in the 1950s when his studies were published, but not until recently has his work been interpreted and popularized in the mass media.

Piaget is best known for his finding that intelligence—adaptive thinking and action—develops in sequence and is related to age. However, the ages at which children can understand different concepts vary from child to child, depending on his native endowment and on the quality of the physical and social environments in which he is reared.

But Piaget's books—*The Origins of Intelligence in Children, The Psychology of Intelligence*, and *The Construction of Reality*—based on his research on how children learn, also proved that it is a waste of time to tell a child things that the child cannot experience through his senses. The child must be able to try things out to see what happens, manipulate objects and symbols, pose questions and seek their answers, reconcile what he finds at one time with what he finds at another, and test his findings against the perceptions of others his age. Activity essential to intellectual development includes social collaboration, group effort, and communication among children. Only after a good deal of experience is the child ready to move on to abstract conceptualizations. Piaget is critical of classrooms where the teacher is

the dominant figure, where books and the teacher's talking are basic instructional media, and where large group instruction is the rule, and oral or written tests are used to validate the whole process. Clearly from his findings, traditional teaching techniques are ineffectual. But for children who must depend on the school environment as the richest they are to encounter, it can be downright damaging; denied a chance to grow, their minds may actually atrophy.

Can the open classroom approach transform American primary education as it is doing in England? To Lillian Weber, this is the basic question. As assistant professor of early childhood education at City College, she feels there is a ground swell of interest.

"When I started placing student teachers, after coming back from England, there wasn't one classroom in New York City that I could put a teacher into where she had the slightest chance of being able to apply the theories of how children learn that she was studying at the college." Now, as the result of three years of intensive effort, there are thirty-seven, mostly on the Upper West Side and in Harlem, and Mrs. Weber is swamped with requests for help in introducing these theories in more schools.

Considerable progress has also been made in Philadelphia, where the reform school administration of Mark Shedd got behind this approach as one element of its attempt to "turn on the system." Under the guidance of Lore Rasmussen, eighteen teachers are using the open classroom approach in five schools, and twenty more are trying it on their own.

On the national level, the Educational Development Center, a nonprofit curriculum-development agency in Newton, Mass., sponsors workshops, provides advisory and consultant services, and develops materials under grants from the Ford Foundation and the federal government's Follow Through program. To spearhead the movement in this country, EDC has brought over experienced British educators, such as Rosemary Williams, who directed the Westfield Infant School, portrayed so vividly by Joseph Featherstone. Through these activities, EDC advises teachers in more than 100 classrooms in eight states.

Three questions are asked most often by educators and parents first exposed to open classrooms in operation. What problems loom largest? Do the children do as well on standardized tests? And what about cost? Do the additional training and the wealth of materials add greatly to the cost of schooling?

The problem cited most frequently is the fad psychology of educational reform. The trajectory was documented by Anthony Oettinger in *Run, Computer, Run.* An innovation comes roaring in on a wave of rhetoric, there is a bustle to get on the band wagon, things seem to be burgeoning, and then suddenly disenchantment occurs when reality falls short of the glowing press releases.

"The biggest threat is that the approach will catch on and spread like wildfire," insists Ann Cook, who has served widely as a consultant on open classroom projects. "Then it would fall into the hands of faddists who are unwilling to give it sufficient time to evolve and mature. Developing the necessary talent to make this work is time-consuming, and Americans are an impatient people."

For this reason, advocates of the approach want to win their battle classroom by classroom, rather than by convincing educational administrators to install the new approach through ukase. "Careful work on a small scale," Featherstone has written, "is the way to start reform worth having. . . . The proper locus of a revolution in the primary schools . . . is a teacher in a classroom full of children."

Another common problem is the tendency to confuse the self-conscious freedom of the open classroom with mere "chaos" and disregard of the children. Conventional educators observing an open classroom for the first time are often so fixated on the children's informality and spontaneity that they fail to note the diligent planning and individual diagnoses by the teachers and the intellectual and sensuous richness of the prepared environment. These latter qualities, however, are hard-won, and to "open" the classrooms without having developed these strengths is to invite mere mindlessness and frustration.

How do the children score on standardized tests? That question is regularly asked by parents and teachers, as if it gets to the heart of the matter with hard-nosed exactness. But open classroom theorists refuse to accept the assumption behind the question. They insist that our new understanding of how children learn and grow makes the present standardized tests obsolete.

"In England there is never any pressure to test in infant schools," explains Rosemary Williams, "but since there is pressure here, someone must come up with realistic tests. We've got Princeton's Educational Testing Service at work on tests that will measure original thinking, independency, and creativity—the kind of thing our program is out to develop."

The available evidence indicates that, even measured by the present tests, open classroom children progress normally in reading and arithmetic scores. But an increased *desire* to read and write is also evident, and children score higher, on the average, in math comprehension. This is startling, since traditional classrooms focus principally on reading and arithmetic the first two years, while open classrooms accord them equal status with such activities as painting and block building.

The question of cost also arises in many people's minds when they see the richness of materials and equipment in the classroom. And indeed there are considerable start-up expenses. David Armington of EDC estimates that to fill an open classroom with the most elaborate equipment available in a situation where money is no object costs $1,100 or $1,200, making an initial investment of $36 per child the first year. However, roughly half the equipment is highly durable and does not have to be replaced in subsequent years, and operating costs can be reduced by using parents and older children as aides. For educational value received, its advocates argue, the open classroom is a bargain—but, like good buys, it can often be least afforded by those who most need it.

In the present climate of American education, the open classroom approach sometimes seems like a flower too fragile to survive. The demands on the schools today are harsh and often narrow. Many black parents demand measurable reading achievement and other test scores to assure that they are no longer being given short shrift. At the same time, white parents are often concerned that the schools continue to give their children an advantage in status over someone else's children.

In such a climate, the open classroom seems precariously based on a kind of trust little evident in education today. Teachers must trust children's imagination, feelings, curiosity, and natural desire to explore and understand their world. They also must learn to trust themselves—to be willing to gamble that they can retain the children's interest and respect once they relinquish the external means of control: testing, threats, demerits, petty rules, and rituals. School administrators, in turn, must trust teachers enough to permit them to run a classroom that is not rigidly organized and controlled but, rather, is bustling, messy, flexible, and impulsive. Parents must trust school people to do well by their children, without the assurance provided by a classroom atmosphere recognizable from their own childhoods and validated, however emptily, by standardized tests.

Much recent experience suggests that the basis for trust such as this may not exist in American education at present. But perhaps the existence of classrooms where learning based on such trust is taking place will itself help create the beginnings of a new climate.

What words would you use to define an open classroom? Would you be more likely to find an open classroom in ghettos or suburbs? What are the differences between an open classroom and a traditional classroom?

Readings

Barth, Roland, and Rathbone, Charles. A comprehensive bibliography on British schools and open education, *The Center Forum* 3, no. 7 (July 1969), 2–8. The Center for Urban Education, 105 Madison Ave., N.Y., N.Y.

Blackie, John. *Inside the Primary School.* British Information Services, Sales Section, 845 Third Avenue, New York 10022.

Bowlby, John. *Child Care and the Growth of Love.* New York: Pelican-Penguin, 1961.

Brown, Mary, and Precious, Norman. *The Integrated Day in the Primary School.* New York: Agathon Press, 1970.

Featherstone, Joseph. "Schools for Children," *New Republic*, Aug. 19, 1967, pp. 17–21.

———. "Experiments in Learning." *New Republic*, Dec. 14, 1968.

———. "Report Analysis: Children and Their Primary Schools. *Harvard Educational Review* 38, no. 2 (Spring 1968).

Gardner, D. E. M. *The Children's Play Centre.* New York: Agathon Press, 1970.

Glagau, M., and Fassel, L. *The Non-Graded Primary School: A Case Study.* Englewood Cliffs, N.J.: Prentice-Hall, 1967.

Johnson, H. *School Begins at Two.* New York: Agathon Press, 1970.

Peters, R. S. *Perspectives on Plowden.* New York: Humanities Press, 1969.

Plowden et al. *Children and Their Primary Schools.* British Information Services, 845 Third Ave., New York 10022.

Rathbone, Charles. *Open Education: Selected Readings.* New York: Citation Press, 1970.

The reader may wish to write to the Education Development Center, 55 Chapel St., Newton, Mass. for further information. Refer to their Early Childhood Education Study.

Barbara Shiel's Class Journal

March 5, We Begin:

A week ago I decided to initiate a new program in my sixth-grade classroom, based on student-centered teaching—an unstructured or nondirective approach.

I began by telling the class that we were going to try an "experiment." I explained that for one day I would let them do anything they wanted to do—they did not have to do anything if they did not want to.

Many started with art projects; some drew or painted most of the day. Others read or did work in math and other subjects. There was an air of excitement all day; many were so interested in what they were doing that they did not want to go out at recess or noon!

At the end of the day I asked the class to evaluate the experiment. The comments were most interesting. Some were "confused," distressed without the teacher telling them what to do, without specific assignments to complete.

The majority of the class thought the day was "great," but some expressed concern over the noise level and the fact that a few "goofed off" all day. Most felt that they had accomplished as much work as we usually do, and they enjoyed being able to work at a task until it was completed without the pressure of a time limit. They liked doing things without being "forced" to do them and liked deciding what to do.

They begged to continue the "experiment," so it was decided to do so, for two more days. We would then re-evaluate the plan.

The next morning I implemented the idea of a "work contract." I gave them ditto sheets listing all our subjects with suggestions under each. There was a space provided for their "plans" in each area and for checking upon completion.

Each child was to write his or her contract for the day—choosing the areas in which he would work and planning specifically what he would do. Upon completion of any exercise, drill, review, etc., he was to check and correct his own work, using the teacher's manual. The work was to be kept in a folder with the contract.

I met with each child to discuss his plans. Some completed theirs in a very short time; we discussed as a group what this might mean, and what to do about it. It was suggested that the plan might not be challenging enough, that an adjustment should be made —perhaps going on or adding another area to the day's plan.

Resource materials were provided, suggestions made, and drill materials made available to use when needed.

I found I had much more time, so I worked, talked, and spent the time with individuals and groups. At the end of the third day I evaluated the work folder with each child. To solve the problem of grades, I had each child tell me what he thought he had earned.

Also at this time the group wrote a second evaluation of the experiment, adding comments their parents had made. All but four were excited and enthusiastic about the plan and thought school was much fun. The four still felt insecure and wanted specific assignments. I talked with them about giving the experiment time—sometimes it took time to adjust to new situations. They agreed to try. The rest of the class was thrilled at the prospect of continuing the rest of the year.

The greatest problem I've encountered is discipline. I have many problem individuals in my class, and there was a regression in terms of control when the teacher's external controls were lifted. Part of the difficulty stems from the fact that I let the children sit where and with whom they liked. The "problems" congregated together, spent much of their day fighting (verbally and physically), "bugging" each other, and generally accomplishing very little, which brings to mind another problem for me—internally. I am having a difficult time watching them do nothing and am concerned at times about their progress, achievement, etc. I have to remind myself constantly that these pupils were "failing" under the old program, and never turned in completed assignments under the old regime either. They only *looked* like they were doing something!

I've considered the possibility of moving some of the seats in the problem area, but I realize that I would be defeating an important aspect of the program if I re-established my control. If we can survive this period, perhaps in time they will develop greater *self*-control.

It is interesting to me that it is upsetting to them too. They all sit close to my desk and say it is too difficult this new way. The "temptation" is too great. This would indicate that they are not as recalcitrant as they seemed.

The class has been delighted in general. They even carry their projects and work outside and have the whole school interested and talking about the idea. And I've heard the story that they think I've really changed (since I've stopped trying to make them conform to my standards and rules, trying to make them achieve *my* goals!!).

The atmosphere is a stimulating, relaxed, happy one (discounting the problem area upheaval).

An interesting project has developed. I noticed that some of the boys were drawing and designing automobiles. I put up a big piece of paper for them to use as they wished. They discussed their plans and proceeded to do a mural on the history of cars, incorporating their designs as cars of the future. I was delighted. They used the encyclopedia as a reference, as well as books on cars they

brought in. They worked together, and some began models and scrapbooks, boys who had produced very little, if anything, so far this year.

Other ideas began to appear in other areas; the seed of initiative and creativity had germinated and began to grow.

Many children are doing some interesting research in related (and unrelated) areas of interest. Some have completed the year's "required" work in a few areas, such as spelling.

Most important, to me, is the evidence of initiative and self-responsibility manifested.

March 12, Progress Report:

Our "experiment" has, in fact, become our program—with some adjustments.

Some children continued to be frustrated and felt insecure without teacher direction. Discipline also continued to be a problem with some, and I began to realize that although the children involved may need the program more than the others, I was expecting too much from them, too soon—they were not ready to assume self-direction *yet*. Perhaps a gradual weaning from the spoon-fed procedures was necessary.

I regrouped the class—creating two groups. The largest group is the nondirected group. The smallest is teacher-directed, made up of children who wanted to return to the former teacher-directed method, and those

who, for varied reasons, were unable to function in the self-directed situation.

I would like to have waited longer to see what would have happened, but the situation for some disintegrated a little more each day—penalizing the whole class. The disrupting factor kept everyone upset and limited those who wanted to study and work. So it seemed to me best for the group as a whole as well as the program to modify the plan.

Those who continued the "experiment" have forged ahead. I showed them how to program their work, using their texts as a basic guide. They have learned that they can teach themselves (and each other) and that I am available when a step is not clear or advice is needed.

At the end of the week they evaluate themselves in each area—in terms of work accomplished, accuracy, etc. We have learned that the number of errors is not a criterion of failure or success. Errors can and should be part of the learning process; we learn through our mistakes. We also discussed the fact that consistently perfect scores may mean that the work is not challenging enough and perhaps we should move on.

After self-evaluation, each child brings the evaluation sheet and work folder to discuss them with me.

Some of the members of the group working with me are most anxious to become "independent" students. We will evaluate together each week their progress toward that goal.

I have only experienced one parental objection so far. A parent felt her child was not able to function without direction.

Some students (there were two or three) who originally wanted to return to the teacher-directed program are now anticipating going back into the self-directed program. (I sense that it has been as difficult for them to readjust to the old program as it would be for me to do so.)

March 19, Progress Report:

Today, from my point of view as a teacher, has been the most satisfying since we began our new program.

It began with an individual evaluation with each child in the teacher-directed program. (I had had conferences with the non-directed group the preceding day.) Several of the children in the former group felt that they were ready to go back into the non-directed group. They had decided they liked the freedom after all and thought they understood the responsibilities involved. It was decided that they would try it for one week to see if they really were ready. I would help them at any time they needed help with their work plan or actual work.

At this point I have only six in the teacher group. One wants to be in the other group, but since her mother was the one parent who complained I told her she must discuss it at home first.

We had an oral evaluation, one of the topics discussed being parental reaction. One boy said his mother said it sounded as if I had given up teaching! Another boy said his father told him that he had tried self-responsibility with him before, and he thought I was nuts to try it with so many at once!

We discussed what we could do to help our parents understand the program. It was suggested (by the children) that we could take our weekly work folders home to show what we were actually accomplishing and that since the intangible work was on the work contract it could be discussed as well.

The rest of the day was spent with as little interference as possible by me. Groups and individuals proceeded with their plans; it was a productive, rewarding day.

The days have fluctuated between optimism and concern, hope and fear. My emotional temperature rises and falls with each rung climbed on the ladder of our adventure. Some days I feel confident, buoyant, sure that we are on the right track—on other days I am assailed by doubts. All the teacher training, authoritarian tradition, curriculum, and report cards threaten and intimidate me.

I must exercise great control when I see a child doing nothing (productive) for most of a day; providing the opportunity to develop self-discipline is an even greater trial at times.

I've come to realize that one must be se-cure in his own self-concept to undertake such a program. In order to relinquish the accepted role of the teacher in a teacher-directed program, one must understand and accept oneself first. It is important as well to have a clear understanding of the goals one is endeavoring to work toward.

April 9, Progress Report:

I prefer the term "self-directed" to "non-directional" in describing our program. I believe it better describes the goals, as well as the actual implementation, of the program.

It is directed, in the sense that we must work within the structure of the curriculum, the specific units of study. It is self-directed in that each child is responsible for his own planning within this basic structure.

At this point, I have only four pupils who are not in the program. I try to provide a period each day for them when they are able to assume some responsibility, make some decisions. They are children who need much additional help and are insecure and frustrated without my guidance.

As I went through the process of putting grades on report cards, I began to realize that the most valuable aspects of the children's growth could not be evaluated in terms of letter grades. For some there is no observable change, or it is intangible—yet one senses growth, a metamorphosis taking place.

Day to day one can sense the growth in

communication, in social development. One cannot measure the difference in attitude, the increased interest, the growing pride in self-improvement, but one is aware that they exist. And how does a teacher evaluate self-discipline? What is easy for me, may not be easy for you!

The report cards are only an indication, but I know the children will be as pleased as I am at the improvement in their grades, and the great decrease in citizenship checks.

In evaluating their work I find them to be fairly perceptive, aware of their capacity and how it relates to their accomplishment. I rarely need to change grades. When I do, sometimes I must upgrade!

I mentioned earlier how many "problems" there have been in this class—both disciplinary and emotional. This program in fact developed out of an attempt to meet the challenge that the "problems" presented. At times I felt whipped, defeated, and frustrated. I felt I was making no headway and resented my role as a policeman.

Since our program has been in full swing I've found that I've undergone change, too. Early in the year I could but bide my time until I could send the "gang" onward and upward—at least see them off to seventh grade.

I find now that I see these children with different eyes, and as I've watched them, I've begun to realize that there *is* hope. I have asked to take this class on, in a self-contained situation, to seventh grade. Scheduling may prevent this becoming an actuality, but I feel these children would continue to progress toward self-actualization within the framework and freedom of the self-directed program.

I feel that now that the mechanics of the program are worked out, now that there is greater understanding and rapport between the children and myself (since I have discarded the authoritarian role), there is greater opportunity for self-growth, not only creativity, initiative, imagination, but self-discipline, self-acceptance, and understanding.

At times when I see children who are not doing what I think they ought to be doing, I must remind myself, again, of the ultimate goals and the fact that they did not produce "required" work when it was assigned previously. They may be drawing something that is not esthetically pleasing to me, but they *are* drawing, and it *is* imaginative! They may not be "busy," but they may be *thinking*; they may be talking, but they are cooperating and learning to communicate; they may fight and respond with signal reactions—abuse one another verbally—but it may be the only way they know. They may not do as much math, but they understand and remember what they do do.

Best of all, they are more interested in school, in their progress. I would venture that this program might result in fewer dropouts, "failures" in school.

It is not the panacea, but it is a step forward. Each day is a new adventure, there are moments of stress, concern, pleasure—they are all stepping stones toward our goal of self-actualization.

There are many different ways of helping students learn and grow. Barbara Shiel found one way. Do you know any other approaches? Have you ever been a student in a nondirective class or an experimental class of some kind? Describe that class. Was it successful? Some teachers let children form partnerships with other children. Each pair studies together, sharing the same tests and grades. So-called slow learners improve. Why? Who is the real teacher?

"The Rise of the Free School"
by Bonnie Barrett Stretch

For the past five years, critics have been telling parents and teachers what is wrong with the public schools. Such writers as John Holt, Herbert Kohl, Jonathan Kozol, George Dennison, and Paul Goodman have described the authoritarianism that structures many classrooms, the stress on grades and discipline at the expense of learning, and the suppression of the natural curiosity and instinct of the young. Many parents and teachers have begun to see for themselves the boredom, fear, and grievous lack of learning that too often accompany schooling—not only for the poor and the black, but for suburban white youngsters as well—and they have begun to ask what can be done about it.

The revolt is no longer against outdated curriculums or ineffective teaching methods—the concerns of the late fifties and early sixties. The revolt today is against the institution itself, against the implicit assumption that learning must be imposed on children by adults, that learning is not something one does by and for oneself, but something designated by a teacher. Schools operating on this assumption tend to hold children in a prolonged state of dependency, to keep them from discovering their own capacities for learning, and to encourage a sense of impotence and lack of worth. The search is for alternatives to this kind of institution.

In the past two years, increasing numbers of parents and teachers have struck out on their own to develop a new kind of school that will allow a new kind of education, that will create independent, courageous people able to face and deal with the shifting complexities of the modern world. The new schools, or free schools, or community schools—they go by all these names—have sprung up by the hundreds across the country. Through a continuous exchange of school brochures and newsletters, and through various conferences, the founders of these schools have developed a degree of self-awareness, a sense of community that has come to be called "the new schools movement."

The new schools charge little or no tuition, are frequently held together by spit and string, and run mainly on the energy and excitement of people who have set out to do their own thing. Their variety seems limitless. No two are alike. They range from inner city black to suburban and rural white. Some seem to be pastoral escapes from the grit of modern conflict, while others are deliberate experiments in integrated multicultural, multilingual education. They turn up anywhere—in city storefronts, old barns, former barracks, abandoned church buildings, and parents' or teachers' homes. They have crazy names like Someday School, Viewpoint Non-School, A Peck of Gold, The New Community, or New Directions—names that for all their diversity reflect the two things most of these schools have in common: the idea of freedom for youngsters and a humane education.

As the Community School of Santa Barbara (California) states in its brochure: "The idea is that freedom is a supreme good; that people, including young people, have a right to freedom, and that people who are free will in general be more open, more humane, more intelligent than people who are directed, manipulated, ordered about . . . ."

The Santa Barbara Community School is located in a converted barracks on a hill above the town. The fifty or so children (ages three to fourteen) almost invariably come from wealthy, white, fairly progressive families who want to give their children "the nicest education possible," as one teacher put it. Inside the building are a large meeting room; some smaller rooms for seminars, discussions, and tutorials; a wood and metal shop; classrooms for the younger children; and a small library. Classes for the younger children are based on the Leicestershire model. Rooms are organized by activity centers—a math corner here, a reading corner there. Parents' money has helped provide a remarkable amount of creative learning materials. Children are free to move from one thing to another as their interest shifts, and children of all ages frequently work and play together. For the older kids, the method is largely tutorial: one, two, or three youngsters working with a teacher. Although there is a "core curriculum" of literature, science, and social studies, the classes follow the interests and preferences of the students.

Outside and behind the building is enough space for a large playground, a pile of wood and lumber, a large pile of scrap metal including bicycle and car parts, and an old car, whose motor the older children are dismantling as a lesson in mechanics or physics (depending on whom you talk to). Children of all ages use the wood and metal to carve or weld into sculpture, as well as to fix bikes and build toys. "It's important for kids to learn about tools," explained a teacher. "Most kids don't know how things work. You really have to see a six year old in goggles with a welding torch to appreciate what it means."

The parents like the school, although they sometimes worry about how much the children are learning. By "learning" they mean the three Rs, social studies, etc. Parent pressure has led the Community School to place more emphasis on traditional subject matter than many free schools do. Teachers, on the other hand, are more concerned about another kind of learning. They would like to help these white middle-class youngsters develop a better sense of the world, to expose them to styles of life and work besides those of their families. There are frequent trips to ranches, factories, local businesses, and other schools. But these experiences, being interludes, remain essentially artificial to children.

What are real are the comforts and concerns that inform their daily lives and that are shared with their friends.

In contrast to this isolation is the Children's Community Workshop School in New York City. Situated in an economically and racially integrated neighborhood, The school makes a conscious effort to keep its enrollment one-third white, one-third black, and one-third Puerto Rican. Because it is intended specifically as an alternative to the public schools, the Community Workshop charges no tuition. It is supported primarily by foundation grants and private donations, but the scramble for money is a continuous one that taxes a great deal of the energy of the school's director, Anita Moses.

Like the Santa Barbara Community School, the Community Workshop bases its structure on the Leicestershire method. And, again like Santa Barbara, it does not hold strictly to that method. There is a great deal of emphasis on the children's own interests, and new directions and materials are being tried all the time. A visitor to the school may find one group of children at a table struggling to build arches out of sugar cubes; another two or three children may be working with an erector set, others with tape recorders and a typewriter. In the midst of all this independent activity may be found one teacher helping one child learn to write his name.

Except for the use of Leicestershire techniques, there is little similarity between the Children's Community workshop and the school in Santa Barbara. The heterogeneity of the student body makes the educational and human problems far more complex. Where achievement levels and cultural backgrounds vary widely, there is a great deal of accommodation necessary on the part of teachers and parents. At the same time, there can be no question that the children are learning more than the traditional three Rs.

Both the Community Workshop and the Santa Barbara Community School, however, have more structure than many free schools. The tendency in these schools is not to stress conventional intellectual training, to offer it if and when the children want it, and in general to let the youngsters discover and pursue their own interests. The new schools agree fully with Piaget's statement that "play is the serious business of childhood," and a child may as easily spend whole days in the sandbox as in the reading center. The lack of structure, however, leads to a lot of noise and running around, and all this activity may seem like chaos to a visitor. Often that's exactly what it is. It is a difficult skill to attune oneself to individual children, and to build on their individual needs and concerns, and few teachers have mastered it. Often, too, older youngsters, suddenly released from the constraints of public school, will run wild for the first few weeks, or even months, of freedom. but gradually, as they work the pent-up energy out of their system, and as they learn that the adults really will allow this freedom, they begin to discover their own real interests and to turn their energy to constructive tasks.

"The longer they've been in public school, and the worse their experience there is, the longer it takes for them to settle down, but eventually they all do," says Bill Kenney, who has taught at Pinel School in Martinez, California, for ten years. Pinel is an essentially Summerhillian school where classes in subjects such as reading and arithmetic are offered, but the children are not compelled to attend. Based on his experience at Pinel, Mr. Kenney believes that in a school that is solidly middle-class it can be expected that any happy, healthy child will eventually learn to read, write, and do basic arithmetic, whether or not he is formally taught. The experience of other middle-class free schools tends to corroborate this assumption

The appeal of this philosophy is enormous, judging from the number of students and teachers applying to the new schools—all these schools report more applicants than they can handle—and from the constant flow of visitors who come to watch, ask questions, and sometimes get in the way. A few schools have had to set up specific visiting days in an effort to stem the tide. Three major conferences on "Alternatives in education" took place this spring—in Cuernavaca, Mexico; in

Santa Barbara, California; and in Toronto, Canada—and people flocked to them by the hundreds to talk to such "heroes" as John Holt and George Dennison, and to talk to one another and learn who's doing what and how. Representatives from foundations, universities, and the U.S. Office of Education also came, eager to know whether the critics' ideas can be given life.

Through the conferences and through correspondence and exchanges of school newsletters, a self-awareness is developing among the new schools, a sense of themselves as part of a growing movement. Much of this increased consciousness is due to the work of the New Schools Exchange, an information clearinghouse that grew out of a conference of 200 schools a year ago. During its first year, the exchange set up a directory of new schools, put teachers and kids in touch with schools, and schools in touch with teachers, kids, materials—and even, occasionally, money. In that year, too, 800 new names were added to the exchange list, and the exchange helped many through the labor pains of birth by offering nuts-and-bolts information about how to incorporate a school, and ways to get through the bureaucratic maze of building, fire, and health regulations.

But the mortality rate among these new schools is high. Harvey Haber of the Exchange estimates about eighteen months is the average life span. This includes those that endure for years and those that barely get off the ground. Money is universally the biggest hassle and the reason most commonly cited for failure. Even those schools that endure are seriously hampered by the constant struggle for fiscal survival that too often must take precedence over education. Most schools are started by people who are not rich, and charge little or no tuition, in an effort to act as an alternative for the common man (the rich have always had alternatives). Teachers work for pennies, when they are paid at all. "How do I survive?" one teacher laughed a bit anxiously. "I found a nice landlord who doesn't bug me about the rent. I dip into my savings, and get my parents and friends to invite me to dinner—often. Then, there are food stamps, of course. Mostly we rely on each other for moral support and help over the really rough places."

This kind of dedication, however, is too much to ask of anyone for any length of time. Working with children in an open classroom with few guidelines makes tremendous demands on teachers, Anita Moses of the Children's Community Workshop points out. Furthermore, teachers must often give their time for planning, for parent conferences, or for Saturday workshops with new teaching techniques and materials. There are intrinsic rewards for this, of course, but extrinsic rewards are also necessary, Mrs. Moses stresses, and those rewards should be in terms of salary.

There are other hurdles besides money—red tape, harassment by various state and city bureaucracies, and hostility from the community at large. In Salt Lake City, for example, a citizens committee tried to close a new Summerhill school on the grounds that the school was immoral and the teachers were Communists.

But perhaps the most fundamental factor for survival is the degree of commitment on the part of the teachers and parents. For brochures, newsletters, and other public pronouncements, it is possible to articulate the concept of freedom and its importance to the emotional and intellectual development of the child. But basically the appeal is to a gut-level longing for love, joy, and human community, and often the schools are run on this romantic basis. "If you stop putting pressure on the kids, the tendency is to stop putting pressure on the staff, too," one teacher observed. Schools that fail within a few months of opening tend to be those begun by people merely interested in trying out a new idea. When the idea turns out to be more complex, and its implementation more difficult than anticipated, the original good feeling evaporates and a deeper determination is required.

Parents and teachers who have worked out their ideas together, who have similar goals, who know what they want for their children and why, have a better chance of keeping their school alive. Nonetheless, almost every school follows a similar pattern. If they make it over the physical hurdles of getting money, finding a building, and meeting bureaucratic regulations they run into the spiritual struggle. Usually, somewhere in the first three to six months, according to Harvey Haber, comes the first great spiritual crisis: "structure" vs. "nonstructure." Having experimented with the idea of freedom, and having discovered its inherent difficulties, many parents and teachers become impatient and anxious. Are the children learning anything, they wonder, and does it matter? Frequently there is a slowdown in acquisition of traditional academic skills. Children, it turns out, would rather play than learn to spell, and the blossoming forth of innate genius in a warm, benevolent atmosphere fails to occur. Anxious adults begin to argue for more structure to the school day, more direction for the kids, more emphasis on the familiar three Rs. Others insist upon maintaining the freedom, and upon learning to work with children on a new freer basis that really tests its limitation and possibilities.

As Robert Greenway, whose sons were enrolled in the Redwood Association Free School in Sonoma County, California, wrote:

It seems to me that this anxiety that gets aroused about "what's happening to our kids" is understandable and inevitable. In a public school, we turn our children over to the wardens; there is no illusion about the possibility of influence to torture us.

. . . But a truly cooperative venture arouses every possible hope about involvement in the growth of our children —and probably every latent frustration about what we think *didn't* happen to us as well. . . . I suggest that, unless we find a way of dealing with the real anxieties and concerns that this type of enterprise arouses, then we'll fail before we've hardly started (I'm responding to my own growing sense of frustration and anxiety, and to the sign of sudden and/or premature withdrawals from the school, and to the growing hue and cry for "more organization").

The Santa Fe (New Mexico) Community School went through this crisis in the middle of its second year, a bit later than most. Parents were willing to go along with the school as long as the teachers seemed confident about what was happening with the children. But when one teacher began to articulate the fears many parents had tried to suppress, the situation came to a head. There was a period of trying to impose more order on the kids, and the kids rebelled and refused to take it. Some staff menbers were fired, and parents demanded more teachers with bachelor's and master's degrees, but found they could not get them for a salary of $200 a month. There were endless pedagogical debates, and finally some of the parents simply took their kids back to the public school. "Unfortunately, those who left were the ones with the most money," sighed one teacher. "We're poorer now, but the people here are here because they're dedicated."

After the crisis, the school was reorganized. Previously ordered by age clusters, it is now divided into activity centers, and children of all ages move freely from one center to another. On a bright Southwestern day a visitor may find a couple of boys sitting in front of the building, slumped against a sunwarmed wall, eating apples and reading comic books. Inside, in the large front room, a group of children may be painting pictures or working with leather or looms. In a quiet, smaller room, someone else is having a guitar lesson. A room toward the back of the building is reserved as the math center; a couple of teachers are math enthusiasts, and many of the older children pick up from their own excitement for the subject.

In the playground behind the building is an Indian kiva built by students and teachers learning about the culture of local Indian tribes. The Southwest is a multicultural area, and the Community School has tried to draw on all these cultures. There are Indian and Spanish children enrolled, as well as white, and each is encouraged to respect and learn from the cultures of the others.

But despite its efforts to reach into the Indian and Spanish communities, the Santa Fe Community School remains essentially a white middle-class school. The Chicanos and Indians, mainly poor or working-class, tend to shy away from such experiments, partly because their cultures are traditionally conservative with highly structured roles for adults and children, and partly because the poor cannot afford to take a chance on the future of their young. Middle-class whites can always slip back into the mainstream if they choose. But for the poor, neither the acquisition of such intellectual tools as reading and writing nor a place in the economy is guaranteed.

These fundamental differences show up clearly in the community schools operated by and for black people. Black people on the whole bring their children to these schools, not merely because they believe in freedom for self-expression or letting the child develop his own interests, but because their children are not learning in the public schools, are turning sullen and rebellious by the age of eight, and are dropping out of school in droves. The ideology in many of these schools is not pedagogical, but what one school calls "blackology"—the need to educate the children in basic skills and in pride of race. In the black schools there is much more emphasis on basic intellectual training and much more participation on the part of parents. By and large, parents are the founders of these schools; they are the main source of inspiration and energy. They have the final say in selecting both teachers and curriculum, and their chief criterion is: Are the children learning?

As in the white schools, classrooms for the younger children are frequently patterned after the Leicestershire model. But the approach is deliberately eclectic, providing closer guidance and more structured activities for youngsters who need it. The academic progress of the children is carefully observed and quietly but firmly encouraged. "We want teachers who will try a thousand different ways to teach our children," said one mother.

Equally important is a teacher's attitude toward race. Although some schools would like to have all-black faculties—and in a number of cities, parents are in training to become teachers and teacher aides—they must still hire mainly whites. "When I interview a teacher," said Luther Seabrook, principal of the Highland Park Free School in Boston, "I always ask, can you think of a community person as an equal in the classroom?" Many teachers cannot, either because of racial bias, or because of notions about professionalism. Even after a teacher is hired, the going is still rough where feelings run high on the part of blacks and whites, but there is a determination to confront these problems directly through open discussion and group sessions.

The same approach applies to daily work in the classroom. Teachers and aides are encouraged to talk openly about their successes and problems in weekly planning sessions, to admit mistakes, and to try out new ideas.

Such sessions are frequently the keystone of the teaching process in these schools. They are the times when teachers can get together and evaluate what has been happening in the classroom, how the children have responded to it, and how the teachers have responded to the children. "It's a tremendous place to grow," one teacher remarked. "You're not tied to a curriculum or structure, and you're not afraid to make mistakes. Everyone here is in the same boat. We get support from each other and develop our own ways of handling things."

There is little doubt that the youngsters prefer the community schools to traditional schools. The humane and personal atmosphere in the small, open classrooms makes a fundamental difference. The children work together writing stories or figuring math problems, working with Cuisenaire rods or an elementary science kit. They are proud of their work and show it eagerly to visitors. There is virtually no truancy, and many youngsters hate to stay home even on weekends, according to their mothers.

But perhaps the greatest achievement of these schools is with the parents. They develop a new faith, not only in their children but in themselves. "Now I know," said a New York City mother, "that, even though I didn't finish high school, it is possible for me to understand what they are teaching my child." In changing their children's lives, these parents have discovered the power to change their own lives, as well. Parents who are not already working as aides and coordinators in the classrooms drop by their schools often to see how Johnny is doing. At the East Harlem Block Schools in New York, stuffed chairs and couches and hot coffee put parents at ease, while teachers talk with them as equals and draw them into the education of their children.

Nonetheless, black schools share many of the problems with the community that white schools have. People are suspicious of new ways of teaching, even though their children obviously are failing under the old ways. Parents who enroll their children out of desperation still grow anxious when they see the amount of freedom allowed. In integrated schools, like Santa Fe or the Children's Community workshop, there is the added problem of race and class, as middle-class parents learn that all the children are not necessarily going to adopt middle-class values and lifestyles, that cultural differences are valid and must be accepted.

Some schools are fed up with "parent education"; it takes too much time away from the children. A number of schools already are taking only children whose parents are in sympathy with their aims, parents who won't panic if the child doesn't learn to read until he is eight or nine.

But as a school grows more homogeneous, it faces the danger of becoming an isolated shelter against the reality of the outside world. Instead of educating kids to be strong and open enough to deal with a complex world, the schools may become elitist cloisters that segregate a few people even further from the crowd.

Once again the free schools must ask themselves what they are all about. If one assumes (as many free schools do) that any healthy, happy youngster will eventually learn to read and write, then what is the purpose of school? Is it enough simply to provide one's children with a school environment more humane than the public schools, and then stay out of nature's way?

At a California high school in the Sausalito hills, teachers and students think that that in itself is quite a lot. After going through a typical cycle of kids getting high on freedom and doing nothing for six months, getting bored, and finally facing the big questions—What am I doing? Where am I going?—students and teachers think they have learned a lot about themselves and each other. But as the youngsters return to studying and start to seek answers to those questions, they find the teachers have little to offer besides a sympathetic ear. Some kids return to the public school feeling better for their experience with freedom. (Feeling, too, perhaps, that it didn't work, that they really do need all the rules and discipline their parents and teachers demanded.) Gradually,

those who remain have forced the teachers back to the traditional textbooks as the chief source of knowledge.

The humane atmosphere remains, but missing is a curriculum that truly nurtures the independence of thought and spirit so often talked of and so rarely seen. It takes extraordinary ingenuity to build on students' needs and interests. A few brilliant teachers, such as Herbert Kohl, can turn kids on, meet them where they are, and take them further—can, for example, take a discussion of drugs and dreams and guide it through the realms of mythology, philosophy, and Jungian psychology. But what do you do if you're not a Herb Kohl? According to Anita Moses, you "work damn hard." There are other things, too: You can hire a master teacher familiar with the wide range of curriculum materials available. Little by little you can change the classroom, or the school itself, to make it do the things you want it to do. And little by little, through working with the children and hashing out problems with help from the rest of the staff, you begin to know what it is you want to do and how you can do it.

But even this does not answer the deeper questions—questions that are implicit in every free school, but that few have faced. Is it only a new curriculum or new ways of teaching that we need? Or do we need to change our ideas about children, about childhood itself, about how children learn, what they learn, what they need to learn, from whom or from what kinds of experience? It is clear that our ideas about teaching are inadequate, but is it possible that they are simply false? For example, children can often learn to read and write without any formal instruction. This is not a miracle; it is a response of an intelligent young being to a literate milieu. It is also clear that children learn many cognitive as well as social abilities from their peers or from children but a few years older than themselves. What, then, is the role of the adult in the learning of the child?

In simpler times, children learned from adults continually, through constant contact and interchange, and through their place close to the heart of the community. Today, the society has lost this organic unity. We live in times when children often see their fathers only on weekends. We live in a world that separates work from play, school from the "real" world, childhood from personhood. The young are isolated from participation in the community. They seem to have no integral place in the culture. Too often schools have become artificial environments created by adults for children. How is it possible to forsake these roles?

Young people are trying. Many will no longer accept without question authority based solely on tradition or age. They are seeking alternatives to The Way Things Are.

But the venture into unfamiliar territory generates enormous anxieties. The young are painfully aware of their own inexperience; they lack faith in themselves. But who can help them in their conflicts both within themselves and with the outside world? Surely, this is a function of education. But in today's world there are few adults who can do this for themselves, far less for their children. For who can respond with assurance to the anxieties of young people over sex, drugs, and the general peril in which we live? Who knows how to deal with others when the traditional roles are gone?

And yet it should be possible for adults to relate to young people in some constructive way. It must be possible because the young, in their alienation and confusion, and the culture, in its schizoid suffering, demand it. In the words of Peter Marin, former director of the Pacific High School, a free school in California:

> Somebody must step past the children, must move into his own psyche or two steps past his own limits into the absolute landscape of fear and potential these children inhabit. . . . I mean: we cannot *follow* the children any longer, we have to step ahead of them. Somebody has to mark a trail.

Is this what the free schools are all about? Few of them have asked these questions. Few will ever want to. But the questions are implicit in the movement. The free schools offer

alternatives—alternatives that may be shaped to meet new needs and aims. At least, they offer a first step. At least, the possibility is there.

If you would like to learn more about free schools, here are some ways.

Find out what alternatives to traditional schools are available in your community. Who is marking a trail? Visit some of these schools. Talk to the students and teachers. What do they think of their school? What problems are there? What attitudes do adults hold toward students and students toward adults in these schools? Do you see these schools as model educational systems for the rest of society in the near future? Why or why not? Would you like to be a student in a free school or send your child to one?

Read *Summerhill* by A. S. Neill.

See "People, Places, and Things" in the back of the book for further information on free schools and other new developments.

The Real Teacher

What do you think a real teacher is? A real teacher _____

A real teacher is on my side.
A real teacher lets me be me and tries to understand what it's like to be me.
A real teacher accepts me whether he likes me or not.
A real teacher doesn't have expectations of me because of what I've been or what he's been.
A real teacher is more interested in how I learn than what I learn.
A real teacher doesn't make me feel anxious and afraid.
A real teacher provides many choices.
A real teacher lets me teach myself even if it takes longer.
A real teacher talks so I can understand what he means to say.
A real teacher can make mistakes and admit it.
A real teacher can show his feelings and let me show mine.
A real teacher wants me to evaluate my own work.

Read *On Becoming a Person* and *Freedom to Learn* by Carl Rogers, two books which have influenced many teachers who are trying to be real.

From *Students Without Teachers*
by Harold Taylor

When Theodore Roethke came into class he brought with him everything he was, his passions, his love of poetry, his tenderness, his awkwardness, his irrationality, his habits of scattered thought and scattered reading, his terrible jokes, his good ones, his clowning, sometimes his showing-off, and his deep and compelling wish that his students write, read, speak, and listen to poetry, speak it to each other and learn from it. No one in his class could mistake his meaning or intent no matter what they thought of his style. His assignments of reading were the outcome of what his meetings with the class suggested to him, what he thought would work for them, and they were of all kinds. His purpose in making assignments, as his purpose in teaching, was to tie his students to a love of poetry forever. Then there would be no need for assignments. They are only the means by which the teacher can help to give his students a beginning from which they will never turn back, and that is the ground on which the assignments should be chosen.

Roethke told one class at the beginning of the term what he meant to do with them and how he meant to teach them.

> To find out something about your life: that will be the purpose. It may be necessary to change some of your ways of acting and thinking in the course. The burden will lie on you a good deal more; but it also, I wish you to understand, will lie on me a good deal more. It is much easier for me to lecture than it is for me to store up your various reactions, attitudes, keep turning them over in my mind, letting my unconscious, my creative capacity evolve something, make a synthesis, come through with the right nudges, jeers, japes, kind or harsh words which will bring you into fuller being. Crudely put, it is like this: I am willing to give you a chunk of myself—my time, my patience, my talent—*if* you want it. . . . Faith. That's it. This course is an act of faith. In what? In the imagination of us all, in a creative capacity—that most sacred thing—that lies dormant, *never* dead, in everyone.

What Roethke says in this is very close to the heart of what it means to teach and how an artist in the medium goes about his work. There is no talk here about theories of education, "ground to be covered," or assignments to be met, only about man teaching.

A Teacher

A teacher's got a temper
like a bull.
He growls and roars
like a tiger,
he stamps and gets mad
and sometimes he's glad
he did it.

Bruce McGregor,
Age 11,
Australia

From "The Zaddik"
by Sheldon Kopp

The *relationship* between the zaddik and his disciple was the crucial factor in . . . [the] attempt to give spiritual help, just as the relationship between therapist and patient is crucial. The personality of the teacher takes the place of doctrine. He *is* the teaching. As one student said: "I did not go to my zaddik to learn Torah from him, but to watch him tie his bootlaces."

The zaddik is a helper who extends his hand to a follower and, if the follower will take it, guides him until he is able to find his own way. Yet, the zaddik must never relieve his follower of the responsibility of doing for himself whatever he is strong enough to do. As Rabbi Baer points out, "What you don't get by your own work, you don't have."

At the same time, the zaddik must participate in a way that risks his own deep personal involvement. He must be willing to be close to another and to get caught up in his troubles. "If you want to raise a man from mud and filth . . . you must not hesitate to get yourself dirty."

In a curious way, what the zaddik has to offer is himself. If someone really can learn to be with him, he will have learned what he needs to know. Sometimes the zaddik is caught between what he feels he must do and what he thinks he ought to do. Rabbi Bunam tells of a time when he felt the need to tell a certain story but was tempted not to because it was so worldly and would surely arouse vulgar laughter. He feared that his followers would no longer consider him a rabbi. He decided, nevertheless, to follow his inner feelings and tell the story. The result, he said, was that "the gathering burst out laughing. And those who up to this point were distant from me attached themselves to me." The zaddik risks simply being himself through trusting his feelings and acting on them, thereby engaging a like commitment from his followers.

Have you ever known a zaddik, a Hasidic teacher? Have you ever known a Zen Master? A guru?

If the teacher is not willing to risk new feeling, surely the students will be reluctant to take similar risks. Risk is a contribution that existential analysis has made to traditional psychotherapy. It puts the emphasis on action as the best way of demonstrating to an individual that his expectations and fantasies about his own behavior and response to that behavior may be inaccurate. As a teacher, I have found that I can be more open about my difficulties with a text, my discomfort in a particular atmosphere . . . than I ever imagined. Indeed, I find that those classes are the ones students appreciate most and the ones in which students give most of themselves.

From H. R. Wolf, "Teaching and Human Development: Truth's Body" in *New Directions in Teaching*

From *Perceiving, Behaving, Becoming*
ASCD 1962 Yearbook Committee by Arthur W. Combs, Chairman

SIGNS OF CREATIVE TEACHING

Too many of a child's experiences in too many school situations say to him that he is not enough. When the teacher directs, controls, motivates, questions and evaluates, demands the excuse and asks the reason for behavior, the child must feel that it is wrong to be what he is. When teachers permit children to be what they are and not just what teachers want them to become, openness to experience and a self-directed moving into learning are possible. In such classrooms the following evidences of creative teaching and learning may be observed:

Less teacher domination; more faith that children can find answers satisfying to them.

Less teacher talk; more listening to children, allowing them to use the teacher and the group as a sounding board when ideas are explored.

Less questioning for the right answer; more open-ended questions with room for difference and the exploration of many answers.

Less destructive criticism; more teacher help which directs the child's attention back to his own feelings for clarification and understanding.

Less emphasis on failure; more acceptance of mistakes—more feeling on the part of the child that when he makes a mistake it is done, accepted and that's it. As one child said, "She doesn't rub salt in."

Children's work is appreciated, but praise is not used to put words in the mouths of children.

Goals are clearly defined; structure is understood and accepted by the group.

Within appropriate limits, children are given responsibility and freedom to work. "For once a teacher told us we could do it ourselves and really meant it."

Children are free to express what they feel and seem secure in their knowledge that the teacher likes them as they are.

Ideas are explored; there is an honest respect for solid information, an attitude of "let's find out."

There is a balance of common tasks and individual responsibility for specific tasks which are unique and not shared.

The teacher communicates clearly to children that learning is self-learning. Faith is demonstrated that all children want to become and pupils show satisfaction as they become aware of their growth.

Evaluation is a shared process and includes more than academic achievement.

Motivation for learning is high and seems inner-directed; pupil activity seems to say, "I've got a job I want to do."

From "Teaching in a Vacuum"
by Theodore W. Hipple

One day last year in a lounge conversation I had with a fellow teacher, the subject strayed from the customary baseball bets and salary gripes to something unusual: teaching. We were exploring the area of how we perceived our jobs, a topic we began by simply naming what we did. To my comment that I believed that I was a teacher of high school youth who happened, primarily because of interests of mine, to teach them English, my friend replied that he was, first and last, a chemistry teacher. So strongly convinced of the ultimate importance of his subject was he that any efforts of mine to make him see that the youth he taught were at least equally important, and really vastly more important, failed miserably. He could not see it.

Finally, I hit upon what I thought would be a successful ploy. Slyly I slipped into the conversation this question: "I suppose, then, that you could teach chemistry in a vacuum?"

He gave my question more serious consideration than it deserved and then overpowered me with his answer. "Yes, I could. The kids in my classes are helpful as I can use them as sounding boards and let their responses be a means of progressing with the lesson, but I could handle these matters differently if there were no students present. I could still teach chemistry."

I was shocked. I had taught next to this man for some time and did not know how much his views differed from mine. I then began asking other teachers, high school and college, how they felt and discovered that my friend, far from being a minority of one, voiced a fairly common opinion. It seemed to me that I had the germ of something here: later questioning and further observation of teachers and teaching have convinced me of it. Today's high school and college teachers, large numbers of them at least, could, like my friend, teach in an empty classroom and be comfortable doing it. The next step, then, was to satisfy myself about who, if either of us, was out of step. Possibly, I thought, there is room for both kinds of thinking in teaching.

I am now convinced that I was wrong even to consider that teachers may regard their students as so many inanimate blotters and be allowed to get away with it. Teaching is ternary: X teaches Y to Z. Without a large amount of demonstrated consideration of the needs and interests of both X and Z, not much teaching is going to go on.

"Oh, of course," my friend would argue, "I don't teach in a vacuum, there are students there and I try to gear my course to what I think they can handle. But I still insist that what I teach is, and ought to be, chemistry. The discussing of some general topic, no matter how interesting, I would have to regard as an unjustified intrusion into the classroom lesson."

I disagree. Today's high school or college teachers cannot have this attitude and do the kind of job society has every right to expect of them. We teachers are not simply imparters of knowledges and skills, however we may glorify these with our acronymic curricula and Socratic methods of inquiry. We are, rather, the shapers of living, breathing human beings, and unless we ourselves endeavor to come across to our students as equally living and breathing, our efforts to shape this behavior may not reap the potential benefits available to us; we can, though, by being willing to reveal our widespread interests, be of significant service to our students.

Consider another point for a minute. Why is it that elementary school teachers are almost universally liked by their pupils? They do the same sorts of things that we teachers of high school and college students do: they give assignments and tests, pass and fail students, keep some after school, smile at some, frown at others. The reason their pupils like them is, I think, that these teachers are seen by their students as whole human beings. We, simply but sadly, are not so regarded by our students.

The elementary teacher is knowledgeable about many things: she teaches art, English, math, singing, social studies, science. She discusses current events from the weekly news magazines her students subscribe to, plays tag with them as she monitors the playground, admonishes them to wear boots as "It's cold-catching weather."

We, on the other hand, are seen as masters of one trade, but jacks of none. We know ancient history or Latin or microbiology or Shakespearean tragedy, but, it appears, nothing else. It may very well be that we have our students much at heart, but not, I fear, as whole people, but rather as so many consumers of ancient history or Latin or microbiology or Shakespearean tragedy.

Just as we fail to demonstrate that we see our students in their totality as vital, dynamic human beings, so also do we forbid them to see us as anything but the masters of that which we profess to know: our subject. Our seeming reluctance to talk of anything other than these artificially organized pieces of knowledge militates against fruitful discussion and reinforces the television image of the competent-in-but-one-area teacher. . . .

Were your elementary teachers "whole human beings" and your secondary teachers competent-in-but-one-area?

Education derives from the Latin verb *educare*, to train, to instruct, to put in, or from the verb *educere*, to draw out, to lead forth. Recall a teacher who was important to you. Did this teacher draw from you ability you did not realize you had? Or did he give you something you did not already have? Did he do both? What did he draw out? How did that ability get there originally? What did he choose to put in? Is the emphasis on the student or on the subject matter? Is it a question of either/or?

From *The Child and the Curriculum* by John Dewey

"Discipline" is the watchword of those who magnify the course of study; "interest" that of those who blazon "The Child" upon their banner. The standpoint of the former is logical; that of the latter psychological. The first emphasizes the necessity of adequate training and scholarship on the part of the teacher; the latter that of need of sympathy with the child, and knowledge of his natural instincts. "Guidance and control" are the catchwords of one school; "freedom and initiative" of the other. Law is asserted here; spontaneity proclaimed there. The old, the conservation of what has been achieved in the pain and toil of the ages, is dear to the one; the new, change, progress wins the affection of the other. Inertness and routine, chaos and anarchism, are accusations bandied back and forth. Neglect of the sacred authority of duty is charged by one side, only to be met by countercharges of suppression of individuality through tyrannical despotism.

Such oppositions are rarely carried to their logical conclusion. Common sense recoils at the extreme character of these results. They are left to theorists, while common sense vibrates back and forward in a maze of inconsistent compromise. The need of getting theory and practical common sense into closer connection suggests a return to our original thesis: that we have here conditions which are necessarily related to each other in the educative process, since this is precisely one of interaction and adjustment.

What, then, is the problem? It is just to get rid of the prejudicial notion that there is some gap in kind (as distinct from degree) between the child's experience and the various forms of subject matter that make up the course of study. From the side of the child, it is a question of seeing how his experience already contains within itself elements—facts and truths—of just the same sort as those entering into the formulated study; and, what is of more importance, of how it contains within itself the attitudes, the motives, and the interests which have operated in developing and organizing the subject matter to the plane which it now occupies. From the side of the studies, it is a question of interpreting them as outgrowths of forces operating in the child's life, and of discovering the steps that intervene between the child's present experience and their richer maturity.

Abandon the notion of subject matter as something fixed and ready-made in itself, outside the child's experience; cease thinking of the child's experience as also something hard and fast; see it as something fluent, embryonic, vital; and we realize that the child and the curriculum are simply two limits which define a single process. Just as two points define a straight line, so the present standpoint of the child and the facts and truths of studies define instruction. It is continuous reconstruction, moving from the child's present experience out into that represented by the organized bodies of truth that we call studies.

On the face of it, the various studies, arithmetic, geography, language, botany, etc., are themselves experience—they are that of the race. They embody the cumulative outcome of the efforts, the strivings, and successes of the human race generation after generation. They present this, not as a mere accumulation, not as a miscellaneous heap of separate bits of experience, but in some organized and systematized way—that is, as reflectively formulated.

Hence, the facts and truths that enter into the child's present experience, and those contained in the subject matter of studies, are the initial and final terms of one reality. To oppose one to the other is to oppose the infancy and maturity of the same growing life; it is to set the moving tendency and the final result of the same process over against each other; it is to hold that the nature and the destiny of the child war with each other.

Define "continuous reconstruction" or make a drawing of the relationship of the child to the curriculum. Why are school learning and experience often separated from life?

I submit that learning is relational, that it can occur only in the context of a relationship and that a relationship cannot occur unless those involved with it consciously commit themselves to it. This conscious commitment condemns the fixed patterns that are the historical mode of education because the essential dynamic of a relationship insists that the self of one person communicate with the self of another person, and it means that neither person withholds the participating self. The existentialist argues that man is a meaning-disclosing being, and it is that shared commitment to self-disclosure that unifies the student-teacher and learning-teaching relationships. Thus, the self of the teacher is as central to the development of the curriculum which is the environment of those relationships as is the course the "teacher" is asked to teach.

From Scott Hope, "Relations Stop Nowhere" in *New Directions in Teaching*

How does the *way* teachers and students relate to each other affect *what* each learns?

The Cairn

When I think of the little children learning
In all the schools of the world,
Learning in Danish, learning in Japanese
That two and two are four, and where the
  rivers of the world
Rise, and the names of the mountains and
  the principal cities,
My heart breaks.
Come up, children! Toss your little stones
  gaily
on the great cairn of Knowledge!
(Where lies what Euclid knew, a little grey
  stone,
What Plato, what Pascal, what Galileo:
Little grey stones, little grey stones on a
  cairn.)
Tell me, what is the name of the highest
  mountain?
Name me a crater of fire! a peak of snow!
Name me the mountains on the moon!
But the name of the mountain that you climb
  all day,
Ask not your teacher that.
Edna St. Vincent Millay

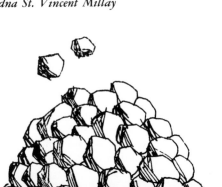

A teacher can withhold life from children by failing to give freely to them the truths he thinks he has learned in his lifetime. Some of us may feel teaching should be a very impersonal, objective thing, that the teacher's role is to get children to interact with materials of instruction. Thus, children are deprived of their greatest heritage—the knowledge secured the hard way by the teacher's generation. Adults are responsible for seeing that the new generation receives the benefit of what it took them decades to learn. If we teach little children what we were taught as children, but no longer believe, then human potentiality will drag along on the old myths and superstitions . . . there has been entirely too much emphasis on objectivity in teaching, on the safe, impersonal use of instructional material. This is the hygienic approach; no one gets infected this way, and no one gets excited either.
Donald McNassor

Would you agree that the teacher teaches his own "infection" and "excitement" rather than course content? Or that "what the teacher is, is more important than what the teacher teaches" as stated by Karl Menninger in *Love Against Hate*? Is it either/or?

One way to learn about oneself is to read books written by teachers who have made some progress in their own struggle to know themselves and their students.

Readings

Ashton-Warner, Sylvia. *Spinster*. New York: Simon & Schuster, 1959.

——. *Teacher*. New York: Simon & Schuster, 1963.

——. *Myself*. New York: Simon & Schuster, 1964.

Bliss, Perry. *And Gladly Teach*. Boston: Houghton, Mifflin Co., 1935.

Braithwaite, E. R. *To Sir with Love*. Englewood Cliffs, N.J.: Prentice-Hall, 1960.

Chase, Mary Ellen. *A Goodly Fellowship*. New York: MacMillan Co., 1939.

Decker, Sunny. *An Empty Spoon*. New York: Harper & Row, 1969.

Dennison, George. *The Lives of Children*, New York: Random House, 1969.

Gordon, Julia Weber. *My Country School Diary*. New York: Harper & Bros., 1946; Dell, 1970.

Herndson, James. *The Way It Spozed to Be*. New York: Bantam Books, 1968.

——. *How to Survive in Your Native Land*. New York: Simon & Schuster, 1971.

Holt, John. *How Children Fail*. New York: Dell Publishing Co., 1964.

——. *How Children Learn*. New York: Pitman Publishing, 1967.

Kaufman, Bel. *Up the Down Staircase*. Englewood Cliffs, N.J.: Prentice-Hall, 1964.

Keller, Helen. *The Story of My Life*. New York: Doubleday & Co., 1903.

Kohl, Herbert. *36 Children*. New York: New American Library, 1967.

Kozol, Jonathan. *Death at an Early Age*. Boston: Houghton Mifflin Co., 1967.

Lane, Homer. *Talks to Parents & Teachers*. New York: Schocken, 1969.

Mayhew, K. C., and Edwards, A. C. *The Dewey School*. New York: Atherton Press, 1966.

Neill, A. S. *Summerhill: A Radical Approach to Child Rearing*. New York: Hart Publishing Co., 1960.

Patton, Frances. *Good Morning, Miss Dove*. New York: Dodd, Mead & Co., 1954.

Postman, Neil, and Weingartner, Charles. *Teaching as a Subversive Activity*. New York: Delacorte Press, 1969.

——. *The Soft Revolution*. New York: Delacorte Press, 1971.

Richardson, Elwyn S. *In the Early World*. New Zealand Council for Educational Research, 1964. New York: Pantheon Books, 1969.

Russell, Bertrand. *Education and the Good Life*. New York: Liveright, 1931.

Stuart, Jesse. *The Thread that Runs So True*. New York: Charles Scribner's Sons, 1949.

Tharp, Louise Hall. *Until Victory*. Boston: Little, Brown & Co., 1953.

Yates, Elizabeth. *Nearby*. New York: Coward-McCann, 1947.

Teachers speak to teachers. What do these teachers say to you?

Learn to keep your perspective. Nothing that happens on any one day in any one classroom is a world-shaking event—remember that when it temporarily shakes *you*. A sense of humor helps; especially when the joke's on you.

Learn to do your own thing. Your teaching personality has to be your every-day personality, or the children will tear your ego to shreds. They may even give you some insights into what you really are. If you can't take that—working with children is not for you.

Learn to live with failure. You'll never do as much for any child as you hoped to do, and you'll know you've failed completely with some. Be able to fail without feeling yourself a failure; and to measure yourself by what you can accomplish and not what you cant'.

Margaret L. Barkley
A second-grade teacher

At my table looking out the windows I wonder what to say to you . . . to a young teacher. Across the spring garden, above the cineraria, through the trunks of the towering trees; over the silk water of the inner harbor I see the ships' entrance, beyond which is

A teacher affects eternity;

the tall Pacific and beyond that, your country. Only to find I have no advice.

I look back on 50 years, you look forward on 50 years. This world is yours, not mine. It was mine when I was young and I strongly knew it. True, there's a war on now but there was one on then; the world still belongs to you. For ever the world belongs to youth. Do you also strongly know it?

From 50 I have no advice. But from 30 I have! In the splendid authority of youth to youth I quote from those blurring pages, written in fierce swift pencil-passion: "You must be true to yourself. Strong enough to be true to yourself. Brave enough, to be strong enough, to be true to yourself. Wise enough, to be brave enough, to be strong enough, to be true enough to shape yourself from what you actually are. What big words, O my Self: true, strong, brave and wise! But that's how it is, my Self. That's how it must be for you to walk steadily in your own ways, as gracefully as you feel, as upright as you feel, a ridiculous flower on top of your head, a sentimental daisy. For therein lies your individuality, your own authentic signature, the source of others' love for you.
From Sylvia Ashton-Warner, *Myself*

The painting is called "Primeval Wall," and it represents the ancient cave paintings where the drama of teaching began a hundred million years ago.

From Henry Adams, *The Education of Henry Adams*. Artist William Baziotes. Courtesy of Container Corporation of America.

he can never tell where his influence stops

The Gestalt Prayer

I do my thing, and you do your thing.
I am not in this world to live up to your
  expectations
And you are not in this world to live up
  to mine.
You are you and I am I,
And if by chance we find each other, it's
  beautiful.
If not, it can't be helped.
Frederick S. Perls

Be The Teacher

You know how to do something others
don't. Teach all or some students how. You
know about something others don't. Get
others interested in learning about it. Find out
what other students are interested in exploring. Teach each other. Choose a game or
exercise, one of your own or any of the following. Remember your childhood favorites.
Warm-up, if you wish, by first teaching the
game to a small group of students. When you
are ready, teach it to the class. Games help
people relax and relate to each other. Games
keep us in the here and now. Games can help
you be you. Do you dare?

Warm-up Games

There is one seat available
in a class. Four people
want it. Present yourself
orally or in writing, giving
the arguments why you
should have the place.

Form two lines facing each
other. Each person carefully look
over the person opposite.
Then shift the line one position
so that each has a new partner.
Again examine the person
opposite, then shift until the group has
rotated completely and you
are back to your original
partner.

Carry on a conversation with your partner using
declarative statements only—no questions.
Comments may be nonconsequential or serious.
Ex: "I like peanut butter." "I love my wife."

Say your name.
Now make a movement
to express that name. The
group imitates the movement
and says the name.
Turn to another student
and say, "And who are you?"
Continue the exercise with
each person in the group.

Hold a pencil or pen
and say, "This is Peter."
"I'm Phyllis and who are you?"
Hand the pencil to the next person
who says, "This is Peter.
You're Phyllis. I'm Bill,
and who are you?"
Each person adds his own name
to the others around the circle.

Choose another person in the class, preferably someone you don't know. Take turns finding out as much about the other person as possible, knowing you will have to introduce him to the class later. Take a walk together or find a quiet corner.

Introduce yourself saying, "And now I'd like you to meet . . .

Introduce yourself saying, "My name is Dick and I feel . . . (tired, silly)

Pretend you're at a cocktail party. Get up and walk about the room, meeting people informally and making small talk, the sillier the better.

Carry on a conversation with another person using only that person's name. See how great a range of meaning you can experience through sounds, facial expressions, and gestures.

Get in touch with a sound inside of you, make that sound, then say your name. Then say, "Now I am aware of . . ." Tell the group what feelings or sounds you are aware of. Keep your eyes closed, then open your eyes, look at the group, and say your name.

Share bread together. Look, smell, and pass the loaf around the circle. One person slowly breaks the loaf in half and passes both halves around the circle. Look in one another's eyes as the loaf is passed. Break off a piece and place it in your mouth with your eyes closed. Take your time. Chew slowly. Taste the bread. Open your eyes and see the group. Share your feelings.

Close your eyes. Listen to what is going on inside of you. Slowly extend your hands and explore the space in front of your chair, under your chair, behind your chair, above your chair. Feel all around, even touching the person next to you. Slowly open your eyes and share this experience with the class.

Sit or lie down. Close your eyes and concentrate on the sounds around you, your breathing. Tense up as much of the body as possible, then relax. Repeat several times, tightening and relaxing.

Close your eyes, touch, tap, or slap your face, neck, shoulders, arms, hands, chest, stomach, buttocks, thighs, legs, and feet. Open your eyes.

Be gentle as you touch, tap or slap another person, his head, face, neck, shoulders, and arms. Have him bend over as you continue the exercise on his back, buttocks, legs. Exchange.

Close your eyes. Touch, tap, or slap with fingers relaxed and gentle your head, one area at a time for several seconds—the top, sides, back, forehead— all over your head. Stop and put your hands down. Open your eyes.

Take a voyage through your body with your eyes closed. Breathe easily. Be aware of your feet resting on the floor; don't move them. Continue the trip slowly moving through your body: your toes, your heels, the top of your feet, the calves, the knees, the thighs, the buttocks, your lower back, your back leaning against the chair, your shoulders, upper arms, elbows, wrists, hands, fingers, your neck, the back of your head, the top of your head, the forehead, your cheeks, nose, and mouth; be aware of your breathing, the sounds in the room. Then slowly open your eyes.

Other Games

Place your left hand on your own face while placing your right hand on your partner's face. Your partner does the same. Touch—explore each other's faces.

Sit in a circle. Choose a conductor. Everyone create a sound and rhythm using voice and/or hands, feet etc. which the conductor orchestrates.

Close your eyes. Let a leader guide you to a partner. Explore each other's hands until the leader separates you. Mill around the room. Open your eyes and try to find the person who was your partner.

Be the teacher, the guru, the wise man. Throw a ball, pencil or any small object to someone in the circle. Ask him to be the teacher and tell all he knows about shoes, a wall, the sky, a candle, etc. Let each person assume the role of teacher.

Write as much as possible on a subject chosen by the "teacher for the day." Don't worry about spelling, punctuation, or grammar. If you are the "teacher," select anything evocative or provocative: a news clipping, a quotation, a musical selection, a poster etc. Then collect the papers, write comments on them, return them and invite discussion.

Position yourself comfortably on the floor or on a chair. Sit relaxed. Don't lean against anything. Take a deep breath moving your head toward the floor. Let the breath out as you lift your head back up. Pay attention to your breathing. Rock gently back and forth. Find a spot on the floor about four feet in front of you. Look at it. Let your eyes go slightly out of focus. Let your hands rest, palms up on your knees about a foot apart. Be in an open, receptive position. Let all the sounds come and go. Let your thoughts come and go freely. Do not try to block them. Do not dwell on them. Let them flow like water through your mind. Let the teacher tell you when to stop. Return gradually to the group. Make eye contact with all persons. Where are you now? Are you centered?

Speak extemporaneously (three to five minutes) on subjects chosen by the "teacher for the day." Use a tape recorder for playback.

Walk about the room in all directions. Start shaking the hands of persons you meet. Now shake elbows, then shoulders, hips, legs, ears, nose. Spend at least 15 seconds with each area. Close your eyes and experience your feeling.

Stand facing your partner with palms touching, elbows up. Have a hand dance, one person leading the other, until you're dancing without a leader. Be playful, argumentative, seductive. Move about the room. Slowly stop the dance, remaining still, palms together. CLose your eyes. One partner take a step back and lean his weight against the other. Reverse. Both partners lean against each other. Slowly stand up and separate.

Be Frank Laubach, who taught adults how to read throughout the world. Choose a partner, one to play the teacher, the other to play the student. Go through a reading lesson without once saying "no" or "wrong." Vary your approach. Avoid any negative statements. Try to teach reading without saying "yes" or "right" either. Be nonjudgmental. Switch roles.

Walk about the room shaking right hands. Upon direction stop and touch and feel someone's right hand. Walk about the room shaking left hands. Then stop and get to know a left hand. Move about the room shaking both hands, quickly, slowly, gently, angrily, sadly, tenderly. Then stop and explore two hands with eyes closed. Have an argument, make up, play, dance. Still holding hands, open your eyes. See your partner.

****

Start a sound. The person next to you picks it up and repeats it with you until he mimics your sound exactly. Then he alone keeps the sound until he transforms it into a sound of his own. The next person picks up that sound, mimics it, makes it his own, and then passes it on.

Stand an arm's length apart. Concentrate your eyes at the stomach level of your partner. Bring your right hands very slowly into the space between. Let your hands relate to each other without touching. After a time, introduce the left hand. Let all hands relate without touching unless teacher suggests this. Bring hands to rest.

117

With your eyes closed back slowly toward the center of the room. As you touch others, find a back, stay for several seconds, then move on. After a few minutes of back touching, separate while you explore another person's back with your hands. Change places and repeat. Then have a back conversation. Be gentle, happy, angry, sad, affectionate. Slowly separate and open your eyes.

Choose a partner. Sit facing him. Relax. Concentrate on his face, feature by feature, trying to mold your face to mirror his. Someone else should side coach by moving around the room and suggesting quietly, "The eyes need widening" or "The mouth is narrower" etc. When the side coach calls "switch," reverse roles and let your partner mold his face to match yours. Whoever side coaches, should call "switch" at shorter and shorter intervals so that changes must be made more and more rapidly. Do you feel as if you have the same face as your partner?

Decide who is the leader and who is the mirror. Stand facing each other at about an arm's length, feet apart, eyes on the floor. Move your eyes slowly up the other person's body until you make eye contact. Initiate movement very slowly while your partner mirrors that movement exactly. Keep eye contact throughout. When "switch" is called, let your partner continue the movement. Keep eye contact. Rely on peripheral vision to follow the body movement. As you become skillful at changing back from one role to another, you may be able to synchronize movements so there is no leader and no follower.

Find a small object to hold. Look at it from every angle as if you were seeing it for the first time. Feel its weight. Toss it up and down. Roll it on the floor. Squeeze it. Taste it. Close your eyes and feel it against your face, your eyelids, your lips. Place it on top of your head. Become that object. Open your eyes. Tell someone about that object.

In couples, one person is the sound maker and one is the mover. The mover keeps his eyes closed while the sound maker sings out three syllables, such as Oh, Ah, Ee. The mover begins to move as he feels these sounds in himself. The sound maker can vary the rhythm, pitch, intensity of the syllables.

Play artists and blobs. The artist forms his partner into some kind of statue. The blob relaxes as much as possible until the statue is formed. Artists give their works a name and examine each other's statues. Then blobs become artists.

Choose a partner. One of you is the student, the other the teacher. Imagine a situation. Carry on a conversation in gibberish for three to five minutes. Exchange roles. Then meet again as equals. The conversation is entirely in gibberish and pantomime.

How does it feel to be a teacher? What did you learn? Did students understand your directions? Did you invite evaluation? The following books have many more suggestions for games and exercises:

Brown, George I. *Human Teaching for Human Learning*. New York: Viking Press, 1970.

Burgess, Bonita. "A Working Bibliography on Games." Intensive Learning Center and Office of Affective Development, Philadelphia Public Schools, Intensive Learning Center, 15th and Luzerne Streets, Philadelphia, Pa.

DeMille, Richard. *Put Your Mother on the Ceiling: Children's Imagination Games*. New York: Walker & Co., 1967.

Forbush, W. B., and Allen, H. R. *The Book of Games for Home, School and Playground*. New York: Holt, Rinehart, and Winston, 1954.

Gunther, Bernard. *Sense Relaxation below Your Mind*. New York: Macmillan Co., Collier Books, 1968.

Howard, Jane. *Please Touch*. New York: McGraw-Hill Book Co., 1970.

Huxley, Laura A. *You Are Not the Target*. New York: Farrar, Straus & Giroux, 1963.

Lederman, Janet. *Anger and the Rocking Chair*. New York: McGraw-Hill Book Co., 1969.

Lewis, Howard R., and Streitfeld, Harold S., *Growth Games*. New York: Harcourt Brace Jovanovich, 1970.

Marshall, Bernice S. *Experiences in Being*. Belmont, Calif.: Brooks/Cole, 1971.

Perls, Frederick S. *Gestalt Therapy Verbatim*. Lafayette, Calif.: People Press, 1969.

Schutz, William C. *Joy: Expanding Human Awareness*. New York: Grove Press, 1967.

Spolin, Viola. *Improvisation for the Theater*. Evanston, Ill.: Northwestern University Press, 1963.

The Listening Chamber René Magritte, Collection of William N. Copley

"The Listening Chamber"

CHAPTER FIVE

THE COMMUNITY OF THE CLASSROOM

How can you know me
Or I know you
In the vast cosmos
Of P.S. 42?

When biologists talk about an ecosystem, they are talking about living things and how we relate to each other and to our environment. We can look at schools as a kind of ecosystem with people relating to people in a shared space within a certain time. We share our lifespace for better or for worse. How can we make it better?

All this knowledge about the individual is fine. But so what? We never work with the "individual" in midair; school classes are groups. The moments in a teacher's life when he has one child at a time in his room are rare. His daily role is that of a leader of groups. It is true that the teacher wants to reach each individual by what he does and by what he makes the individual do. But his direct action is in and through the group. He meets individuals mainly embedded in groups, that is, as parts of some group pattern or other. . . . For a long time we did not know what this idea meant. Even now many people seriously believe that a group is simply an arithmetical accumulation of so many individuals and that the whole problem is one of numbers. . . . The management of group behavior and the cultivation of group atmospheres that are supportive of, rather than detrimental to the tasks of learning and growing constitute special areas in their own right.

From Fritz Redl, *When We Deal with Children*

How would you define the word "group"? What groups have you been a part of? How did you feel in these groups? Were there differences between the groups? What is a role? What kinds of roles did you or do you play in groups? Do you have a favorite or unfavorite role? Is it possible to be roleless? How can a group experience bring out your individuality? How can a group experience squelch it?

I've always liked groups that I've been in, otherwise, I wouldn't have been in them.

A GROUP IS AN INTERACTION OF IDEAS

I'd like to learn some new roles.

group: a specified number of any given material or substance or items.

A group is a state of mind. Today, this class is a group. On the first day, we were not. When my hair is clean, the strands are not a group. When it is dirty, the strands are a group. Get it!?

I've been the passive, "good little student."

All my life I've played leader, organizer, director.

a group is two or more individuals working together for a common end.

I never became a group leader because of lack of interest.

Family: This is the one important group to belong to.

I'm not that group oriented.

A group is a specific number of people who come together to talk, work, etc. Some groups may just exchange ideas, while other groups may solve problems, make decisions.

A GROUP IS A GATHERING OF PEOPLE.

NAIL SOUP

*A Folktale For Our Time As Retold by Bonnie
Rubinstein and Mary Greer*

Once upon a time a tramp was making his
way over a steep mountainside. He was
hungry and tired and longed for a good meal
and a soft bed for the night. At last, near
dusk he reached the summit of the mountain
where he could look down upon the valley
below. There, nestled quietly at the mountain's foot, he saw a small village. He thought
to himself as he hurried toward the huts,
"Surely some kind soul will offer me bed
and board for the night, and I will be able
to travel on again in the morning."

But the villagers of the little hamlet did
not look kindly upon strangers and when
the tramp arrived, dusty and dirty from the
road, one after another they shut their doors
in his face. The butcher swept him out of
his shop with a broom, calling after him,
"We are poor hard-working people with
scarcely enough to feed our own. We want
none of you and your kind hereabouts." And
the baker would not open his door but called
from his window sweet with the scent of
fresh bread, "I can barely make ends meet
and you ask me for a handout. Be on your
way! The candlestickmaker, having seen the
stranger in town, hurried home and locked
his door, so that when the tramp came
knocking, he hid in the bedroom to give
the appearance that nobody was at home.

By this time, the day had passed into twilight and the tramp had just about given

up hope. Then he saw one house newly
painted with a red dutch door standing
slightly apart from the others at the far edge
of the village. His hopes brightened a bit,
and he hastened to pull the brass bell that
hung shiny and polished over the door. He
rang and rang and nobody came. At last,
he called out in desperation, "Hello, is anybody home?

    I am a poor man seeking a bit of bread
      and cheese.
    I am a poor man seeking a little rest
      and ease.
    I have travelled far and wide
    Keeping my secrets locked inside.

Then the tramp heard soft footsteps approaching, and the dried-up face of an old
widow woman in a blue bonnet peered out
at him from the top half of the door.

"Who are you and what do you want,
stranger?" she asked tersely.

Again the tramp repeated his rhyme, and
then from his pocket he pulled a rusty nail.
"You see this nail, my dear lady. This nail
comes directly from the king's own kitchen,
where it has made many a fine pot of soup."

The woman stared incredulously at the old
bent nail. "Indeed," she huffed. "Since when
do the king's cooks use rusty nails for cooking?"

"Let me in and I will demonstrate its
powers before your very own eyes."

Her curiosity aroused, the widow woman
opened the bottom half of the door, and the

tramp entered a comfortable but modest sitting room.

"I can give you a pot, a hot fire, and water,
but I have little else to add to your soup,"
said the old woman. "It has been a long hard
winter and my larder is almost gone."

The tramp smiled to himself for he was
wise in the ways of people. "Bring me a
pot filled with water and light the fire, and
I shall make a soup for you such as the king's
own cook would brew."

The old lady hurriedly brought in the
water and lighted the fire under the great
iron pot. Then she watched the tramp drop
in the rusty nail with great flourish and saw
it float slowly to the bottom. The tramp
hummed and stirred, stirred and hummed:

    "I have travelled far and wide
    Keeping my secrets locked inside."

After tasting the water with a long wood-
en spoon, he said, "We could use a bit of
salt and pepper and perhaps a few grains
of barley. But if you don't have it, we'll do
quite well without it and not think at all
about it."

"Oh, that I have," replied the widow and
hurried off to her pantry. When she returned
she brought with her not only the salt and
pepper and barley but also a few carrots.

"My gracious," said the tramp. "This is
more than I expected. This will indeed be
a soup fit for a king." And he added them
to the pot.

A child, who had watched the tramp's
unsuccessful progress through the town and

had followed him to the widow lady's house, peeked over the half-opened door.

Taking another taste the tramp said, "Young one, our soup is already tasty and fragrant but a bit of beef and a drop of milk would add a little something special. But if you think your mother does not have it, we'll do quite well with what we have."

The child hastened to her home and pulling on her mother's apron said, "Oh, mother, do give me a piece of meat and a drop of milk to add to a marvelous soup that the tramp is making for the widow lady all from a nail!"

The mother opened her larder door and found some meat and milk and even an end of sausage, which she handed to her daughter. "I'll go myself and see this soup!" she exclaimed. And so both of them hurried back to the widow's house.

Now, in the meanwhile, some of the villagers who had seen the tramp go into the widow lady's cottage gathered curiously outside her door. Smelling the wonderful aroma wafting through the open window, they knocked on the door. The old lady invited them in to see the miracle of the soup made from a nail.

They stood amazed before the steaming pot and hastened back to their own homes to gather something to add while the tramp stirred and smiled, smiled and stirred and sang to himself:

"He who travels far and wide
   Keeps many a secret locked inside."

When the villagers returned they brought parsley and sage and chives, fresh from their gardens, turnips and beets from their stores, and the baker, who had joined the group, donated fresh bread, cheese, and a bottle of wine. "What is soup without these?" he laughed, as he helped the old woman pull out her long table and prepare it for the feast.

The tramp took one last taste of his soup and pronounced it ready. The steaming bowls were passed around and the villagers were exuberant in their praise of the soup and its maker.

"Imagine," said the old woman, "and all from a nail."

They feasted and laughed and drank and danced through the evening until not a drop of the soup was left. The tramp, taking the nail from the bottom of the pot, said to the widow woman:

"Here, for your kindness, good lady, is the wonderful nail. Keep it and use it. And now, I must be on my way."

"Oh, no," cried the woman, pulling his dusty sleeve. "There are bears that prowl our forest in the dark. Such a man as you should have a warm, safe bed for the night. Upstairs in my loft you may sleep, and when you awake travel on your way refreshed and safe."

So the tramp stayed the night and, after a hearty breakfast, he opened the red door and stepped out into the sunny morning. He bid the widow woman a warm goodbye as she pressed a bright coin into his palm and handed him a carefully wrapped package for lunch. Then they embraced like old friends.

"Many thanks for what you have taught me," said the woman. "Now, I shall never go hungry again. Such people as you are rare as swallows in winter."

The tramp shrugged his shoulders. As he started down the road he called:

"It's all in the knowing how."

Is the tramp in the tale a teacher, a con man, a psychologist, an artist, a facilitator? How did he gain trust? How did he keep it? Why is trust important in a group? In a classroom? What promotes it? What interferes with it? Have you ever known anybody like the tramp? What nails did he use? What nails could you use? Did you come to this class empty or full? What are you prepared to give? Try the "Nail Soup" ritual.

Drop a nail in the pot
Stir it and whir it
Add something to it
Taste it and see what you've got.
Find a pot, pan, or bowl.
Drop a nail in it.
Add a little something of yourself.
Talk about what you're putting in
And what it means to you.
When everyone's added a bit,
See, hear, feel, taste what you've got.

More Nails for the Soup

Mark duplicate sets of numbers on slips of paper.
Draw a slip and find your partner with the same number.
Talk together about "Nail Soup" for five minutes.
Join another couple and continue the discussion
for another five or ten minutes. Then all join another
foursome and discuss for another five or ten minutes.
You can continue to expand until the smaller groups
become one large group if you want.
The subject for discussion can be predetermined or
left open.

Have a chalk-in on the board,
on the tennis court,
or on a sidewalk.
Have a paint-in
or a draw-in.

Take a walk around campus
together. Fly kites.
Build something together
out of cardboard, paper,
or whatever you can find.
Break it up and rebuild.

One person starts a sound.
It travels around the circle
so that it becomes a ribbon of sound.
Pick it up and pass it on as
quickly as possible. After awhile,
someone acts as the changer or transformer
and makes a new kind of sound and sends it on.

Courtesy of *Family Circle* Magazine

Go to a local theater together and
see a movie that relates
to class.
There have been lots of them:
The Prime of Miss Jean Brodie
To Sir with Love
Up the Down Staircase
Goodbye, Mr. Chips
The Wild Child
The Miracle Worker
There will be more.

or Make a movie strip together.
Unroll a long strip of blank
film. Use flow pens to draw
or write on the film.
Run the film through the pro-
jector backed up by 33 rpm
music played on 45 rpm speed.

or Take Polaroid shots of the
class. Collage them, paste
them up. Write captions
under them.

Half the class plans a "happening"
for the other half on one day.
Then the other half
returns the gift the next day.
Get outside the room,
use the whole campus.

or Try a scavenger hunt.
Divide into small groups.
Each group makes a list of
things for another group to
find around campus. Exchange
lists. Set a time limit.
Return with what has been
scavenged. Choose one object
in each group. Create an
improvisational skit around it.

Bring a baby picture of yourself.
Mix them up.
Everybody guess who is who.

Half the group lies
limp on a carpet or grass. The
others walk around,
gently lifting arms, legs, heads,
shoulders, hips. Reverse.

Break into groups of
six or eight. Form a tight
circle. One person
stands in the center,
eyes closed,
feet together, body
stiff. He begins to
fall toward the circle.
Catch him
as he falls and
gently pass him to the
person next to you.
Pay attention. You
are responsible for
another person. Don't
talk. Let everyone
have a turn in the center.

Gently lift a person from the floor, putting your hands under
his stiff body. Swing him
easily, turn him, throw him up
and down a little. Lower him
carefully. Let him gradually
open his eyes. Stay with him
quietly until he breaks
the silence.

Figure out how the entire class can form a circle by
each person lying down with his head on another
person's stomach. Once the problem is solved try a
group giggle, cough, word. What happens to the vibrations?

Lie down on your stomachs, heads
toward the center of the circle.
Close your eyes and start crawling
toward the center. When you make
contact with someone, gently crawl
over or under, continuing toward the
center. Make a big body pile. Open
your eyes and slowly unpile.

or

Form a long chain of hands with a leader
who goes in, around and under,
taking everyone with him until a
human knot is formed. Then, he
retraces his steps and unties the knot.

Form small groups of six or eight with one
person in the center who is blindfolded.
Move around in a circle until
the center person calls out, "Still
Pond." Stop all movement while the center person tries to identify someone
by feeling his face and hands. If
he is correctly named, he goes into
the center with the blindfold over his
eyes and the game begins again.

Find a private place in the room.
Hide yourself under a paper bag or a sheet.
Listen to quiet music. Stay in yourself.
Gradually let yourself
emerge. Meet a few people at a time.
Keep your eyes closed until you're
ready to open them. Don't talk.
Move with someone. Join others until
the whole group is together. Play
lively music. Have a be-in.

Generally speaking, we must find a way to
organize schools and classrooms horizontally
rather than vertically. That is to say,
classroom and school atmospheres need to
be created in which human beings relate to
each other on a horizontal plane rather than
a vertical scale. In a horizontal organizational
structure, people learn to be useful as unique
and different individuals and yet relate as
equal human beings. In a vertical organizational structure, difference is used to determine status and people relate as superior and
inferior human beings. A horizontal organizational structure seems more likely to encourage active, responsible and trustworthy
behavior. Since almost all participants in a
vertical organizational structure are subordi-
nates, such an atmosphere actually promotes
passive and irresponsible behavior. We need
to learn to create an atmosphere of freedom
without license—in which people are free to
be themselves and in which they have a feeling of identification with others who are free
to be their unique selves.

From ASCD 1962 Yearbook Committee
Arthur W. Combs, Chairman
Perceiving, Behaving, Becoming

CHAPTER SIX
THE GROUP AS A WAY OF EXPLORING IDEAS

While Lewin, Lippitt and White were conducting their classic experiment on the effect of climates of leadership (*laissez faire*, authoritarian, democratic) in Iowa, Charles H. Judd of the University of Chicago, one of the leading professors of education in the country, visited one of the experimental groups. According to George D. Stoddard, who was in charge of the experimental station, Judd remarked to Lewin, "Professor Lewin, this class is the most accurate representation of the typical American schoolroom I have ever seen." Lewin was embarrassed and replied, "But, Dr. Judd, you have been observing our rendition of an *authoritarian* situation." Evidently Judd, like most Americans, did not recognize the autocratic element in the conduct of a class by a teacher using common methods who, though kindly, was throughout directive. It should be noted that the experimenters found something like 32 times as many expressions of hostility in the so-called authoritarian groups as in the democratic groups.

From James Marshall, "Conflicting Educational Interests" in *Teaching and Learning*

A vertical order is more authoritarian and autocratic; a horizontal order is more egalitarian and democratic. Can *you* recognize the difference? With which organization are you more familiar? Which do you prefer? In what kind of classroom do you want to be a student? A teacher? Which are you *ready* for? If you shift from a vertical to a horizontal arrangement, what happens to the teacher? To the student? Is there a difference between how you think you *ought to feel* and how you *really do feel*? Can you accept where you are and then try to move to where you may want to be? Can you change? Find out where you are coming from and where you are now. Are the following questions true or false for you?

I don't work hard unless I am forced to.

I often ask "Why."

You shouldn't expect me to like school.

I am resourceful when decisions are left up to me.

I need competition to feel motivated.

Teachers should never admit they don't know something or that they're wrong.

I feel more comfortable when I am told what to do.

I am more motivated by success than by failure.

I believe too many teachers place too much emphasis on maintaining order and control.

Today's schools are too soft on kids.

I like to do my own planning in school.

I prefer to be seen and not heard.

I prefer to be heard and not seen.

I prefer not to be seen or heard.

I prefer to be seen and heard.

I tend to be unruly unless I'm carefully supervised.

I think most students lack imagination and drive.

It is important for me to feel that "teacher knows best."

I believe that students and teachers can cooperate in planning experiences.

I am not certain whether teachers and students can cooperate in planning experiences.

I think students and teachers can cooperate in planning experiences but I've never really participated in the process.

I do not believe that teachers and students can cooperate in planning experiences.

William Steig

I have no control over him

Readiness for Democracy and Teacher Training by David N. Aspy

People tend to treat others as they have been treated because models are more significant than mere cognitive understanding in determining our behavior. This is reflected in the old adage, "Your actions speak so loud, I can't hear your words." In light of this, it is important that those who believe in democratic processes in the educational context demonstrate their beliefs by their practices. We are, in fact, teaching process whether we choose to or not. This is true for *all* courses. All of us affect the students' ability to implement democratic processes in the classroom, and we either facilitate or retard this learning.

Educators who prepare people to deal with other human beings must choose the skills they hope to teach their trainees. Many educators believe that the ability to apply democratic processes is one of those essential skills. Others believe that this approach results in highly ineffective teaching. Another position, the one adopted by this paper, is that a graduate of a teacher education program should be able to relate to her students in many different ways—just one of which is a democratic approach.

It seems important to emphasize two aspects of this position. *First*, democratic practice constitutes only one of several effective ways to operate in a classroom, and *second*, in the context of our society, democratic processes are so important that graduates of teacher education programs should be able to use them in their teaching when appropriate. Additionally, the desirability of democratic processes in a given learning context is rightfully a professional decision of the teacher.

As a first step in this approach, the concept of *readiness* should be applied. Students who enroll in teacher education courses are not equally ready to participate in democratic processes, and classes which hope to create democratic atmospheres will encounter difficulties which can be lessened by providing differential experiences commensurate with the students' levels of readiness. This article proposes four levels of readiness for the democratic process and presents procedures for diagnosing these levels as well as differential treatments for them.

Those who choose to enter teacher education courses have received about the same kind of classroom experience as those who select other professional schools. That is, they have had the same teacher models as other students and have formed similar ideas about the role of the teacher in the classroom. We may assume, therefore, that the implicit role conceptions held by teacher trainees very probably reflect classroom practices currently popular in the school setting. Research by Flanders and Ryans sheds a great deal of light on this topic. They found that the typical teacher spends most of her time directing student behavior. Certainly, direction of behavior is a predominant form of teacher-student interaction even at the undergraduate and graduate levels. As a result, our teacher trainees are most apt to believe that teaching is a process in which the more knowing person transmits his accumulated knowledge to those designated as less knowing . . . in this instance, the students. Thus, most of our students come to us with an attitude that teaching is directing student behavior.

For those of us who believe that teaching is a facilitative or liberating function, our task is twofold. *First*, we must help our students redefine the teacher's role, and *second*, we must demonstrate the effectiveness of the facilitative role. This, of course, makes our task doubly difficult, since the first phase creates antagonism and uncertainty among many students while the second involves asking them to try behaviors with which they are often unfamiliar.

The typical levels of readiness for a democratic approach are: (1) opposers, (2) doubters, (3) cognizers, and (4) flourishers.

The *opposers* are those who have been so steeped in autocratic tradition that they are unable to cope with the democratic atmosphere and must try to get the leader to structure the situation. The *doubters* have been heavily influenced by autocratic functioning, but have received enough democratic experience to wonder if it is not really a better process. They are willing to try to understand it. The *cognizers* are those who intellectually understand and believe that democracy can be a preferred mode of functioning, but, since they have never tried to implement it themselves, they want to understand it experientially. They are more than willing to try it. The *flourishers* are the fortunate group experientially. That is, democracy is an implicit part of their being, and they frequently fail to understand the doubts of their classmates.

In order to test the validity of these levels of readiness for democracy, the following questionnaire was administered to 250 undergraduate education majors:

If a democratic classroom is one in which the students and the teacher plan their experiences cooperatively, I . . .

    I. do not believe that democratic processes are applicable to a classroom.

    II. am willing to investigate the use of democratic processes in the classroom, but I have some doubts about it.

    III. believe democratic processes can and should be used in the classroom, but I need to learn more about them before I use them in my teaching.

    IV. plan to use them extensively in my own teaching.

The results were as follows:

Level	N	Percent
I. Opposers	2	1
II. Doubters	45	18
III. Cognizers	180	72
IV. Flourishers	23	9
TOT N = 250		

Of course, this simplistic approach does not meet tests of statistical rigor, but it has the advantage of straightforwardness. The most interesting aspect of the results is that the overwhelming majority of students expressed a willingness to proceed with democratic practices in their classrooms if they just knew how. Our chief task seems to be implementation by example rather than convincing students cognitively. This finding is consistent with other studies which indicate that education courses transmit theory better than they upgrade actual classroom practice.

Determining the levels of readiness for democratic classroom procedure may be completed during the first meeting or within a short number of meetings. The earlier diagnosis permits more time for the process described, while the later diagnosis may insure more accuracy. However, accuracy is not crucial if the process of moving from group to group is flexible.

First session diagnosis could be accomplished by the administration of any one of several instruments which tell us something about a person's orientation to democratic procedures in the classroom. The California F-Scale has some promise in this direction. Another process is that suggested by Machover and Travers in which the student is asked to draw a picture of the teacher at work in the classroom.

This writer combined these procedures and found: (1) that students whose drawings place the pupils in straight rows with the teacher at a considerable distance from them tend to have authoritarian attitudes about the classroom, and (2) that drawings which depict the teacher among her students arranged in a sort of circular fashion are completed by students with relatively less authoritarian attitudes.

Later diagnosis may be completed by operating democratically in the first few meetings and then asking students how they feel about the class proceedings. It seems that those who are enthusiastic about the class are more able to cope with democratic processes than those who feel extremely uncomfortable in it. Further diagnostic groups may be composed of those who feel uncertain and those who think this may be a good approach. Of course, if it is possible to observe the trainees in teaching situations, this would give indispensable insight into their operationalized attitudes toward democracy in the classroom. However, since the trainee is rarely observed in this situation during the beginning courses in education, this information usually will be obtainable only at the conclusion of the training program.

The four groups are at different stages of readiness for democratic interaction and should receive differential treatment.

The *opposers* should first be given the opportunity to express their attitude toward democracy in the classroom and then to examine the impact of various procedures upon students. When these alternatives are examined freely and thoroughly, the students should have a cognitive understanding of some of the results of both democratic and nondemocratic interaction. If they demonstrate an inability to implement democratic processes, it seems necessary to suggest either (1) they enter some other teacher training program consistent with their attitudes, or (2) they drop out of teacher training and enter some other area of training.

The *doubters* must be able to express their conflicting views and to assess both the advantages and disadvantages of democratic interaction in the classroom. After their discussions and evaluations, they will probably move in one of two directions, (1) toward democratic processes, or (2) away from them. Those who move toward democratic processes are ready to experience them, while those who move away should be given the same alternatives as the opposers. This may seem harsh treatment for the opposers, but unless they are willing to experience democratic practices themselves, it is relatively certain that they cannot provide them for their students. The doubters constitute the most sensitive group because they may easily move in either direction. Thus, they must be allowed a longer time to make their choices. But at some stage they must involve themselves in the process rather than remain at the choice point. Only involved people have the opportunity to learn to effectively operationalize democratic practices in the classroom.

It seems necessary to reiterate a previous assumption that if and when the professional personnel in a teacher training program concluded that democratic practices were one of the preferred modes of classroom management, then the graduates of that program should be able to perform democratically in their classrooms. Of course, if that assumption is not made, then no such requirement should exist. Perhaps the crux of this position is that if we think democratic procedures are significant, we ought to treat the matter sincerely and not conflict our students through a contradiction between our theory and our practice.

The *cognizers* should be allowed to experience a democratic classroom, and the process should be clearly described as the class interacts. The main thrust for the cognizers will be that of mutual reinforcement as they experience the opportunity to do something meaningful from their frames of reference. However, the emphasis at this stage is upon internalizing the process rather than on production. That is, the students' primary task is to become familiar experientially with classroom democracy in process.

The *flourishers* are ready to move ahead with their use of democratic processes. The biggest problem for this group will most likely be that of structuring and implementing the task they select. Their completion of a meaningful study may well lead to sustaining democratic behavior and translating it into teaching behavior.

This article adopts the position that the concept of readiness must be applied to the teaching of democratic processes to teacher training candidates. It proposes four levels of readiness for democratic classroom process, (1) opposers, (2) doubters, (3) cognizers, and (4) flourishers. Additionally, diagnostic procedures and differential treatment for the levels are described.

The underlying assumption is that each of the students who completes a teacher training program should be able to apply democratic procedures in the classroom. The concomitant assumption is that teachers are reluctant to employ processes in their teaching that they have not experienced as students. That is, teacher training programs can best assure that teachers will operate democratically when they have demonstrated their facility with this approach as students.

Of course, the final test is the teacher's actual classroom behavior. The approach outlined in this paper may enable us to help more teachers become comfortable with the use of democratic processes.

If we preach democracy in our schools but we practice autocracy, what are we really teaching? Do we learn what we live? Donald Aspy says that democratic practice is one of a number of effective ways to teach and learn.

Larry Cuban speaks of the need for "diverse learning situations" in schools. Have you had the opportunity of experiencing many modes of learning in school or has diversity been lacking? How willing are you to experiment with new and different ways?

Games show human relationships.
Have you ever thought that some games are autocratic and some are democratic? Play some of these. Guess which are which.

Form a line
behind a leader.
Follow him wherever he goes,
doing whatever he does.
Take turns being leader.

One person begins a
mechanical movement.
Another person attaches
to him and adds a movement.
Continue to add yourselves
to the machine, using sounds
and moving through space.
If there are too many people
for one machine, make
several and let them meet
each other and interact.

Line up in front of the leader
or form a circle around him.
Do what the leader does
when he says "Simon says"
(or the leader's own name
can be used: "Freddie says")—
"Simon says put hands on head,"
"Simon says put hands on foot."
But if he says, "Put hands on nose"
and you do it, you're out because
Simon didn't say to do it.
The faster the pace
the funnier the game.

Make a mural together.
Fingerpaint a fresco.
Do tangrams together.
In small groups. (See page 223.)
See how many different
figures you can create
with the five shapes.

You are the leader.
Tell others to take a
specific number of steps forward.
They must ask, "May I?"
or they are penalized. The
first one to tag the leader wins.

One person goes to the
front and begins an
activity nonverbally.
Others enter once the
first person establishes what he's
doing. Form a scene
without words doing your
thing together and let
it play itself out.

One person stands up.
Another stands behind him
and plays on him as if he were
a musical instrument,
quietly humming a melody.
A third person makes the second
his musical instrument.
Continue until the line
is long enough to form a circle.
The first person then closes the circle
by playing on the back of the last person.
Enlarge the sounds, sing out loud.
Move the musical circle around the room
or stay in a line and navigate.

Use a ball or bean bag.
One person is the teacher, who
stands in the center.
Everyone else is a pupil and stands in
his numbered circle.
The teacher throws the ball
and if a pupil fails to
catch it, he goes to the
last circle and everyone
else moves up. If a pupil catches
the ball, he throws it back to
the teacher. If the teacher
misses the return throw, all the
pupils move up one circle and the
teacher takes the last circle.

Somebody is "It" and
leaves the room.
The rest of the group
stands in a circle.
Choose a leader who begins
and changes all movements.
Be aware of the leader
without looking directly
at him. Change movements
when he does.
Call back the person who is
"It." Tell him to stand
in the center and guess who
the leader is. If he
discovers the leader, the
leader becomes "It."

Lie down on the floor in
a wheel, faces up, heads toward the
center. One person begins a story
and, when ready, passes it
on to the next person.
Let the story travel around
the circle until it is finished.
What does it tell about the group?

Two partners begin a mirror.
Two more partners attach
themselves at some point to the
same part of the bodies of the
first set and begin their own mirror.
A third set attaches to the second set
until the entire group is involved
doing mirrors, still maintaining
contact with persons on both sides.
Use sounds if they come naturally.

". . . A Worthy Task, a Plan, and Freedom."

The X.Y.Z. is a wonderful place,
The organization's a shocking disgrace.
There's Snowy, and Boco, and Dit Thomas too,
With their hands in their pockets and nothing to do.
They stand on the field and they rave and they shout
On subjects they know sweet nothing about;
For all that I learn here I might as well be
Where the mountains of Mourne sweep down to the sea.
Children's rhyme

The goal must be plain; one must have a sense of where one is trying to get to in any given instance of activity. For the exercise of skill is governed by an intention and feedback on the relation between what one had intended and what one has achieved thus far—"knowledge of results." Without it, the generativeness of skilled operations is lost. What this means in the formal educational setting is far more emphasis on making clear the purpose of every exercise, every lesson plan, every unit, every term, every education. If this is to be achieved, then plainly there will have to be much more participatory democracy in the formulation of lessons, curricula, courses of study, and the rest. For surely the participation of the learner in setting goals is one of the few ways of making clear where the learner is trying to get it.

From Jerome S. Bruner, "The Skill of Relevance or the Relevance of Skill"

Donald Aspy stressed that ". . . teachers are reluctant to employ processes . . . they have not experienced . . ." An entire course of study can be organized democratically around shared concerns. Write down three of your own most serious concerns in education, problems you want to explore. How many others share one or more of these concerns? Or get together with five or six others in class and *discover* what educational interests you have in common. Read the following selection on working in groups. Try out the approach. What problems do you encounter? What is your real teacher? What benefits do you receive? What do you learn? Is "the medium the message"? Share your experience of process with other groups. See the Kaiser Industries film *Why Man Creates*. How does the group process resemble the creative process?

From *The Workshop Way of Learning* by Earl C. Kelley

A true learning situation is a problem-solving situation. It is common in life outside of school on an individual basis. The individual starts with wanting to do something. He has a goal which is his own and therefore worthy, in his opinion. He figures out how he wants to go about it. Then he proceeds to try to do it the way he decided would be most likely to succeed. If he seems not to be achieving his goal, he stops and asks himself whether or not there was anything wrong with his plan. He revises his plan and tries again. This time he may succeed, or he may have to change his plans again. If he cares enough about his goal, he will continue to contrive until he reaches it. It is simply a matter of having a goal held to be worthy, making a plan which seems likely to achieve the goal, trying the plan, evaluating the failure, replanning, trying it again, revised in the light of experience and achievement. This is what we all do all of the time, and it is the essence of the learning situation.

The only place in life where we do not follow the typical learning procedure, oddly enough, is in school, where people are presumably assembled for the express purpose of learning. This defection is complete, from the first grade to the doctor's degree. In school the goal is furnished by the teacher, and may or may not be worthy to the learner.

Whether the learner holds it to be worthy or not is a matter of little or no concern to the teacher. The plan of attack is given by the teacher, and the teacher watches to see that the plan is carried out as directed. There is no need for evaluation along the way because the plan is sure to work, since it has worked many times before. Achievement is automatic as long as the tested plan is followed, but satisfaction of achievement is lacking because the goal was not one which the learner really cared about in the beginning. He has been denied the adventure of contriving. The learner has come in for the least interesting part of the process, and there is little in it for him except work. He has missed the exhilaration of holding a worthy goal and achieving it.

Successful group work would be easy if it were not for the fact that other people are involved; in other words, it would be easy if it were not group work. Arriving at a common goal and releasing the energies of several people in a concerted attack on the problem is the difficulty. It is also the point of greatest reward, because each individual enriches all of the others, and the profit to each member of the group is far greater than in solitary action. But the steps are the same, and are simple. If they are kept in mind, the complexity of joint action will be the only complexity involved.

THE GOAL. No group can accomplish anything until it has figured out what it wants to do. This seems elementary, but many a group has failed because it never clarified

its goal. This, then, becomes the first order of business. The group must stick to the clarification of its goal until everyone in the group knows what the group wants to do and accepts it as worthy.

Establishing a goal which all can accept is not easy. It may call for a good deal of compromise. There is the advantage that the people in the group are together because they have a common general interest. But what one individual sees in a general topic may be quite different from what another sees, and this needs to be carefully worked out. It may come about that one person is unable to accept the goals of the great majority. This person may need to withdraw from the group and join another, or get the counsel of a staff member as to where in the total workshop there may be a spot where his present felt needs are apt to be met.

The topic which has brought the group together is often too general to put people to work. It needs to be made specific, so that each member can see something that he can do about it. Energy is released on specifics, not on generalities. We usually have one or more groups meet together to work on the problem of democracy in the classroom. The popularity of this topic, which nearly always emerges from the total group and is never injected by the staff, shows that many teachers earnestly desire to learn how to get rid of the autocratic methods they have inherited, and teach more democratically so that their children will have some preparation for citizenship in a democracy. But the topic itself will never motivate anyone to action.

One group, met together around this topic, made it specific by listing some questions which gave the members places to take hold. Some of these questions follow. "How can I organize my class so that every member will have a chance to contribute? How can I find out what goals my learners can accept? When and how can I use small group techniques? How do I go about teacher-pupil planning? How can I work with my pupils democratically without having them get out of control? What kind of planning can young children do?" This list of questions made the general topic meaningful, and gave the members of the group ideas as to how they could begin. It sent them to books, to staff members, and to colleagues for information.

The specific goal of the group should be arrived at through consensus. This means that it is talked through and modified until every member of the group can accept it as worthy. No group can succeed if there is a minority which cannot accept what the group is going to do. Such minorities will exist if the chairman resorts to voting as a means of gaining a decision. Parliamentary practice—the motion, the second, the vote—can ruin any group that is planning to work together, because it divides the group instead of bringing it together. Full discussion, understanding, and compromise can achieve goals which all can accept and on which all can spend themselves. This is consensus.

Once the specific goal or goals have been agreed upon, they need to be put into writing, and copies need to be supplied each member. These written goals should be constantly in front of the group and regularly referred to; all planning should be done with these goals clearly in mind.

THE PLAN. Having agreed upon what the group is to do, the next step is to plan how it is going to do it. This will probably involve a long-time plan and a short-time plan. The group can lay down ways of going about the whole thing so that the semester will end with achievement. This is essential, but it does not tell each individual what he can do about it tomorrow.

The short-time plan has to do with what the group is going to do next Thursday evening, and what each member can do between meetings so that he can be a more useful member of his group. Without this short-time plan, the members will come back in a week just the way they went out, so far as the group project is concerned. They will have missed the opportunity to increase their value to their fellows.

What members do between meetings so that the goals will be brought nearer will take on many forms. The first thing many of us think of is reading. And indeed it may be that the member may profit by looking up some literature on the topic to be considered This is only one way of preparing to be a good member the next week, however, and may not be the most fruitful way. Some other and more promising experiences are that he may try something in his class, or he may talk to others whose experience and judgment offer something, or he may consult his students who are the consumers. He may profit most of all, on occasion, by thinking about the problem himself, and coming to some tentative conclusions in that way. When he feels that he has made progress in that way, he will gain respect for his own thinking. Many of us have been trained not to respect our own thinking but to feel that we have to depend on the thinking of others. This leads us to acceptance on authority, whether what the authority says makes sense or not. We are particularly inclined to accept if the "authority" has succeeded in getting his ideas printed. We have undue reverence for the printed page, not realizing that the author is usually just another person like ourselves who has accumulated material and had it printed.

The long-time plan needs to be put in writing. The short-time plan need not be. The last few minutes of every session should be devoted to what the group is going to do at the next meeting, and what individual members can do to make the next meeting successful. Of course if the group already knows what it is going to do, then this short planning session is not needed, but in most instances it will be.

THE TRY. Now we put into operation the plans we have made. Here contriving which bears directly on the goal begins. This will probably extend over a number of meetings.

THE CHECK-UP. All members of the group, and particularly the chairman, must watch the try, to see whether the goal is likely to be reached by what is going on.

It is not altogether a matter of approaching the goal, although that is important. There are other factors and conditions to be watched. Is there general participation? Has every member been involved? Is the morale of the group good? Are the members becoming better acquainted and coming to enjoy each other's company more? Is the attendance of the group good? Do they work their full time at each meeting, or do they usually adjourn early? Do members of the group begin to find that there are errands they have to do which cannot be done any time except when the group meets? Are they at a loss as to what to do when the meeting starts?

Some of these symptoms may reveal the fact that the plan is not working. The members of the group had at one time expressed interest in what was projected, and if that interest has evaporated, it seems likely that the plan needs to be reconsidered.

THE PLAN REVISED. When symptoms indicate that all is not well, a session is needed to discuss the reasons. This discussion should be as frank and free as possible. To the degree that it can be done, every member's ideas should be brought out. If poor attendance is a problem, it might be helpful if the recorder would notify each member by mail that a gripe session has been scheduled. Disaffected members are more likely to show up for a gripe session than a work session, especially if the work sessions have been unrewarding.

In this session, the weaknesses of the plan as it has operated can be brought out, and revision can be made so that the members will feel that it will now work. It may be necessary to discard the old plan and substitute a new one. The defects of some of the personalities may come out in such a way that they can be accepted, and these persons may learn from this how to become better group members. Some may have driven others away by their talkativeness, others may have failed to do anything to make the group succeed.

This check-up meeting ought to have the help of a staff member unless the presence of the staff member reduces freedom and frankness. This should not be the case if the staff has succeeded in establishing the proper relationships with the workshop members. If the members of the group feel that a particular staff member is the cause of the breakdown, then the group will do better by itself or with another member of the staff. The chairman should be in the best position to decide whether a staff member should attend and who it should be.

TRY AGAIN. Further contriving is not in order, in the light of what has been learned and through the use of the revised plan.

THE ACHIEVEMENT. There is no way to tell how many times the plan of action may need to be revised. As in life, we can never be sure that any projected action will take us where we want to go. No plan can ever be said to be a good plan until it is put to the test through concrete action and has brought the results which the plan was intended to bring.

In the contriving, which is the putting of a projected plan into action—with the struggle and frustration which is usually entailed—the greatest amount of learning occurs. In order for real learning to come about, the group must have freedom to plan wrongly, and to learn through action that they have planned wrongly. More is to be learned by making mistakes in planning and execution than in perfect performance.

Of course this can be carried too far. If a group makes so many mistakes in planning and execution that it never gets anywhere, never makes any progress, feelings of futility will eventually dissipate the energies of the members and the group will disintegrate. This will not ordinarily happen. If a group pursues a fruitless path for a time, this experience should show it a better path, not a worse one. But there is nothing to be

138

gained by artificially forcing better planning. There is more learning to be gleaned from finding out that the group cannot do what it projected than there would be in having an outsider do its planning for it.

In most cases, when the end of the semester comes, the goal will have been achieved, and the satisfaction which comes from ultimate success after much contriving will be felt. The significance of the goal will lose some of its importance, because the process will assume greater importance. The possession of the achieved goal will bring satisfaction, to be sure, but no specific set of materials or ideas can become as important, once achieved, as the contriving which brought the goal into being. The skill acquired in working with other people will abide with the individual members of the group long after the materials constituting the goal become outgrown and insignificant. This skill is the one thing we can be sure will be needed by all human beings in a social world, and this is especially true of teachers.

One of the human values to come out of successful group operation is that the members will continuously grow in their respect for each other. They will continuously get to know each other better, and to find value in each other. Out of their contriving and frustration there will grow a group solidarity, with everyone belonging. The members will discover, often to their surprise, that these are really remarkably fine people they have been thrown with. A sort of "one for all, all for one" blood brotherhood comes, which often means much to people who by habit and training have been solitary workers, and who have felt growth stunted through the loneliness of the human spirit. . . .

Criticisms of the group process are frequently heard. They come from people who have been members of groups which have failed to achieve their goals and have therefore failed to bring satisfaction to the participants, and from those who have never tried to be members of groups. They sometimes come from people who drop in on a group once, and, being unable to see where the group started or where it is going, go away without any notion of what has been going on. It is doubtful that such people are really motivated by an honest desire to see what is going on, since they would never want their own work to be judged by such a brief spot sample without orientation.

Many of the criticisms are true in specific cases. We cannot guarantee a successful experience to anyone, any more than he can guarantee it to himself when he attempts something outside of school. Some groups never do get anywhere. The main consolation is that all teachers must work on a percentage basis, and there is no teacher anywhere who has no students who did not profit.

The critics say that there is a great deal of confusion in the group process. This is true. There is confusion wherever real learning, with genuine contriving, goes on. This is true even when people are working by themselves, and it is multiplied when it involves a number of people. The only time there is no confusion is when one person establishes the goal for all, and enforces the action toward it. Democratic procedures require the involvement and consultation of many people, and this results in confusion, or what may appear to be confusion to the superficial observer. The more people involved, the more contriving, the more confusion, and the more learning. In education, beware the machine which runs too smoothly!

Sometimes we hear that group work is nothing more than a bull session, where everybody has his say and nothing eventuates. Some groups do this, and while there is some profit in such sessions, they are likely to play themselves out, and become less and less fruitful. The difference between good group work and a bull session is that in group work the group has an agreed-upon goal, a plan, and is working toward the goal as best it can. A bull session has no goal and no plan.

Some feel that if thrown upon their own, students, even mature teachers, will not work. No one will ever do anything unless someone makes him do it. This is a very commonly held belief among teachers at all levels, and often a teacher who is a student at the university believes this of his own students while resenting it when it is applied to him as a student. The democratic faith calls for a belief in the general rightness and goodness of people, and one who lacks faith in other people lacks the first requisite for democratic teaching. It is true that a person will balk, or be lazy, when forced to pursue the purposes of another. But it makes no sense to assume that he will not spend his energy in the pursuit of his own purposes. The trick to getting people to spend their energies, then, is in finding ways by which purposes acceptable to them can be arrived at. When we hear a teacher proclaiming that other people are lazy while he is not, we are puzzled to know where and how he came into possession of such virtue, while others were denied it. The only tenable position on this matter for anyone to take, it seems, is that no one has a corner on virtue, that people will move when they see something which to them seems worth moving on, and that if they are lazy and perverse, it is best to look to see what goals fail to move them.

Some say that when a group works together all they get is pooled ignorance, and that nothing times nothing is still nothing. There is more than one fallacy revealed by such a statement. In the first place, the members of the group are not ignorant. Each has a lifetime of unique experience back of him, and each has a unique contribution to make. People have been adversely conditioned for so long that the student himself may be persuaded that he is of no value.

It may therefore take time and patience to bring him out so that his experiential background can become useful to his fellows. The person who believes in democracy must believe in the unique worth of every individual and must seek ways of making that worth come out, and only an autocrat could possibly say that a whole group of people have nothing to contribute.

In the second place, the contributions of the members of the group may seem trivial to an outsider, particularly if he holds himself to be superior. But no problem is trivial if it is of concern to the individual at the time. This is precisely the place to start, and it is indeed the only place where a start can be made. As growth takes place, and as the self-confidence of the members grows, the nature of the problems under consideration will also grow, and they will become more and more significant when judged in relation to the total educational scene.

This discussion of the groups has been an oversimplification, but is written in the hope that it will be of help to struggling groups. If group members will watch just two things, a great part of their trouble and the danger of failure will be obviated. The first is to have a specific goal stated in writing for the semester, to which they frequently refer and in the light of which they do their planning. The second is never to adjourn a meeting without knowing what they are going to do at the next meeting, and what each individual can do between meetings so that

he will come back prepared to do his part for its success.

A well-known principle of mental hygiene is that the individual must have a worthy task, a plan, and freedom. This was expounded twenty-five years ago by Burnham, and probably many times before by others. This is what the group must have, and the enthusiasm of group members who have come through a successful group experience is due, we believe, to that fact.

In discussing group process, Kelley says: "The only time there is no confusion is where one person establishes the goal for all and enforces the action toward it." In other words, autocratic organization may run more smoothly than democratic organization. Does this mean we must prefer the one to the other? If you are working in *small* groups, what kinds of difficulties and confusions are you experiencing? Can anything be learned from confusion? How do you feel about the *large* group called a class? What skills do you need to be an effective member of a democratically run group? A good work of art creates harmony out of variety. Is a good group similar? Here are some games and suggestions that might help you to focus on some problem of group process. Take time after an exercise to share your feelings with each other.

Group Process Games

LIFE SPACE

Take a piece of paper and a colored crayon. Draw a circle in the center of the paper to represent you, with your initials in the center of the circle. Make circles to represent as many other people in the group as you want to recognize. Put their initials in the centers. The size of the circle symbolizes how important or unimportant that person is to you.

Find out where you feel you are today in class. Chalk an X in the middle of the room for "IN." Find your own spot on the floor in relation to the center. Mark it with an X and your name. Stand back and take a look at the whole class relationship. Now move to where you usually feel in a group. Mark another X. How far is your first X from your second? Move and find the spot that symbolizes where you *usually* feel in this class. Is today unique? Do you usually feel close to the center, out in the hall, or somewhere in between?

GROUP GRIPE

Tell the group what's bothering you. Let off steam. Sometimes changes have to be made. Sometimes they don't. Ventilation can improve circulation.

Scapegoat or Bear in the Pit Form a tight interlocking circle. One person stands in the center and tries to break out any way he can. Taunt each other.

FEEDBACK SHEETS

After a group discussion make up a sheet that sums up the issues, feelings, attitudes discussed. Ditto it, pass it around. State if anything was resolved. Describe plans for the future if they were made.

MURDER OR DIVIDE AND CONQUER

Cut out pieces of paper equal to the number of people in the group. If there are more than ten, break into several groups and sit on the floor in circles. On one piece of paper in each group, place an X. Fold the papers; each person picks one piece. The person getting the X is the murderer who kills off people by winking at them. The object is for the murderer to eliminate as many people as possible without being identified. A person who is "murdered" must wait a few seconds and then fall over "dead." He is then out of the game. If someone who is "alive" thinks he knows the murderer, he can "accuse," but only if he has actually seen him winking at someone. A false accusation eliminates the accuser. How do you feel playing this game? Do you trust each other? Are you a group?

Exclusion-Inclusion Games:

Miss Tilly likes "kittens, not cats."
Miss Tilly likes "walls, not ceilings."
If you understand the basis of her likes and dislikes, you're in. (See page 223.) for secret.)

Form a tight circle with one or two people on the outside. Outsiders try to get in by whatever means they can.

Form a tight circle. Dance, talk, fool around. Let each person take a turn wandering around outside the circle.

LISTENING, NOT JUDGING

Form small groups. Discuss a topic of general interest. Before you respond to another's comments put his ideas in your own words. If they're not acceptable to him, try again. Discussion is slower but understanding is greater.

STYLES OF LEADERSHIP

Create an apathetic committee of four or more people. Three people volunteer to act as leaders and go out of the room. One re-enters at a time and tries to energize the group. After each has had a turn without seeing the other in operation, open up class discussion on the three approaches. Which leaders were most effective and why? Try videotaping the three leaders in action and play it back to the class for evaluation.

STEREOTYPED ROLES

Decide on some discussion question. Create a demonstration group. Put the title of typical group roles on a slip like "The Dominator," "The Receder," "The Warrier," "The Peacemaker." Six people draw from a hat and form a group playing out their roles. The whole group guesses who they are. Then replay the discussion, reversing roles; then try to be roleless. Do you recognize yourself? Are you stuck in a role? Are you imprisoned by it? How can your group help you? How can you help yourself?

A part of the group, the "joiners," form a line or circle. Play a game or do a dance together. Try to include as many "nonjoiners" as you can by talking, encircling, singing, wheedling, compromising, etc.

Many of us have been trained not to respect our own thinking but to feel that we have to depend on the thinking of others. This leads us to acceptance of authority, whether what the authority says makes sense or not.

From Earl C. Kelley, *The Workshop Way of Learning*

Dependency on authority figures is a necessary part of childhood. Independence and the freeing of the self from dependencies is a necessary part of growing up. Interdependence is a necessary part of true fellowship and community. Unfortunately, the education in our homes and schools does not always provide us with the experiences of transition from dependency on outside authority to respect for our own inner authority leading to true communion with others. Although there is often hidden or overt anger about being dependent and passive, opting for more freedom and personal responsibility is not painless. Becoming one's own teacher is the task of a lifetime.

In attempting to democratize the classroom through the formation of smaller groups, pay attention to the creation of little autocracies, which are recreations of the authoritarian classroom in miniature. Instead of the usual teacher, have a student take over and tell others what to do and when to do it, relieving everyone else of personal responsibility. Here are a few dependency games. Lean, dump, blame, demand. Now what?

Set up three chairs, the one in the center representing the teacher or authority figure. A large mask, a bag, or a sack can be placed there but not an actual person. Let the teacher's pet sit on one side. Let the teacher's rat sit on the other side. Both attempt to get and maintain attention. Is either one *free* of the teacher? Who else besides the teacher does the chair symbolize?

Put a chair in the middle of a circle. Let someone play teacher or leader but without saying anything at all. Members of the group make demands on the leader. You need not be rational. Take turns sitting in the center. Talk about how you feel in that position.

Because passivity is an inevitable response to latent fears of authority and represents a recreation of childhood feelings towards adults, because passivity may well represent an archaic mode of dealing with fears of reprisal, it is wise, I think, for the teacher, from time to time, to address himself to the enactment of passivity in the classroom. Although I am not making, at this point, a case for the fusion of psychoanalysis and teaching, there is a great deal to be learned from an understanding of, and responsiveness to, "transference" in teaching. A careful reading of Freud's twenty-seventh lecture in *A General Introduction to Psychoanalysis* will enable the teacher to take some profound steps towards freeing himself and his students from bondage to the past. Once the student knows that the teacher is a "stand-in" as it were, for past figures of authority, he may well be able to assert himself.

From H. R. Wolf, "Teaching and Human Development: Truth's Body" in *New Directions in Teaching*

TEST

Cover your nose. Now cover your mouth. If you ever get in a test like that dont do what the people say. Becuase if you dont do what they say they will think you are smart. Because if you do it you won't be able to breath. And if sombody tells you to take a LSD pill dont take that to. And if sombody tells you to jump off the bay bridge dont do that eather.

When do you lead? When do you follow? When do you do neither? Can you differentiate?
This little girl is beginning to know the difference.

... The Spirit of Cooperation

Much of school life seems to be built upon the principle of independence and mutual isolation. For example, what are teachers teaching children when they call for recitations with the preface, "Now Johnny, I want to hear what *you* have to say. Don't anybody else help him!" Homework is given out with the admonition: "Make sure it's your *own* work." Exams are given with children separated as widely as possible. Punishments are severe for those who either give or receive help. I realize that a purpose of this isolation is to enable the teacher to evaluate and rank her pupils. But every day? And at such a cost?

From Rachel M. Lauer, "General Semantics and the Future of Education"

From *Culture against Man*
by Jules Henry

Boris had trouble reducing "12/16" to the lowest terms, and could only get as far as "6/8." The teacher asked him quietly if that was as far as he could reduce it. She suggested he "think." Much heaving up and down and waving of hands by the other children, all frantic to correct him. Boris pretty unhappy, probably mentally paralyzed. The teacher, quiet, patient, ignores the others and concentrates with look and voice on Boris. She says, "Is there a bigger number than two you can divide into the two parts of the fraction?" After a minute or two, she becomes more urgent, but there is no response from Boris. She then turns to the class and says, "Well, who can tell Boris what the number is?" A forest of hands appears, and the teacher calls Peggy. Peggy says that four may be divided into the numerator and denominator. Thus Boris' failure has made it possible for Peggy to succeed; his depression is the price of her exhilaration; his misery the occasion for her rejoicing. This is the standard condition of the American elementary school, and is why so many of us feel a contraction of the heart even if someone we never knew succeeds merely at garnering plankton in the Thames: because so often somebody's success has been bought at the cost of our failure. To a Zuñi, Hopi, or Dakota Indian, Peggy's performance would seem cruel beyond belief, for competition, the wringing of success from somebody's failure, is a form of torture foreign to those noncompetitive redskins. Yet Peggy's action seems natural to us; and so it is. How else would you run our world? And since all but the brightest children have the constant experience that others succeed at their expense they cannot but develop an inherent tendency to hate—to hate the success of others, to hate others who are successful, and to be determined to prevent it. Along with this, naturally, goes the hope that others will fail. This hatred masquerades under the euphemistic name of "envy."

Looked at from Boris' point of view, the nightmare at the blackboard was, perhaps, a lesson in controlling himself so that he would not fly shrieking from the room under the enormous public pressure. Such experiences imprint on the mind of every man in our culture the *Dream of Failure*, so that over and over again, night in, night out, even at the pinnacle of success, a man will dream not of success, but of failure. *The external nightmare is internalized for life.* It is this dream that, above all other things, provides the fierce human energy required by technological drivenness. It was not so much that Boris was learning arithmetic, but that he was learning the *essential nightmare. To be successful in our culture one must learn to dream of failure.*

Group participation and agreement remove all the imposed tensions and exhaustions of the competitiveness and open the way for harmony. A highly competitive atmosphere creates artificial tensions, and when competition replaces participation compulsive action is the result. . . . Therefore, in diverting competitiveness to group endeavor, remembering that process comes before end result, we free the student-actor to trust the scheme and help him to solve the problems of the activity.

From Viola Soplin, *Improvisation for the Theater*

In some games it's each one for himself, me against you and you against the next guy. In some games we form teams against other teams, us guys against you guys together. In some games we band together to help each other. Otherwise nobody wins. Play these games. Which are cooperative? Which are competitive? Which are both?

Choose partners.
Sit back to back,
legs straight out in front.
Interlock arms by pushing
against each other's backs.
Try to stand up together as
one unit. Find your common
center.

Form two teams based on sex,
age, random grouping, or
chosen by team captains.
(Choosing the team is a
game in itself—how does
it feel to wait?)
Fight for a cloth, a ring, a rope.
Pull together against the
other team.

You've got "it"; I want "it."
"It" is never defined in this game.
One person can have "it,"
others try to get "it."
Or one group has "it," and
other groups try to get "it."
If one method doesn't work,
use another. But get "it!"

A. "Here we come!"
B. "Where from?"
A. "New York."
B. "What's your trade?"
A. "Lemonade."
B. "Give us some!"
A. "We have none."

Team A decides on some kind of trade or occupation and then approaches team B at a center point in a large room or field calling, "Here we come!" Both teams engage in the call and response. When it is finished, team A acts out its profession and team B tries to guess it. When the correct word is called out team A runs back to home base. Anyone caught defects to team B, which then takes its turn.

Pair off.
Sit facing each other,
feet against each other.
Hook fingers together.
Pull against the hands.
Push against the feet.
Repeat over and over.
Relax and do it again.

Play some lively music.
One of you start a dance
movement in the center of a
circle. Dance up to someone
who imitates your movement while
the group claps a rhythm. Then
return to the circle, while your
partner gradually transforms your
dance movement into something of
his own. Continue the process of
giving, imitating and transforming
movements until everyone has had
a turn.

Use your bodies
to build a house or
domicile of some kind.
Let people become furniture—
tables, chairs, telephones.
Others live in the house.
Then huff and puff and
blow it all down.

Form two teams.
The first person in each
line places an orange
under his chin.
On the word "go" pass
the orange from person
to person using no hands.
The first team to pass
the orange to the end of
the line and back to the
front, wins.
(Can also be done by passing
a lifesaver from a toothpick.)

Make a chair seat.
Grasp your own left wrist
with your right hand,
your partner doing the same.
With your free left hands
grasp each other's forearms.
Now carry a third partner
around in space.

Two partners share one pillow.
Experiment with different ways
of giving and taking the pillow.
Make it something very valuable
and precious, make it something
vile and distasteful, make it
something heavy and something
light. Play around with variations.

Partner 1 stands at the feet of partner 2. Partner 1 leans over and holds the hands of partner 2 who is lying as stiff as a board. Pull up partner 2. Reverse.

IOIOIOIOIOIOIOIOIOIOI

A good old-fashioned spelling bee.
Form two teams or form
one line where each one
is "for himself."
Let the "teacher" give a word
to one person at a time.
If he misses, he's out.
If he's correct, he stays in,
scoring a point for himself
or his teammates.

From "The Skill of Relevance or the Relevance of Skill"
by Jerome S. Bruner

. . . education must concentrate more on the unknown and the speculative, using the known and established as a basis for extrapolation. This will create two problems immediately. One is that the shift in emphasis will shake the traditional role of the teacher as the one who knows, contrasting with the student who does not. The other is that, in any body of men who use their minds at all, one usually gets a sharp division between what my friend Joseph Agassis calls "knowers" and "seekers." Knowers are valuers of firm declarative statements about the state of things. Seekers regard such statements as invitations to speculation and doubt. The two groups often deplore each other. Just as surely as authority will not easily be given up by teachers, so too will knowers resist the threatening speculations of seekers. Revolution does have difficulties!

With respect to encouraging speculative extrapolation, I would particularly want to concentrate on "subjects" or "disciplines" that have a plainly visible growing edge, particularly the life sciences and the human sciences; human and behavioral biology, politics, economics, sociology, and psychology organized around problems, solutions to which are not clearly known. The reward for working one's way through the known is to find a new question on the other side, formulated in a new way.

Form a tight circle. Brainstorm for new questions "on the other side, formulated in a new way." If you are a person called "the teacher," guide, don't "God" the discussion. Spend as much time as possible exploring for questions. How could you develop an entire curriculum from some of these questions? Are questions as important as answers? Is there always a right answer to questions? What can you teach each other? What can you learn from each other? Are you a "knower" or a "seeker"? Read Dr. William Glasser's account of an "open-ended meeting" as a way of group teaching-learning.

From *Schools Without Failure*
by William Glasser

Probably the cornerstone of relevant education is the open-ended classroom meeting. It is the type of meeting that should be used most often, even where behavior problems are common. When behavior and other social problems are minimal, social-problem-solving meetings will be used infrequently. The open-ended meeting, however, is always applicable; the more it is used, the more relevance can be added to education. In the open-ended meetings the children are asked to discuss any thought-provoking question related to their lives, questions that may also be related to the curriculum of the classroom. The difference between an open-ended meeting and ordinary class discussion is that in the former the teacher is specifically not looking for factual answers. She is trying to stimulate children to think and to relate what they know to the subject being discussed.

For example, in meetings with second-grade classes, I have introduced the subject of blindness. In answer to my question, "What is interesting to you?" one class said they would like to talk about eyes and ears. Although the five senses are not a specific part of the second-grade curriculum, from this introduction an open-ended meeting was held that provided a way for the students to gain greater motivation to read and to take more interest in the world around them.

In the central-city school where I first held this discussion, the second graders usually did not show much intellectual curiosity. What they didn't know about the world didn't seem to interest them; at least, it appeared that way. Yet, when an unknown was introduced in a way that made sense to them, they become excited and showed as much curiosity and as much good thinking as children who come from more stimulating environments. I asked the children what they did with their eyes, and they all said, "See"—a good, simple, factual answer. In a discussion with small children, it is best to let them begin at a simple level where they have confidence in their ability to give a good answer.

Going to a more complex question, I asked, "What do you see with your eyes?" They mentioned many things, including "the words in our books." Again they were succeeding in answering a question; they enjoyed it and were becoming involved. At the same time, I was able to direct them toward books and reading in a way new to them. Children are just as stimulated by new approaches as we are, and they are just as bored with sameness as we are. One value of the open-ended meeting is to give new ways a chance to be used. I then asked them about people who can't see, and they said, "They are blind." A short discussion on what blindness means followed. Despite an apparent understanding of blindness, most of the children believed that blind people could really see if they tried hard. We worked at

length before everyone understood that blind people could not see at all. The children closed their eyes tight and kept them closed. Slowly, through this participation and discussion, it began to dawn on the class that if you are blind, you cannot see.

By now the children were all involved, but so far they hadn't done much thinking or problem solving. It was important at this time to introduce a problem related to their school work that they could solve if they worked hard. I asked, "Could a blind man read?" The reaction I received from the second graders was laughter, puzzlement, and incredulity. To think that a blind man could read, after they had just confirmed that a blind man couldn't see, was absurd. I asked them to keep thinking to see if someone could figure out some way that a blind man could read. Of course, I implied that there was an answer. I wouldn't ask second graders a question that had no answer, although in this case the answer was not easy. I insisted that they keep trying to solve the problem; their first reaction when the going got tough was to give up. In school the children had rarely used their brains to solve problems. Accustomed to simple, memorized answers, they gave up when these answers didn't work.

The discussion so far had piqued the children's interest and awakened their faith in their brains. They kept trying, but they were in trouble. The leader must judge when to give them help; he must not do so too soon. I decided to help them at this time by asking if someone would like to take part in a little experiment. We had an immediate raising of hands; they were all eager to help, partly because they sensed that the experiment was a way to keep the discussion going. I selected a boy who, I detected, was not one of the better students or better behaved members of the class. He was waving his hand, eager to volunteer. Calling him over, I told him to shut his eyes very tight and hold out his hands. I asked him if he were peeking; he said, "No." Putting a quarter in one of his hands and a dollar bill in the other, I asked him if he could tell me what I had put in his hands. The entire class was now glued to the experiment. Some of the brighter students immediately began to glimpse the idea. The boy was able to tell me what was in his hands. I asked him how he knew. Although he wasn't very verbal, he finally said that anyone could tell a dollar bill from a quarter. When I took the dollar bill away and put a nickel in his hand instead, he was still able to distinguish the nickel from the quarter. I then asked him to sit down. Again I asked the class, "How could a blind man read?" Thoughtful students now began to express the idea that if a blind man could feel the letters on a page, he might be able to read. I said, "How could he feel the letters on a page? The page is smooth." And I ran my fingers over a page. One bright child said, "If you took a pin and poked it through the page, you could feel where the pin poked through." From that, most of the class—and they were very excited—was able to get the idea: you could feel the letters on a page!

I still wasn't satisfied, however. I said, "Suppose you *could* feel the letters on the page; I still don't think you could tell one from another." They said they could. I said they couldn't. Suggesting another experiment to try to prove whether or not they could recognize a word by tracing the letters without seeing them, I asked whether they could write their names on the blackboard with their eyes closed. During this discussion I had noticed a little girl sitting next to me trying desperately to follow what was going on. Now she raised her hand vigorously. Every other hand in the class was also raised, but I called on her. Very slowly, somewhat inaccurately although still recognizably, she wrote her name on the board. While she was at the board the teacher, with some alarm, passed me a note saying that the girl was mentally retarded and cautioning me to be prepared for her to fail. Retarded or not, she was fully involved in the experiment. She had managed to scratch something on the board that both she and the class could recognize as her name. Because they were bursting to try, I let some of the other students go to the board to write their names. Most of them did it very well. Through this effort they were able to see the possibility that if they could write their names with their eyes closed, a blind person might feel words in a book. And the smile and eagerness of the "mentally retarded" girl proved that she was as much involved in the discussion as anyone else in the class. Later the class asked what books for the blind look like. They wanted the teacher to bring some in, which she promised to do.

In the discussion after the meeting with the class teacher and several other teachers who were observing, I noted that the meeting could be used as a way to stimulate children to learn to read. The teacher could point out, or have the children point out to her, the advantage of having eyes; reading, difficult as it is for many of these children, is much easier for them than for the blind. The children were deeply involved in the meeting, enjoyed it, and used their brains to think about and solve what seemed at first an insoluble problem. They experienced success as a group and success as individuals. Meetings such as this one in the second grade can be used as motivators in many subjects of the curriculum. In addition, a class that is involved, thinking, and successful will have few disciplinary problems.

In the lower grades, the open-ended meeting may have to be related to the curriculum by the teacher; in the higher grades the class can make the connection. Having a thoughtful, relevant discussion on any subject, however, is more valuable than forcing a connection to the curriculum. In fact, if enough thoughtful discussions are held on subjects not in the curriculum, we should study the curriculum to see where it should be changed. . . .

By treating the whole class as a unit, the same spirit of cooperation can arise as arises on athletic teams. By eliminating failure, by accepting each child's thinking (at least during the time of the meeting), and by utilizing his mistakes as a basis for future teaching, we have a way of approaching the child that supports him. The present system of accentuating his mistakes tears the child down and makes him unable or unwilling to think.

Another advantage of class meetings is the confidence that a child gains when he states his opinion before a group. In life there are many opportunities to speak for oneself. The more we teach children to speak clearly and thoughtfully, the better we prepare them for life. When a child can speak satisfactorily for himself, he gains a confidence that is hard to shake.

Views of the Favorite Colleges

Approaching by the gate, (Class of '79,
All dead) the unimpressed new scholars find
Halls of archaic brick and, if it is April,
Three dazzling magnolias behind bars, like
    lions.

Unsettling winds among the pillars of wis-
    dom
Assure them of harmonious extremes,
However academic. The bells, in key,
Covered with singing birds, ring on the
    hour.

Towering, but without aspiration, the cam-
    panile
Is known to sway an inch in a high wind;
But that, like the statue's changeable com-
    plexion,
Is natural. To find the unnatural,

Gradually absorb the industry
Of ten o'clock: the embryo pig slit through
With the proper instruments by embryos;
And Sophocles cut, for speed, with a blue
    pencil.

Prehensile sophomores in the tree of learning
Stare at the exiled blossoming trees, vaguely
    puzzled,
The lecturer, especially if bearded,
Enhances those druidical undertones.

What is the terminus of books? sing the
    birds.
Tell us about Sophocles! cry the trees.
And a crazy child on rollerskates skates
    through
The campus like a one-man thunderstorm.

John Malcolm Brinnin

Use the "Natural"

"Mary had a little lamb, little lamb, little lamb,
Mary had a little lamb its fleece was white as
snow. And everywhere that Mary went, Mary went,
Mary went, and everywhere that Mary went, the lamb
was sure to go. It followed her to school one
day, school one day, school one day. It followed
her to school one day which was against the rules.
It made the children laugh and play, laugh and
play, laugh and play. It made the children laugh
and play to see a lamb in school. And so the
teacher turned it out, turned it out, turned it
out. . . ." In an open classroom meeting discuss how
you can make the lamb relevant, keep the lamb in
school. What could you do with it in first
grade, eleventh grade, college?

Tomorrow and Tomorrow and So Forth by John Updike

Whirling, talking, 11D began to enter Room 109. From the quality of the class's excitement Mark Prosser guessed it would rain. He had been teaching high school for three years, yet his students still impressed him; they were such sensitive animals. They reacted so infallibly to merely barometric pressure.

In the doorway, Brute Young paused while little Barry Snyder giggled at his elbow. Barry's stagy laugh rose and fell, dipping down toward some vile secret that had to be tasted and retasted, then soaring like a rocket to proclaim that he, little Barry, shared such a secret with the school's fullback. Being Brute's stooge was precious to Barry. The fullback paid no attention to him; he twisted his neck to stare at something not yet coming through the door. He yielded heavily to the procession pressing him forward.

Right under Prosser's eyes, like a murder suddenly appearing in an annalistic frieze of kings and queens, someone stabbed a girl in the back with a pencil. She ignored the assault saucily. Another hand yanked out Geoffrey Langer's shirt-tail. Geoffrey, a bright student, was uncertain whether to laugh it off or defend himself with anger, and made a weak, half-turning gesture of compromise, wearing an expression of distant arrogance that Prosser instantly coördinated with baffled feelings he used to have.

All along the line, in the glitter of key chains and the acute angles of turned-back shirt cuffs, an electricity was expressed which simple weather couldn't generate.

Mark wondered if today Gloria Angstrom wore that sweater, an ember-pink angora, with very brief sleeves. The virtual sleevelessness was the disturbing factor: the exposure of those two serene arms to the air, white as thighs against the delicate wool.

His guess was correct. A vivid pink patch flashed through the jiggle of arms and shoulders as the final knot of youngsters entered the room.

"Take your seats," Mr. Prosser said. "Come on. Let's go."

Most obeyed, but Peter Forrester, who had been at the center of the group around Gloria, still lingered in the doorway with her, finishing some story, apparently determined to make her laugh or gasp. When she did gasp, he tossed his head with satisfaction. His orange hair, preened into a kind of floating bang, bobbed. Mark had always disliked redheaded males, with their white eyelashes and puffy faces and thyroid eyes, and absurdly self-confident mouths. A race of bluffers. His own hair was brown.

When Gloria, moving in a considered, stately way, had taken her seat, and Peter had swerved into his, Mr. Prosser said, "Peter Forrester."

"Yes?" Peter rose, scrabbling through his book for the right place.

"Kindly tell the class the exact meaning of the words 'Tomorrow, and tomorrow, and tomorrow/Creeps in this petty pace from day to day.' "

Peter glanced down at the high-school edition of *Macbeth* lying open on his desk. One of the duller girls tittered expectantly from the back of the room. Peter was popular with the girls; girls that age had minds like moths.

"Peter. With your book shut. We have all memorized this passage for today. Remember?" The girl in the back of the room squealed in delight. Gloria laid her own book face-open on her desk, where Peter could see it.

Peter shut his book with a bang and stared into Gloria's. "Why," he said at last, "I think it means pretty much what it says."

"Which is?"

"Why, that tomorrow is something we often think about. It creeps into our conversation all the time. We couldn't make any plans without thinking about tomorrow."

"I see. Then you would say that Macbeth is here referring to the, the date-book aspect of life?"

Geoffrey Langer laughed, no doubt to please Mr. Prosser. For a moment, he *was* pleased. Then he realized he had been playing for laughs at a student's expense.

His paraphrase had made Peter's reading of the lines seem more ridiculous than it was. He began to retract. "I admit—"

But Peter was going on; redheads never know when to quit. "Macbeth means that if we quit worrying about tomorrow, and just live for today, we could appreciate all the wonderful things that are going on under our noses."

Mark considered this a moment before he spoke. He would not be sarcastic. "Uh, without denying that there is truth in what you say, Peter, do you think it likely that Macbeth, in his situation, would be expressing such"—he couldn't help himself—"such sunny sentiments?"

Geoffrey laughed again. Peter's neck reddened; he studied the floor. Gloria glared at Mr. Prosser, the indignation in her face clearly meant for him to see.

Mark hurried to undo his mistake. "Don't misunderstand me, please," he told Peter. "I don't have all the answers myself. But it seems to me the whole speech, down to 'Signifying nothing,' is saying that life is—well, a *fraud*. Nothing wonderful about it."

"Did Shakespeare really think that?" Geoffrey Langer asked, a nervous quickness pitching his voice high.

Mark read into Geoffrey's question his own adolescent premonitions of the terrible truth. The attempt he must make was plain. He told Peter he could sit down and looked through the window toward the steadying sky. The clouds were gaining intensity. "There is," Mr. Prosser slowly began, "much darkness in Shakespeare's work, and no play is darker than *Macbeth*. The atmosphere is poisonous, oppressive. One critic has said that in this play, humanity suffocates." He felt himself in danger of suffocating, and cleared his throat.

"In the middle of his career, Shakespeare wrote plays about men like Hamlet and Othello and Macbeth—men who aren't allowed by their society, or bad luck, or some minor flaw in themselves, to become the great men they might have been. Even Shakespeare's comedies of this period deal with a world gone sour. It is as if he had seen through the bright, bold surface of his earlier comedies and histories and had looked upon something terrible. It frightened him, just as some day it may frighten some of you." In his determination to find the right words, he had been staring at Gloria, without meaning to. Embarrassed, she nodded, and, realizing what had happened, he smiled at her.

He tried to make his remarks gentler, even diffident. "But then I think Shakespeare sensed a redeeming truth. His last plays are serene and symbolical, as if he had pierced through the ugly facts and reached a realm where the facts are again beautiful. In this way, Shakespeare's total work is a more complete image of life than that of any other writer, except perhaps for Dante, an Italian poet who wrote several centuries earlier." He had been taken far from the Macbeth soliloquy. Other teachers had been happy to tell him how the kids made a game of getting him talking. He looked toward Geoffrey. The boy was doodling on his tablet, indifferent. Mr. Prosser concluded, "The last play Shakespeare wrote is an extraordinary poem called *The Tempest*. Some of you may want to read it for your next book reports—the ones due May 10th. It's a short play."

The class had been taking a holiday. Barry Snyder was snicking BBs off the blackboard and glancing over at Brute Young to see if he noticed. "Once more, Barry," Mr. Prosser said, "and out you go." Barry blushed, and grinned to cover the blush, his eyeballs sliding toward Brute. The dull girl in the rear of the room was putting on lipstick. "Put that away, Alice," Prosser said. "This isn't a beauty parlor." Sejak, the Polish boy who worked nights, was asleep at his desk, his cheek white with pressure against the varnished wood, his mouth sagging sidewise. Mr. Prosser had an impulse to let him sleep. But the impulse might not be true kindness, but just the self-congratulatory, kindly pose in which he sometimes discovered himself. Besides, one breach of discipline encouraged others. He strode down the aisle and squeezed Sejak's shoulder; the boy awoke. A mumble was growing at the front of the room.

Peter Forrester was whispering to Gloria, trying to make her laugh. The girl's face, though, was cool and solemn, as if a thought had been provoked in her head—as if there lingered there something of what Mr. Prosser had been saying. With a bracing sense of chivalrous intercession, Mark said, "Peter. I gather from this noise that you have something to add to your theories."

Peter responded courteously. "No, sir. I honestly don't understand the speech. Please, sir, what *does* it mean?"

This candid admission and odd request stunned the class. Every white, round face, eager, for once, to learn, turned toward Mark. He said, "I don't know. I was hoping *you* would tell *me*."

In college, when a professor made such a remark, it was with grand effect. The professor's humility, the necessity for creative interplay between teacher and student were dramatically impressed upon the group. But to 11D, ignorance in an instructor was as wrong as a hole in a roof. It was as if Mark had held forty strings pulling forty faces taut toward him and then had slashed the strings. Heads waggled, eyes dropped, voices buzzed. Some of the discipline problems, like Peter Forrester, smirked signals to one another.

"Quiet!" Mr. Prosser shouted. "All of you. Poetry isn't arithmetic. There's no single right answer. I don't want to force my own impression on you; that's not why I'm here." The silent question, *Why are you here?* seemed to steady the air with suspense. "I'm here," he said, "to let you teach yourselves."

Whether or not they believed him, they subsided, somewhat. Mark judged he could safely reassume his human-among-humans pose. He perched on the edge of the desk, informal, friendly, and frankly beseeching. "Now, honestly. Don't any of you have some personal feeling about the lines that you would like to share with the class and me?"

One hand, with a flowered handkerchief balled in it, unsteadily rose. "Go ahead, Teresa," Mr. Prosser said. She was a timid, sniffly girl whose mother was a Jehovah's Witness.

"It makes me think of cloud shadows," Teresa said.

Geoffrey Langer laughed. "Don't be rude, Geoff," Mr. Prosser said sideways, softly, before throwing his voice forward: "Thank you, Teresa. I think that's an interesting and valid impression. Cloud movement has something in it of the slow, monotonous rhythm one feels in the line 'Tomorrow, and tomorrow, and tomorrow.' It's a very gray line, isn't it, class?" No one agreed or disagreed.

Beyond the windows actual clouds were bunching rapidly, and erratic sections of sunlight slid around the room. Gloria's arm, crooked gracefully above her head, turned gold. "Gloria?" Mr. Prosser asked.

She looked up from something on her desk with a face of sullen radiance. "I think what Teresa said was very good," she said, glaring in the direction of Geoffrey Langer. Geoffrey snickered defiantly. "And I have a question. What does 'petty pace' mean?"

"It means the trivial day-to-day sort of life that, say, a bookkeeper or a bank clerk leads. Or a schoolteacher," he added, smiling.

She did not smile back. Thought wrinkles irritated her perfect brow. "But Macbeth has been fighting wars, and killing kings, and being a king himself, and all," she pointed out.

"Yes, but it's just these acts Macbeth is condemning as 'nothing.' Can you see that?"

Gloria shook her head. "Another thing I worry about—isn't it silly for Macbeth to be talking to himself right in the middle of this war, with his wife just dead, and all?"

"I don't think so, Gloria. No matter how fast events happen, thought is faster."

His answer was weak; everyone knew it, even if Gloria hadn't mused, supposedly to herself, but in a voice the entire class could hear, "It seems so *stupid*."

Mark winced, pierced by the awful clarity with which his students saw him. Through their eyes, how queer he looked, with his chalky hands, and his horn-rimmed glasses, and his hair never slicked down, all wrapped up in "literature," where, when things get rough, the king mumbles a poem nobody understands. He was suddenly conscious of a terrible tenderness in the young, a frightening patience and faith. It was so good of them not to laugh him out of the room. He looked down and rubbed his fingertips together, trying to erase the chalk dust. The class noise sifted into unnatural quiet. "It's getting late," he said finally. "Let's start the recitations of the memorized passage. Bernard Amilson, you begin."

Bernard had trouble enunciating, and his rendition began " 'T'mau 'n' t'mau 'n' t'mau.' " It was reassuring, the extent to which the class tried to repress its laughter. Mr. Prosser wrote "A" in his marking book opposite Bernard's name. He always gave Bernard A on recitations, despite the school nurse, who claimed there was nothing organically wrong with the boy's mouth.

It was the custom, cruel but traditional, to deliver recitations from the front of the room. Alice, when her turn came, was reduced to a helpless state by the first funny

153

face Peter Forrester made at her. Mark let her hand up there a good minute while her face ripened to cherry redness, and at last relented. "Alice, you may try it later." Many of the class knew the passage gratifyingly well, though there was a tendency to leave out the line "To the last syllable of recorded time" and to turn "struts and frets" into "frets and struts" or simply "struts and struts." Even Sejak, who couldn't have looked at the passage before he came to class, got through it as far as "And then is heard no more."

Geoffrey Langer showed off, as he always did, by interrupting his own recitation with bright questions. " 'Tomorrow, and tomorrow, and tomorrow,' " he said, " 'creeps in'—shouldn't that be 'creep in,' Mr. Prosser?"

"It is 'creeps.' The trio is in effect singular. Go on. Without the footnotes." Mr. Prosser was tired of coddling Langer. The boy's black hair, short and stiff, seemed deliberately ratlike.

" 'Creepsss in this petty pace from day to day, to the last syllable of recorded time, and all our yesterdays have lighted fools the way to dusty death. Out, out—' "

"No, no!" Mr. Prosser jumped out of his chair. "This is poetry. Don't mushmouth it! Pause a little after 'fools.' " Geoffrey looked genuinely startled this time, and Mark himself did not quite understand his annoyance and, mentally turning to see what was behind him, seemed to glimpse in the humid undergrowth the two stern eyes of the indignant look Gloria had thrown Geoffrey. He glimpsed himself in the absurd position of acting as Gloria's champion in her private war with this intelligent boy. He sighed apologetically. "Poetry is made up of lines," he began, turning to the class. Gloria was passing a note to Peter Forrester.

The rudeness of it! To pass notes during a scolding that she herself had caused! Mark caged in his hand the girl's frail wrist and ripped the note from her fingers. He read it to himself, letting the class see he was reading it, though he despised such methods of discipline. The note went:

Pete—I think you're *wrong* about Mr. Prosser. I think he's wonderful and I get a lot out of his class. He's heavenly with poetry. I think I love him. I really do *love* him. So there.

Mr. Prosser folded the note once and slipped it into his side coat pocket. "See me after class, Gloria," he said. Then, to Geoffrey, "Let's try it again. Begin at the beginning."

While the boy was reciting the passage, the buzzer sounded the end of the period. It was the last class of the day. The room quickly emptied, except for Gloria. The noise of lockers slamming open and books being thrown against metal and shouts drifted in.

"Who has a car?"

"Lend me a cig, pig."

"We can't have practice in this slop."

Mark hadn't noticed exactly when the rain started, but it was coming down hard now. He moved around the room with the window pole, closing windows and pulling down shades. Spray bounced in on his hands. He began to talk to Gloria in a crisp voice that, like his device of shutting the windows, was intended to protect them both from embarrassment.

"About note passing." She sat motionless at her desk in the front of the room, her short, brushed-up hair like a cool torch. From the way she sat, her naked arms folded at her breasts and her shoulders hunched, he felt she was chilly. "It is not only rude to scribble when a teacher is talking, it is stupid to put one's words down on paper, where they look much more foolish than they might have sounded if spoken." He leaned the window pole in its corner and walked toward his desk.

"And about love. 'Love' is one of those words that illustrate what happens to an old, overworked language. These days, with movie stars and crooners and preachers and psychiatrists all pronouncing the word, it's come to mean nothing but a vague fondness for something. In this sense, I love the rain, this blackboard, these desks, you. It means nothing, you see, whereas once the word signified a quite explicit thing—a desire to share all you own and are with someone else. It is time we coined a new word to mean that, and when you think up the word *you* want to use, I suggest that you be economical with it. Treat it as something you can spend only once—if not for your own sake, for the good of the language." He walked over to his own desk and dropped two pencils on it, as if to say, "That's all."

"I'm sorry," Gloria said.

Rather surprised, Mr. Prosser said, "Don't be."

"But you don't understand."

"Of course I don't. I probably never did. At your age, I was like Geoffrey Langer."

"I bet you weren't." The girl was almost crying; he was sure of that.

"Come on, Gloria. Run along. Forget it." She slowly cradled her books between her bare arms and her sweater, and left the room with that melancholy shuffling teenage gait, so that her body above her thighs seemed to float over the desktops.

What was it, Mark asked himself, these kids were after? What did they want? Glide, he decided, the quality of glide. To slip along, always in rhythm, always cool, the little wheels humming under you, going nowhere special. If Heaven existed, that's the way it would be there. *He's heavenly with poetry.* They loved the word. Heaven was in half their songs.

"Christ, he's humming." Strunk, the physical ed teacher, had come into the room without Mark's noticing. Gloria had left the door ajar.

"Ah," Mark said, "a fallen angel, full of grit."

"What the hell makes you so happy?"

"I'm not happy, I'm just heavenly. I don't know why you don't appreciate me."

"Say." Strunk came up an aisle with a disagreeably effeminate waddle, pregnant with gossip. "Did you hear about Murchison?"

"No." Mark mimicked Strunk's whisper. "He got the pants kidded off him today."

"Oh dear."

Strunk started to laugh, as he always did before beginning a story. "You know what a goddam lady's man he thinks he is?"

"You bet," Mark said, although Strunk said that about every male member of the faculty.

"You have Gloria Angstrom, don't you?"

"You bet."

"Well, this morning Murky intercepts a note she was writing, and the note says what a damn neat guy she thinks Murchison is and how she *loves* him!" Strunk waited for Mark to say something, and then, when he didn't, continued, "You could see he was tickled pink. But—get this—it turns out at lunch that the same damn thing happened to Fryeburg in history yesterday!" Strunk laughed and cracked his knuckles viciously. "The girl's too dumb to have thought it up herself. We all think it was Peter Forrester's idea."

"Probably was," Mark agreed. Strunk followed him out to his locker, describing Murchison's expression when Fryeburg (in all innocence, mind you) told what had happened to him.

Mark turned the combination of his locker, 18–24–3. "Would you excuse me, Dave?" he said. "My wife's in town waiting."

Strunk was too thick to catch Mark's anger. "I got to get over to the gym. Can't take the little darlings outside in the rain; their mommies'll write notes to teacher." He waddled down the hall and wheeled at the far end, shouting, "Now don't tell You-know-who!"

Mr. Prosser took his coat from the locker and shrugged it on. He placed his hat upon his head. He fitted his rubbers over his shoes, pinching his fingers painfully, and lifted his umbrella off the hook. He thought of opening it right there in the vacant hall, as a kind of joke, and decided not to. The girl had been almost crying; he was sure of that.

How would you describe the group in Prosser's class? Does it resemble any of your own high school classes? Do you ever sense a group mood, the "electricity . . . which a simple weather couldn't generate"? Compare a Monday morning with a Friday morning in class. Compare a hot, sunny day with a rainy day. Should a teacher respond to these moods? How effectively does Prosser deal with the group mood? How well does he relate to individuals? He asks for a show of personal feelings. Is the climate in his classroom conducive to revealing feelings? Trust? How "real" is Prosser with his students? How "real" are they with him? How "real" is Gloria? What games is each playing that aren't for fun? Who is the real teacher?

Do you think Shakespeare should be taught in high school? If so, what could a creative teacher do to make Shakespeare relevant? How could he make use of groups and individual study and paired learning to democratize the class? How could he deal with feelings? Role play alternative approaches to Prosser's teaching. What are some of the "unsettling winds among the pillars of wisdom"?

155

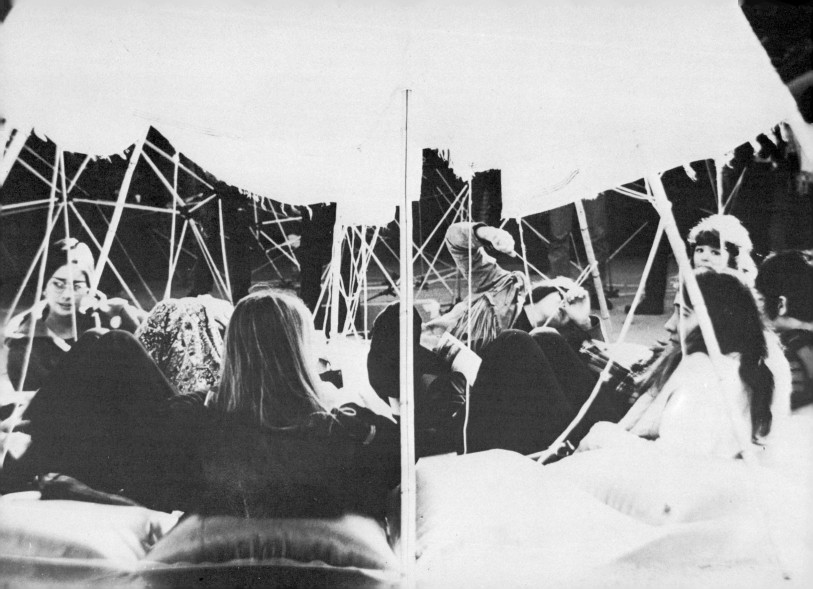

Chapter Seven

The Group as a Way of Exploring Feelings

In this time of great change and personal confusion, we must help children and youth to explore intensively and continuously their roles as individuals growing and changing in increasingly urban communities. Children must be helped to confront and cope with the realities of their own life space—the ways they make and relate to friends, the ways they behave in groups, how they reconcile personal desires with the social good, how they treat individuals who are different in some ways from themselves. It is in such a matrix that they will shape their own identity and character and become positive, constructive citizens rather than self-indulgent, noninvolved individuals.

From Fannie R. and George Shaftel, *Role-Playing for Social Values*

What would you do in this situation?
In early spring two new girls were transferred into the class.

They sauntered into the room and sat together near the rear wall. When I asked them their names, they told me I ought to know since I was the teacher. It was going to be a difficult hour.

I handed out paper, and the girls let it slide to the floor. I asked the class to take out pens; the girls began to crack their gum. They made snide remarks about everything. The other kids never said a word the whole period. They just sat and stared at me, and I had wild visions of the whole group uniting against me—a teacher always makes a good scapegoat.

"I'll bet she thinks she's pretty cute," one of the girls muttered just loudly enough.

"I wonder who thought up that stupid assignment," the other said. I had to ignore them. To compete would have been fatal—I'm just not clever enough. So I said nothing—but they were plenty hard to ignore.

By the time the bell rang, I hated every kid I'd ever met, and decided it might be nice to work in a toy store or something. I was about to dash to the bathroom when Frankie and Bernice approached me. I didn't know what to expect.

"Mrs. Decker," Frankie began. He looked at me very hard. "We've got to get those girls out of here." I couldn't believe it.

"You're gonna not like them, and you won't want to teach us any more," Bernice said.

"We've got something sort of special in this class," Frankie continued, "and we're not gonna let them ruin it."

Great things happen at the funniest times.

I asked what they thought we should do. Frankie said, "Don't you worry about it—I'll take care of them after school."

I explained that dealing with people is tough business, and you can't just kill everyone you don't like. They finally agreed that more subtle tactics might be better. And besides, it wasn't worth it to get yourself in trouble over such jive people. I said I'd leave it to the class to handle the situation.

It was an easy way out. It made them feel good—and I hadn't the slightest idea what to do myself.

From Sunny Decker, *An Empty Spoon*

Turn to page 223 to find out what she did.

The man whose calling it is to influence the being of persons that can be determined, must experience this action of his (however much it may have assumed the form of non-action) ever anew from the other side. Without the action of his spirit being in any way weakened he must at the same time be over there, on the surface of that other spirit which is being acted upon—and not of some conceptual, contrived spirit, but all the time the wholly concrete spirit of this individual and unique being who is living and confronting him, and who stands with him in the common situation of "educating" and "being educated" (which is indeed one situation, only the other is at the other end of it). It is not enough for him to imagine the child's individuality, or to experience him directly as a spiritual person and then to acknowledge him. Only when he catches himself "from over there," and feels how it affects one, how it affects the other human being, does he recognize the real limit, baptize his self-will in Reality and make it true will, and renew his paradoxical legitimacy.

From Martin Buber, *Between Man and Man*

A meeting of two: eye to eye, face to face.
And when you are near I will tear your eyes
  out
And place them instead of mine,
And you will tear my eyes out
And will place them instead of yours.
Then I will look at you with your eyes
And you will look at me with mine.

From J. L. Moreno, *Psychodrama*, vol. I

Could you share the mountain of feelings you climb all day with your teacher or your classmates or were these feelings regarded as irrelevant to school life? How many times have problems at home followed you to school and problems at school been carried back home? We've been pretty effective in teaching technical know-how; we seem to be able to mass produce almost anything but healthy human relationships. Maybe this is the "new frontier." Some people call it "The New Copernican Revolution"; others call it the human potential movement. Whatever you call it, we in the schools are going to have to give at least equal time to creating environments and exploring ways to increase human know-how, openness, flexibility, spontaneity, creativity, problem solving, discovery. In this section are three approaches now in use in schools where people learn to deal with feelings and work with conflict: social-problem-solving meetings, role playing or sociodrama, and Summerhillian type open, school-wide meetings run by students. None of these is radically new. They're just not used enough. Are

you a "knower" or a "seeker"? What's in your toolchest?

Think of a problem related to school with which you are now grappling and where your feelings are deeply involved.

Think of a problem you struggled with when you were younger.

Think of a problem that a friend, relative, or classmate is wrestling with.

What do the following approaches offer you in understanding and working with conflicts or helping others to understand and work with theirs?

From *Schools Without Failure* by William Glasser

When children enter kindergarten they should discover that each class is a working, problem-solving unit and that each student has both individual and group responsibilities. Responsibility for learning and for behaving so that learning is fostered is shared among the entire class. By discussing group and individual problems, the students and teacher can usually solve their problems within the classroom. If children learn to participate in a problem-solving group when they enter school and continue to do so with a variety of teachers throughout the six years of elementary school, they learn that the world is not a mysterious and sometimes hostile and frightening place where they have little control over what happens to them. They learn rather that, although the world may be difficult and that it may at times appear hostile and mysterious, they can use their brains individually and as a group *to solve the problems of living in their school world. . . .*

School children have many social problems, some of which may call for discipline, some not. Under ordinary conditions, because there is no systematic effort to teach them social problem-solving, school children find that problems that arise in getting along with each other in school are difficult to solve. Given little help, children tend to evade problems, to lie their way out of situations, to depend upon others to solve their problems, or just to give up. None of these courses of action is good preparation for life. The social-problem-solving meeting can help children learn better ways.

At another meeting, Mike was introduced as the topic. Physically overweight and not too clean-looking in appearance, with hair in his eyes and a very loud, offensive voice, and holes in all his tee shirts caused from biting and twisting and chewing on them, he was not pleasant to behold! Mike said he didn't like the class because they didn't like him. When asked why they didn't like him, he said it was because he was fat. The children eagerly disagreed. They said that had nothing to do with it. Mike wanted to know why, then. He was given the opportunity to call on those children he wanted to explain to him what they found offensive about him. Someone said it was because he wears funny hats to school, like the pilot's helmet he wore the day before. (Incidentally, he never wore it again.) Some said he dressed sloppily. Martin said it was because he said things that hurt people. For example, when Martin came home from Europe and showed the class several treasures that he brought to share, Mike said he didn't believe they were from Paris and that he bought the same things here. Martin said that hurt his feelings. David said that when he shared things with the class, Mike blurted out similar

derogatory remarks. (Mike still has not cured himself of this, by the way.) John, who had become much more introspective and perceptive, said it was because Mike always made funny faces and looked up at the ceiling with a disgusted look on his face when people tried to talk to him. While he was saying this, Mike was doing just that. John said, "See, Mike, you're doing it right now, and you don't even know it." Mike was asked if anyone, in his opinion, went out of his way to be nice to him. He said, only Alice, whom he liked. Everyone giggled. Alice said she didn't care if everyone did laugh at her, she liked Mike and was not ashamed to be his friend. She liked being nice to him. We talked as a group about the importance of having one friend at least. The others found that no one really tried to go out of his way to be his friend, but each person would try to make some gesture to show they would try in the next week. They really rose to the occasion, but soon forgot about it and were their usual apathetic selves. However, no one seemed to go out of his way to be nasty, which was a change. Alice continued being nice to Mike, and the children stopped teasing her about it. Harriet, who was one of the girls who was teasing Alice, apologized in a class meeting for doing so, and she said she had once been teased for befriending someone without other friends, and that it took more courage to be his friend and yet she wanted to. She told Alice that, even though it had hurt her feelings when the others teased her, she had forgotten and

teased Alice and that she was sorry, as she could really understand how Alice felt. There has been a tremendous change in Mike this semester. He is not lackadaisical about his work or appearance, speaks more quietly, uses more self-control, plays a fairer game in the yard, gets along much better with others, and has more (or some) friends.

From *Summerhill, the Loving World* by Herb Snitzer

General Meeting III

CHAIRMAN: *First business on the agenda. Bob.*

BOB: *I have two things I want to make known. One, somebody borrowed my work gloves about ten days ago, and they haven't returned them. I would like to have them back.*

CLANCY: *I have them, Bob. I'll give them to you at the end of the meeting. Sorry about that.*

BOB: *Okay. The other thing is this. Since last Saturday, just for kicks, I started keeping track of how many times I was asked for money, and between last Saturday and Thursday, when people caught on to what I was doing, I was asked eighty-seven times* [Laughter] *by thirty-two different people. I'm not counting staff, and if I had said "yes" to all requests I would have given out twelve pounds, fourteen and four, which is twice as much as what a teacher makes here in a week, and half the time I said "no," I was called stingy. I know it's funny, looking back on it, but living with it from day to day makes life rather unpleasant.*

ENA: *We've been living with that for twenty years, Bob.*

CHAIRMAN: *Right, so if you don't want to be put down in Bob's book, don't ask him for money. Next business.*

MYRNA: *I'd like to say something about this lost-and-found business, and the rewards. I think this reward business should be stopped. Certain people this week have been taking advantage of this. They have stolen things, and have waited until a reward has gone up, and then they queue up for the reward for finding something they stole in the first place. I'd like to propose that no rewards be given for things found. I just think it encourages people to steal things. We should be honest enough with each other so that if we find anything, we should give it to Carole to post on the board, and not wait until a reward is put up.*

BRENDAN: *Look, that's up to the person who wants to give a reward, isn't it?*

MYRNA: *Well, I think the community has a perfect right to decide what it is worth.*

CAROLE: *Look, Myrna, you may lose something that isn't worth threepence, but may be worth a great deal more in how you feel about it. Why should the community decide how you feel about it?*

MYRNA: *Look, all I'm saying is that people cannot put up a reward without bringing it to the attention of the community. If you lose something, you have to make an announcement before the community before a reward can be posted. Okay?*

CHAIRMAN: *All right, all in favor of that. All against. It isn't carried.*

ROY: *Take another vote.*

WILF: *I don't think a vote is necessary. All Myrna is doing is appealing to the community not to bring up a reward straight away. That's all.*

CHAIRMAN: *Okay. Is that okay with you, Myrna?*

MYRNA: *Yes.*

CHAIRMAN: *Right.*

CAROLE: *You must remember that sometimes it is a good thing. Remember that time that woman lost her keys in the hockey field. She offered a reward, and they were found in about two hours.*

LES: *I propose this meeting is closed.*

WILF: *Now, wait a minute. I think this is an important matter that Myrna has brought up. I think that what she says is quite true—that rewards do encourage people to steal, and it should be dealt with here and now.*

CAROLE: *I think this is a bit much. There have been things that have been genuinely lost, and people put up a reward because they know that everyone keeps their eyes open.*

SCOTT: *Look, Myrna. I don't think you have to propose this. It is a personal thing between the person who lost the article or whatever and what he wants to do about it. Look, I don't think we have a right to say that someone cannot give a reward when he or she wants to. Nobody has the right to say that. It's your life.*

WILF: *I'd just like to reply to Carole here. She is right. People shouldn't be stopped from offering rewards when they want to. It is a suggestion that before this is done, you appeal to the community. No one said you had to do this. You can do what you want.*

MYRNA: *I think the community should decide when a reward is necessary.*

BRENDAN: *Hell, no! If I decide I want to put up a reward, that's my business—not yours.*
CHAIRMAN: *Okay, okay. That's enough now. I think we've talked this subject dead. Anyone else? Neill.*
NEILL: *I want to say something quite serious, and I don't want any laughter about it. I made a law at the beginning of this term about smoking if you are under sixteen. I made this law because the government told all schools to discourage smoking among children, and Summerhill can't stand out against the whole of the schools of England. I had to follow on, and make a law that you can't smoke under sixteen. Now, a lot of people are smoking under sixteen, and quite openly. Well, I'm telling you now, but before I say it, some of you think I'm an old softie. Neill is an easygoing guy. Well, I'm going to tell you all something. You have to choose whether you are going to smoke here or not. If you're going to smoke here, you're not coming back. I'm telling Clancy's parents that. I'm telling others that as well. I've got to carry this law through. I can't punish you. Only the community can punish, but I can say, all right, if you don't want to live the Summerhill way, you're not coming back. You can call this a punishment if you like. And that applies to the Americans too. I'm going to have this law carried out for my own safety and for yours as well. So don't feel you can come here, and do as you like. You can't.*
CHAIRMAN: *Right. We've all heard Neill. You take it from there. Is there any more business? Meeting closed, then.*

Does the Summerhill meeting resemble the social-problem-solving session of Glasser's? In what ways are they similar? Different? Who is the teacher and who are the students? What is being taught and what is being learned? Many people think Summerhill equals freedom, and freedom equals doing anything you want all the time. Yet, Neill's concluding remark is: "So don't feel you can come here and do as you like. You can't."

How can you "do your thing" and I "do my thing" and still "get it all together"? How do we strike a balance between freedom and order?

Thinking is not a monologue. It's a dialogue between parts of ourselves. Thinking is dialogical. Being is dialectical, many voices, many rooms in us talking to each other, a group. Parts of us take over; parts recede. A part of us throws rocks at another part that hides behind the couch. Some voices speak softer than others. Some carry big sticks. Listen to all your voices for a change. Democratize your own head. Choose a controversial subject such as the open classroom, no grades, going to school, communal living. Write down or talk into a tape recorder or use chairs. Talk for the different parts of your-self. Give the parts names, numbers, letters. Listen to what they're saying. Are the voices agreeing? Disagreeing? Cooperating? Competing? How do they resolve their conflicts? Can you run your own Summerhill Saturday night general meeting on Wednesday?

From Fannie R. and George Shaftel, *Role-Playing for Social Values*

Role playing, when properly and skillfully used, is uniquely suited to the exploration of group behavior and of the dilemmas of the individual child as he tries to find a place in the many and increasing groups in his life and at the same time struggles to establish personal identity and integrity. When properly used, role playing permits the kind of "discovery" learning which occurs when individuals in groups face up to the ways they tend to solve their problems of interpersonal relations, and which occurs when, under skillful guidance, young people become conscious of their personal value systems. As a result, young people are helped to develop a sensitivity to the feelings and welfare of others and to clarify their own values in terms of ethical behavior.

Role playing, as employed in this book, is not aimed at achieving therapy; nor is it "creative dramatics" or incidental skits to highlight a discussion or lecture. Rather, it is a group of problem-solving procedures that employs all the techniques of critical evaluation implied in the terms "listening," "discussion" and "problem solvings," and is akin to the research procedures which behavioral scientists term *simulation* and *theory of games.*

ROLE-IT!

Role-playing and Psychodrama

The role-playing described here is the kind often referred to as Sociodrama, when we play out roles of people in society who do not necessarily represent ourselves exactly as we are at the moment. Psychodrama, although closely connected and not always neatly separated from sociodrama, involves a protagonist playing himself assisted by auxiliary egos, people from the audience who may be specially trained to assist him. For example, a student may be in a conflict with his father. *When he plays himself* assisted by someone else playing his father in a simulation of the exact home situation, the role-playing is psychodramatic. When, however, a father-son conflict is played by members of the class who can identify with the roles but who are not producing an exact replica of their own situation, the role-playing more closely approximates sociodrama. The line between the two is a fine one. However, psychodrama, being more personal, involves more training on the part of the director and should, therefore, be used with discretion in a classroom. For both forms, we are indebted to Dr. J. L. Moreno, the pioneer in sociodrama and psychodrama.

Warming Up for Role Playing

Sometimes warm ups are "directed," or planned, developing from an interactional problem that the teacher or students have become aware of. Sometimes, warm-ups are "nondirected" or unplanned, growing spontaneously out of what is being seen, heard or done; they can be a natural extension of a classroom meeting, the discussion of a film, book or story. Whatever gets you on your mark and ready to be involved is a warm-up. Try warming-up right now. Think about situations from your own life that these statements suggest: "I'm always being picked on!" "I want to do it myself!" "Nobody understands me." "Shut up and listen, please!" "There's no way to change society." "He lectures over my head." "I'm black and you're white." "I'm a failure." "Keep out!" "All my friends use drugs." Add some of your own.

Setting up the Scene

Find a director. Choose a "What" or one of the above statements that seems interesting. Determine "Who" is involved, the number of participants needed. Establish "Where" they are and "When" the action is to take place. For example: "I'm black and you're white" might lead into a "What" which would be teaching in the "inner cities." The "Who" could be a young, white, middle class teacher from the suburbs trying to communicate with a class of black students from a poorer socio-economic background. The "Where" and "When" might be a high school social studies class right before lunch. "Nobody understands me" could develop into a "What" of self-exclusion or noncooperation where one person in a group refuses to go on a field trip planned by his group, played by five or six people, and insists on his own way.

The "Where" and "When" might be the lawn outside of a classroom at 2:00 P.M. Once the scene is outlined, find volunteers for the parts who feel "warmed-up" and ready to go. Whoever acts as director should avoid the tendency to rehearse the scene; for this diminishes spontaneity; academy award performances are not the goal but honesty and faithfulness to the feelings of people in these situations. The director should pay attention to the audience, too, for if role playing is effective, the lookers and listeners must become active, critical observers rather than passive receivers of entertainment.

Doing it, Talking about it, and Doing it again
Improvise the scene; use props if necessary. Stop the action when the problem is clearly focused or a solution arrived at. Talk about it, discuss possible alternative directions and then replay with the same actors or new volunteers. Role-players can often suggest new solutions by sharing the feelings they had in a part and revealing how they reacted to others in the scene just finished.

Additional techniques
The soliloquy, mirroring, doubling, and role reversing are other variations which, when introduced into role playing, can deepen and intensify action and meaning. In the soliloquy, a participant (with or without the director's suggestion) stands aside from the action and speaks his inner mind. In mirroring, the director suggests that someone from the audience come up and mirror one of the participants to let him see and hear himself while he looks on. In doubling, people from the audience who feel very much in touch with certain participants in the drama may, with the director's permission, enter the scene, stand behind an actor, and speak for him from time to time. This is often done when a person feels a strong identification with a role and senses something important is being left out or overlooked by a player. The double, however, is a helper; if he interferes with or dominates the scene, he should return to the audience. In role reversing, when the director feels participants are locked too rigidly into their own roles he may ask that the persons in conflict reverse and play each other's parts for a while. Then they reverse back and resume action. Many times, the decision to use one or more of these techniques to alter the action is the director's, but, for the most part, the director should attempt to allow the action its natural unfolding and remain unobtrusive unless a device seems definitely needed. The soliloquy, mirroring, doubling, and role reversing are particularly helpful when action is deadlocked, when participants seem unable to comprehend each other, or when people suffer stage fright.

Sharing, Particularizing, and Generalizing
After the role playing, which may entail several enactments of the same scene, an open sharing session emphasizing "what does this mean to me personally" is very valuable and can help everyone see the universality of the experience. It is important here to stay with "I feel" or "I have experienced" rather than dwell upon "People say" or "One does," etc. Generalizing may then follow and new direction discussed in terms of the class goals and emphases. If an issue is of enough concern, other role playing or discussion sessions might be arranged on the same theme. If the role playing relates to cognitive materials being studied, ways of integrating what's been learned could become the focus. Now you might want to consider how you could role play some of the scenes from stories in this book, such as: "The First Day of School," "Luther," "Tomorrow and Tomorrow and So Forth," and the situation from Sunny Decker's, *An Empty Spoon.*

All of us, students and teachers alike, are disadvantaged to some extent in our spontaneity, in our capacity to open up and share our feelings with others, and in our ability to solve social dilemmas creatively. Role playing or sociodrama is an important tool if we want to understand ourselves and others.

In role-playing sessions we have had occasion to observe that the verbal performance of deprived children is markedly improved in the discussion period following the session. When talking about some action they have seen, deprived children are apparently able to verbalize much more fully. Typically, they do not verbalize well in response to words alone. They express themselves more readily when reacting to things they can see and do. Words as stimuli are not sufficient for them as a rule. Ask a juvenile delinquent who comes from a disadvantaged background what he doesn't like about school or the teacher and you will get an abbreviated, inarticulate reply. But have a group of these youngsters act out a school scene in which someone plays the teacher, and you will discover a stream of verbal consciousness that is almost impossible to shut off.

From Frank Riessman, *The Culturally Deprived Child*

It seems rather paradoxical that the ordinary college class in English, Speech, or Basic Communication should in itself exhibit such a variety of marked problems of human intercommunication. Great, indeed, in these selected groups are the problems of individuals and problems of the group as a whole—problems of communications among members of the class as well as problems of communication by the instructor which bog down the learning and teaching processes at so many points. The coldness, the isolation and indifference, the tension and self-consciousness, the boredom, the stage fright, the shoddy work so frequently exhibited represent problems of communication as real and as important as the student may find elsewhere in his living and in his career. The class as a class, and as individuals, bring almost unlimited materials for laboratory practice in both communication and human relationships. Sociodrama, in these situations, as now available, seems very important if the instructor is concerned with the fundamental development of his students.

. . . [C]ommunication and interpersonal relations cannot be separated and . . . these matters should therefore be taught together.

From Elwood Murray, "Sociodrama and Psychodrama in the College Basic Communication Class" in *Psychodrama and Sociodrama in American Education*

Following is a selection from E. R. Braithwaite's novel *To Sir with Love*. "Sir" in the story is a black man from the West Indies. He graduates from college in England but being unable to find work as an engineer, he decides to teach in a predominantly white school in a poor section of London. How do you feel about the way in which the problem is resolved in the story? Experiment with alternative approaches suggested in this section.

From *To Sir, with Love* by E. R. Braithwaite

I was learning from them as well as teaching them. I learned to see them in relation to their surroundings, and in that way to understand them. At first I had been rather critical of their clothing, and thought their tight sweaters, narrow skirts and jeans unsuitable for school wear, but now that they were taking greater interest in personal tidiness, I could understand that such clothes merely reflected vigorous personalities in a relentless search for self-expression.

Just about this time a new supply teacher, Mr. Bell, was sent to our school as supernumerary to the staff for a few weeks. He was about forty years old, a tall, wiry man, who had had some previous experience with the Army Education Service. It was arranged that he should act as relief teacher for some lessons, including two periods of P.T. with the senior boys. One of Mr. Bell's hobbies was fencing: he was something of a perfectionist and impatient of anyone whose coordination was not as smooth and controlled as his own. He would repeat a P.T. movement or exercise over and over again until it was executed with clockwise precision, and though the boys grumbled against his discipline they seemed eager to prove to him that they were quite capable of doing any exercise he could devise, and with a skill that very nearly matched his own.

This was especially true in the cases of Ingham, Fernman and Seales, who would always place themselves at the head of the line as an example and encouragement to the others. The least athletic of these was Richard Buckley, a short, fat boy, amiable and rather dim, who could read and write after a fashion, and could never be provoked to any semblance of anger or heat. He was pleasant and jolly and a favorite with the others, who, though they themselves chivvied him unmercifully, were ever ready in his defense against outsiders.

Buckley was no good at P.T. or games; he just was not built for such pursuits. Yet, such is the perversity of human nature, he strenuously resisted any efforts to leave him out or overlook him when games were being arranged. His attempts at accomplishing such simple gymnastic performances as the "forward roll" and "star jump" reduced the rest of the P.T. class to helpless hilarity, but he persisted with a singleness of purpose, which though unproductive, was nothing short of heroic.

Buckley was Bell's special whipping boy.

Fully aware of the lad's physical limitations, he would encourage him to try other and more difficult exercises, with apparently the sole purpose of obtaining some amusement from the pitiably ridiculous results. Sometimes the rest of the class would protest; and then Bell would turn on them the full flood of his invective. The boys mentioned this in their "Weekly Review," and Mr. Florian decided to discuss it at a staff meeting.

"The boys seem to be a bit bothered by remarks you make to them during P.T., Mr. Bell."

"To which remarks do you refer, Mr. Florian?" Bell never used the term "sir," seeming to think it "infra dig." Even when he granted him the "Mr. Florian," he gave to this form of address the suggestion of a sneer.

"From their review it would seem that you are unnecessarily critical of their persons."

"Do you mean their smell?"

"Well, yes, that and the state of their clothing."

"I've advised them to wash."

"These are the words which appear in one review." The Headmaster produced a notebook, Fernman's, and read: " 'Some of you stink like old garbage.' "

His tone was cool, detached, judicial.

"I was referring to their feet. Many of them never seem to wash their feet, and when

they take their shoes off the stink is dreadful."

"Many of them live in homes where there are very few facilities for washing, Mr. Bell."

"Surely enough water is available for washing their feet if they really wanted to."

"Then they'd put on the same smelly socks and shoes to which you also object."

"I've got to be in contact with them and it isn't very pleasant."

"Have you ever lived in this area, Mr. Bell?"

"No fear."

"Then you know nothing about the conditions prevailing. The water you so casually speak of is more often to be found in the walls and on the floors than in the convenient wash basin or bath to which you are accustomed. I've visited homes of some of these children where water for a family in an upstairs flat had to be fetched by bucket or pail from the single backyard tap which served five or six families. You may see, therefore, that so elementary a function as washing the feet might present many difficulties."

Bell was silent at this.

"I've no wish to interfere, or tell you how to do your work; you're an experienced teacher and know more about P.T. than I ever will,"—the Old Man was again patient, encouraging—"but try to be a little more understanding about their difficulties." He then turned to other matters, but it was clear that Bell was considerably put out by the rebuke.

Matters came to a head that Monday afternoon. I was not present in the gym, but was able to reconstruct the sequence of events with reasonable accuracy from the boys' reports and Bell's subsequent admissions.

During the P.T. session he had been putting them through their paces in the "astride vault" over the buck, all except Buckley, who was somewhat under the weather and wisely stood down from attempting the rather difficult jump, but without reference to or permission from Bell, who was not long in discovering the absence of his favorite diversion.

"Buckley," he roared.

"Yes, sir."

"Come on, boy, I'm waiting." He was standing in his usual position beside the buck in readiness to arrest the fall of any lad who might be thrown off balance by an awkward approach or incorrect execution of the movement. But the boy did not move, and the master stared at him amazed and angry at this unexpected show of defiance by the one generally considered to be the most timid and tractable in the whole class.

"Fatty can't do it, sir, it's too high for him," Denham interposed.

"Shut up, Denham," Bell roared. "If I want your opinion I will ask for it." He left his station by the buck and walked to where Buckley was standing. The boy watched his threatening approach, fear apparent in his eyes.

"Well, Buckley," Bell towered over the unhappy youth, "are you going to do as you're told?"

"Yes, sir," Buckley's capitulation was as sudden as his refusal.

The others stopped to watch as he stood looking at the buck, licking his lips nervously while waiting for the instructor to resume his position. It may have been fear or determination or a combination of both, but Buckley launched himself at the buck in furious assualt, and in spite of Bell's restraining arms, boy and buck crashed on the floor with a sickening sound as one leg of the buck snapped off with a sound of a pistol shot. The class stood in shocked silence watching Buckley, who remained as he fell, inert and pale; then they rushed to his assistance. All except Potter; big, good-natured Potter seemed to have lost his reason. He snatched up the broken metal-bound leg and advanced on Bell, screaming:

"You bloody bastard, you f—ing bloody bastard."

"Put that thing down, Potter, don't be a fool," Bell spluttered, backing away from the hysterical boy.

"You made him do it; he didn't want to and you made him," Potter yelled.

"Don't be a fool, Potter, put it down," Bell appealed.

"I'll do you in, you bloody murderer." Bell was big, but in his anger Potter seemed bigger, his improvised club a fearsome extension of his thick forearm.

That was where I rushed in. Tich Jackson, frightened by the sight of Buckley, limp and white on the floor, and the enraged Potter, slobbering at the instructor in murderous fury, had dashed upstairs to my classroom shouting: "Sir, quick, they're fighting in the gym." I followed his disappearing figure in time to see Bell backed against a wall, with Potter advancing on him.

"Hold it, Potter," I called. He turned at the sound of my voice and I quickly placed myself between them. "Let's have that, Potter." I held out my hand towards the boy, but he stared past me at Bell, whimpering in his emotion. Anger had completely taken hold of him, and he looked very dangerous.

"Come on, Potter," I repeated, "hand it over and go lend a hand with Buckley."

He turned to look towards his prostrate friend and I quickly moved up to him and seized the improvised club; he released it to me without any resistance and went back to join the group around Buckley. Bell then walked away and out of the room, and I went up to the boys. Denham rose and faced me, his face white with rage.

"Potts should have done the bastard like he did Fatty, just 'cos he wouldn't do the bloody jump."

I let that pass; they were angry and at such times quickly reverted to the old things, the words, the discourtesies. I stooped down beside Buckley, who was now sitting weakly on the floor, supported by Sapiano and Seales, and smiling up at them as if ashamed of himself for having been the cause of so much fuss.

"How do you feel, old man?" I inquired.

"Cor, Sir," he cried, smiling, "me tum does hurt."

"He fell on the buck. You should have seen 'im, Sir."

"Gosh, you should've heard the noise when the leg smashed."

"Mr. Bell couldn't catch Fatty, Sir, you should've seen him."

Most of them were trying to talk all at once, eager to give me all the details.

"Bleeding bully, always picking on Fats." This from Sapiano, whose volatile Maltese temperament was inclined to flare up very easily.

"If I'd had the wood I'd have done the f—er in and no bleeding body would have stopped me." Denham was aching for trouble and didn't care who knew it. Bell had slipped away unharmed after hurting his friend, and Denham wanted a substitute. But I would not look at him, or even hear the things he said. Besides, I liked Denham; in spite of his rough manner and speech he was an honest, dependable person with a strong sense of independence.

"Can you stand up, Buckley?"

With some assistance from Seales and Sapiano the boy got to his feet; he looked very pale and unsteady. I turned to Denham: "Will you help the others take Buckley up to Mrs. Dale-Evans and ask her to give him some sweet tea; leave him there and I'll meet you all in the classroom in a few minutes."

Without waiting for his reply I hurried off to the staffroom in search of Bell.

I was in something of a quandary. I knew that it was quite possible Buckley was all right, but there was no knowing whether he had sustained any internal injury not yet apparent. The Council's rules required that all accidents be reported and logged; the Headmaster should be informed forthwith; and in the light of what he had said to Bell so very recently, there would most certainly be a row.

I went up to the staffroom and found Bell washing his face at the sink.

"I've sent Buckley upstairs for a cup of tea," I said. "I suppose he'll be all right, anyway he was walking under his own steam."

"What happens now?" His voice was querulous.

"You should know as well as I do," I replied. "Shouldn't you see the Old Man and make some kind of report?"

"Yes, I suppose I'd better get over to his office right away. I should have attended to the Buckley boy, but the other one rushed me. Thanks for helping out."

"Oh, that's all right," I replied. "But why did you insist on the boy doing the vault?"

"I had to, don't you see; he just stood there refusing to obey and the others were watching me; I just had to do something." His whole attitude now was defensive.

"I'm not criticizing you, Mr. Bell, just asking. Buckley's a bit of a mascot with the others, you know, and I suppose that is why Potter got out of hand."

"I guess it was the way he jumped or something, but I couldn't grab him. He hit the buck too low and sent it flying."

"He's a bit awkward, isn't he; anyway I'm sure the Old Man will understand how it happened."

"He might be a bit difficult, especially after what he said the other day."

"Not necessarily. After all, it was an accident and thank Heaven it's not very serious."

He dried his hands and moved toward the door. "I suppose they'll really go to town on this in their weekly reviews," he remarked.

"I'll ask the boys to say nothing about it. I don't suppose Potter is now feeling any too pleased with himself at his conduct."

As he left Clinty came into the staffroom.

"What's happening, Rick?" she asked. "I just saw some of your boys taking Fatty Buckley upstairs. What's happened to him?"

I told her about the incident and added: "Bell has just gone to the Old Man's office to report the matter."

"Well, what do you know?" she chuckled. "Fancy Potter going for Bell like that. I always thought that boy a bit of a softie, but you never know with those quiet ones, do you?"

"He was not the only one. Sapiano and Denham were just as wild, I think, but they were too busy fussing over Buckley to bother with Bell."

"He is a bit of a tyro, isn't he. This might make him take it a bit easier."

"I don't think the boys mind his being strict during P.T. It's just that Buckley's a bit of a fool and they resented his being hurt. If it had been Denham or someone like that. I'm sure they would have done nothing."

"Yes, I guess you're right. Bell is a good teacher. I wonder how long the Divisional Office will let him stay here. I hope he hasn't had too much of a fright."

"Oh, he'll get over that. Now I must go and have a word with my boys."

I left her. For some inexplicable reason I felt nervous about being alone with Clinty; I felt that there was something she wanted to say to me, and for my part I did not want to hear it.

In the classroom the boys were sitting closely grouped together, looking rather sheepish. I knew they were feeling aggrieved and, according to their lights, justifiably so; but nevertheless the matter of Potter's behavior had to be dealt with.

"How's Buckley?" I asked.

"We left him upstairs with Mrs. Dale-Evans, sir. He didn't want to stay, he kept saying he was all right. But she told him if he wasn't quiet she'd give him some castor-oil, sir. Ugh!" They all managed a smile at Seales' remark.

"Good," I replied, "I expect he'll be quite all right. But there is something I want to say to you about this unfortunate incident." I sat down on the edge of Fernman's desk.

"Potter, there is nothing I can think of which can excuse your shocking conduct in the gym."

Potter's mouth fell open; he looked at me in surprise, gulped a few times and stammered:

"But it was him, sir, Mr. Bell, making Fatty fall and that." His voice was shrill with outrage at my remark.

"Mr. Bell was the master there, Potter, and anything that happened in the gym was his responsibility. Buckley's mishap was no excuse for you to make such an attack on your teacher."

"But Fatty told him he couldn't do it, sir, and he made him, he made him, sir."

Potter was very near tears. His distress was greater because of what he believed was the further injustice of my censure. The others, too, were looking at me with the same expression.

"That may be, Potter. I am not now concerned with Mr. Bell's conduct, but with yours. You came very near to getting yourself into very serious trouble because you were unable to control your temper. Not only was your language foul and disgusting, but you armed yourself with a weapon big enough and heavy enough to cause very serious harm. What do you think would have happened if everyone had behaved like you and had all turned on Mr. Bell like a pack of mad wolves?" I waited for this to sink in a bit, but Potter interjected:

"I thought he had done Fatty in, sir, he looked all huddled up like, sir."

"I see. So you didn't wait to find out but rushed in with your club like a hoodlum to smash and kill, is that it? Your friend was hurt and you wanted to hurt back; suppose instead of a piece of wood it had been a knife, or a gun, what then?" Potter was pale, and he was not the only one.

"Potts didn't think. He was narked, we was all narked, seeing Fatty on the deck. I wasn't half bleeding wild myself."

"You're missing the point, Denham. I think you're all missing the point. We sit in this classroom day after day and talk of things, and you all know what's expected of you; but at the first sign of bother you forget it all. In two weeks you'll all be at work and lots of things will happen which will annoy you, make you wild. Are you going to resort to clubs and knives everytime you're upset or angered?" I stood up. "You'll meet foremen or supervisors or workmates who'll do things to upset you, sometimes deliberately. What then, Denham? What about that, Potter? Your Headmaster is under fire from many quarters because he believes in you—because he really believes that by the time you leave here you will have learned to exercise a little self-control at the times when it is most needed. His success or failure will be reflected in the way you conduct yourselves after you leave him. If today's effort is an example of your future behavior I hold out very little hope for you."

At this moment Buckley walked in, smiling broadly and seemingly none the worse for wear. I waited until he was seated then went on:

"I've no wish to belabor this matter, but it cannot be left like this. Potter, you were very discourteous to your P.T. instructor, and it is my opinion that you owe him an apology." Potter stared at me, his mouth open in amazement at my remark; but before he could speak Denham leapt to his feet.

"Apologize?" His voice was loud in anger. "Why should Potts apologize? He didn't do him any harm. Why should he apologize to him just because he's a bleeding teacher?" He stood there, legs slighty apart, heavy-shouldered and truculent, glaring at me. The others were watching us, but agreeing with him; I could feel their resentment hardening.

"Please sit down Denham, and remember that in this class we are always able to discuss things, no matter how difficult or unpleasant, without shouting at each other."

I waited, fearful of this unexpected threat to our pleasant relationship; he looked around at his collegues indecisively, then abruptly sat down. I continued, in a very friendly tone:

"That was a fair question, Denham, although you will agree it was put a little, shall we say, indelicately?"

I smiled as I said this, and, in spite of his anger, Denham smiled briefly too. I went on:

"Potter, are you quite pleased and satisfied with the way you behaved to your P.T. teacher?"

Potter looked at me for a moment, then murmured, "No, sir."

"But he couldn't help it," Denham interjected.

"That may be so, Denham, but Potter agrees that his own actions were unsatisfactory; upon reflection he himself is not pleased with what he did."

"How's about Mr. Bell then: how's about him apologizing to Buckley?" Denham was not to be dissuaded from his attitude.

"Yes, how about him?" echoed Sapiano.

"My business is with you, not with Mr. Bell," I replied.

This was not going to be easy, I thought. Denham was getting a bit nasty; the usual "sir" had disappeared from his remarks, and Sapiano was following suit.

"It's easy for you to talk, sir, nobody tries to push you around." Seales' voice was clear and calm, and the others turned to look at him, to support him. His question touched something deep inside of me, something which had been dormant for months, but now awoke to quick, painful remembering. Without realizing what I was doing I got up and walked to where he sat and stood beside his desk.

"I've been pushed around, Seales," I said quietly, "in a way I cannot explain to you. I've been pushed around until I began to hate people so much that I wanted to hurt them, really hurt them. I know how it feels,

believe me, and one thing I learned, Seales, is to try always to be a bit bigger than the people who hurt me. It is easy to reach for a knife or a gun; but then you become merely a tool and the knife or gun takes over, thereby creating new and bigger problems without solving a thing. So what happens when there is no weapon handy?"

I felt suddenly annoyed with myself for giving way to my emotion, and abruptly walked back to my desk. The class seemed to feel that something had touched me deeply and were immediately sympathetic in their manner.

"The point I want to make, Potter," I continued, "is whether you are really growing up and learning to stand squarely on your own feet. When you begin work at Covent Garden you might some day have cause to be very angry; what will you do then? The whole idea of this school is to teach you to discipline yourself. In this instance you lost your temper and behaved badly to your teacher. Do you think you are big enough to make an apology to him?"

Potter fidgeted in his seat and looked uncertainly at me, then replied: "Yes, sir."

"It's always difficult to apologize, Potter, especially to someone you feel justified in disliking. But remember that you are not doing it for Mr. Bell's sake, but your own"

I sat down. They were silent, but I realized that they understood what I meant. Potter stood up:

"Is he in the staffroom, sir?"

Denham and Seales stood and joined Potter and together they went to find Bell. I called Buckley.

"How are you feeling, Buckley?"

"Okay, sir," he replied, as jovial as ever.

"What will your parents say about all this, Buckley?" I was being devious, but, I thought, necessarily so.

"I shan't tell 'em, sir. Must I, sir?"

"It's up to you, Buckley. If you feel fine there's no need to bother; but if in the next few days or weeks you feel any pain, it would be best to mention it so that they'd know what to do."

In a few minutes the boys were back, Potter looking red and embarrased; behind them came Mr. Bell.

"May I speak to your boys for a moment, Mr. Braithwaite?" He came in and stood beside my desk and I nodded to him.

"I want to say to all of you," he began, "that I'm sorry what happened in the gym a little while ago. I think that one way or another we were all a bit silly, but the sooner we forget the whole thing, the better.

"How're you feeling now, boy?" He addressed himself to Buckley.

"Okay, sir," the boy replied.

"Fine. Well, I suppose we'll see each other as usual next week." And with that he was gone, having made as friendly a gesture as his evident nervousness would allow.

The boys seemed not unwilling to let the matter drop, so we turned our attention to the discussion of other things.

Additional materials on group process:

Barnfield, Gabriel. *Creative Drama in Schools*, New York: Hart Publishing Co., 1968.

Bazeley, E.T. *Homer Lane and the Little Commonwealth*. New York: Schocken Books, 1969.

Bradford, L.; Gibb, J.R.; and Benne, K.D., editors. *T-Group Theory and Laboratory Method*. New York: Wiley & Sons, 1964.

Glasser, William. *Reality Therapy*. New York: Harper & Row, 1965.

Gorman, Alfred H. *Teachers and Learners the Interactive Process of Education*. Boston: Allyn and Bacon, 1969.

Greenberg, Ira A. *Psychodrama and Audience Attitude*. Beverly Hills, Calif.: Thyrsus Publishing Co., 1968.

"The Group Leader's Workshop" Newsletter. Published monthly by Explorations Institute. P.O. Box 1254. Berkeley, California 94701.

Haas, Robert B. *Psychodrama and Sociodrama in American Education*. Beacon, N.Y.: Beacon House, 1949.

Haskell, Martin R. "The Psychodramatic Method." Distributed by the California Institute of Socioanalysis, Box 6604, Long Beach, California, 1967.

Henry, Charles E.; Lippitt, Ronald; and Zander, Alvin. "Reality Practice as Educational Method." Beacon, N.Y.; Beacon House, Psychodrama Monographs No. 9, 1947.

Klein, Alan F. *Role Playing in Leadership Training and Group Problem Solving*. New York: Association Press, 1956.

Mann, John. *Encounter: A Weekend with Intimate Strangers*. New York: Grossman Publishers, 1970.

Miles, Matthew B. *Learning to Work in Groups*. New York: Bureau of Publications, Teachers College, Columbia University, 1959.

Moreno, J.L. *Who Shall Survive?* Beacon, N.Y.: Beacon House.

Nichols, H., and Williams, L. *Learning about Role-playing for Children and Teachers*. Washington, D.C., Association for Childhood Education International, 1960.

O'Banion, Terry, and O'Connell, April. *The Shared Journey*. Englewood Cliffs, N.J.: Prentice-Hall, 1970.

Otto, Herbert. *Group Methods Designed to Actualize Human Potential*. Chicago: Stone-Brandel, 1967.

Shaftel, Fannie, and Shaftel, George. *Words and Actions: Role-Playing Photo-Problems for Young Children*. New York: Holt, 1967.

Ruitenbeek, Hendrik M. *The New Group Therapies*. N.Y.: Discus Books, 1970.

CHAPTER EIGHT

THE CONSCIENTIOUS OBSERVER IN SOUND, IN SPACE, IN TIME

The Conscientious Observer In Sound

The need to "listen to nature"—and human nature is nature too—takes priority over the somewhat premature demand to classify it. Now, in theory, most research-minded people go along with the statement. In my own experience, for instance, I have been liberally encouraged to go ahead with a modest "collection" of observations and to gather whatever an experientially well-calibrated mind might see and hear and observe when thrown into the midst of raw life.

Fritz Redl, *When We Deal with Children*

Sense Awareness Games

Close your eyes. Listen to
sounds inside of you.
Listen to sounds outside of
you. Shift back and forth.
Make a tape of sounds and
get others to identify them.

Can you see with your ears
and hear with your eyes?
Can you come to your senses

Everyone closes his eyes except
one person, who taps somebody to
come up to the front, side, or
back of the room and imitate
an animal sound. The rest of
the group listens and guesses
who the sound maker is. Once
he is named, he becomes the
chooser for the next round.

With your eyes closed or open tell the group what you are aware of right now! Say, "Now I am aware of my heart beating," "Now I am aware of a plane passing overhead," etc.

Close your eyes and listen to one sound. Get inside of it, outside of it. Find out where it's from and how it feels. Shift to another sound and do the same thing. Then go back to your first sound if it's still there. Shift to a new sound again. Repeat a few times. What do you hear? How do you feel?

Concentrate for several minutes on something close to you—look at it—how does it fit against its background? Focus on something far away. Come back to something close. Continue the shifting back and forth. What do you see? How do you feel?

Who needs the experience of talking in class? Who gets the most? Several studies that have been done on classroom talk show the teacher ahead by 3 to 1. Keep track of talk in one of your classes for a half hour. Does the 3 to 1 hold true? Why or why not? What effect do you think the chance to put thoughts and feelings in words has on the total learning experience for you? Are you part of the silent majority of your class? Whose responsibility is this? Do John Holt's experiences correspond to yours?

Close your eyes and retreat to some place in your memory that you once enjoyed. Stay there a while and then return to the here and now. Open your eyes. Do you see with more clarity? If not, retreat and return again. See what happens.

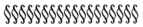

Stage a sudden happening in the class or focus on some action that just occurred. Describe exactly what transpired in your own words. Compare your description with others. Are they the same? Why not?

Form a circle. Place from 15–20 familiar objects on a platter. Look carefully at the objects for a short time or pass the platter around. Write down what you remember seeing.

Pair up. Look carefully at each other. One of you closes your eyes while the other changes something on his person, such as untying his shoelaces. Open your eyes and try to identify the change. Reverse.

Someone gives a short lecture to the rest of the group. Listeners pay attention to the speaker while, at the same time, noting how you listen. In what position is your body? What do you do with your eyes? Where are your hands? How tense are you? Where do you feel it? What do you think about? How do you feel being a listener?

From *How Children Learn*
by John Holt

When I was still teaching fifth grade, I was talking about my class to a twelve-year-old friend of mine. I happened to say that some of the children in my class had been having a conversation. At this my friend looked puzzled. She said, "You mean these kids were talking about this stuff in class?" Yes. She said, "Was this in Show and Tell?" I said, "No, we don't have Show and Tell, but there are lots of times during the day when the kids can talk to each other, if they wish it, about whatever interests them most. Don't you ever have a time in class when you can talk to other people?" She was almost too astonished to answer.

Of course I knew what she would answer even before I asked her. Bill Hull once said to me, "Who needs the most practice talking in school? Who gets the most?" Exactly. The children need it, the teacher gets it. Even in the most supposedly enlightened schools, the usual rule in almost every class is that a child talks only to the teacher, and then only when called on. In many schools children are forbidden to talk between classes or in the corridors. This leaves only lunch, when they are busy eating, and recess, when they are trying to let off a little steam built up during their long periods of enforced stillness and silence. And I have known more than a few children who have gone to schools where often they were not allowed to talk during lunch, and sometimes even during recess. After school children head for home, where their time is likely to be taken up with homework and TV, and where in any case nobody else may be very interested in talking to them. The result of this kind of education is that children of ten or even older may be no better at talking than they were at five. In fact, I have known many ten year olds, in a highly intellectual community, who were nowhere near as good at talking as many five year olds I have known.

This loss of skill and interest in talking affects every subject in the standard curriculum. For example, take writing. A child who does not talk will not have many things that he wants to say, and hence will not know what to write about. He will often feel that nothing he might want to say or write could possibly be of any interest to anyone else, and that if he did say or write something, others would only laugh at it. As fast as thoughts come to him, he censors them, rules them out. When he does try to express his thoughts, he finds it hard, because he has had so little practice in putting words together. Because he has never learned in practice what kinds of things make speech clear, forceful, and effective, he will have no way to judge the worth of his own writing. As they say, he will have a tin ear. The test of good writing, after all, is not whether it obeys "laws of grammar," but what it sounds like. If a student does not know what good talk sounds like, all the rules of grammar in the book will not enable him to write well. And the fact is, as a glimpse at many a learned journal will make plain, that many of our most highly educated men write extraordinarily badly.

Lack of skill in conversation is also likely to make poor readers, at least of many kinds of writing. The good reader enters into an active dialogue with the writer. He converses with him, even argues with him. The bad reader reads passively; the words do not engage his mind; he is like a bored listener at a lecture. Such a reader, studying a text, is very likely to use his mind as if it were a photographic plate, as if by staring hard enough and long enough at words on a page he could fix them in his memory. This never works. In courses like math or science, in which one must often follow instructions, turn other people's words into action, the inarticulate child often finds that he can't do it. Or he may find that he cannot separate in his mind what he understands from what he does not, or state his confusions clearly enough to enable others to help him. In short, the child in school who is not fluent with words is bound hand and foot. No doubt our schools are too symbol-minded, and should give more time and scope to other forms of expression. Perhaps someday they will. Right now, it is fluency that pays. Yet, in almost all schools, hardly anything is done to help children become fluent, precise, and skillful in speech.

The so-called revolution now going on in

education has so far done little to change this. In many classes doing the very latest thing in math, social studies, or whatever, the pattern of talk is what it always was. The teacher does most of the talking, and now and then asks the children questions, to make sure they have been paying attention and understand. Now and then a bold teacher will start what they call a "discussion." What happens then is usually what Bill Hull calls "answer pulling." The teacher asks a series of pointed questions, aimed at getting students to give an answer that he has decided beforehand is right. Teachers' manuals are full of this technique—"Have a discussion, in which you draw out the following points. . . ." This kind of fake, directed conversation is worse than none at all. Small wonder that children soon get bored and disgusted with it.

Even if class discussions were open, honest, unmanipulated, and genuinely interesting to the young, and even if all children took equal part in them, they would not be enough to give most children skill in speech. There are too many children, and too little time. What is the answer? Simple enough, if we have the courage to try it. In many elementary school classes in England, children are free to work in pairs or small groups, and to talk—if they do it quietly—as they work. In classes where the children are not yet allowed to do independent work of their own choosing, there should be plenty of time set aside for children to talk to each other, about whatever interests them, without guidance or interference from the teacher. There might be times when the teacher would have to ask children to talk more quietly. But he should not control what the children talk about.

In my last fifth-grade class, I used to set aside a period every now and then as a free period. In that time the children could read, or draw, or play games (chess became very popular), or do puzzles, or, as they liked best of all, talk to each other. As time went on, I felt more and more that these periods were perhaps the most useful part of the day. Sometimes the girls' conversations would turn into whispering and giggles, or the boys' into shouting arguments. But on the whole, and more and more as the children gained experience, the conversations seemed to be serious, and very useful to all taking part in them. For one thing, at such times the distinctions between able students and less able broke down. Some of the poorest students were very interesting and well-informed talkers, and could talk and argue as equals with the most successful students in the class. To this, some teachers have said that children who were used to being tightly controlled in class would not know what to do with free time if they had it, and would abuse it. The problem is not as serious as they think, but it is real. One way to deal with it is, at first, to make free periods short, perhaps fifteen minutes or half an hour, with the restriction that talk must be quiet. There might even be some periods that could be free but silent. As the children get used to freedom and find interesting ways to use it, they can be given more of it. In such ways we can break out of the school lockstep and make the classroom a place where more and more independent studying, thinking, and talking can go on.

QUIET!!
shhhhhush!
NO TALKING

Silence!
Do not speak unless spoken to!

Do Not Disturb!
Children should be seen and not heard.

I want to record two general thoughts about my own performance with the class. First, the students have carried into the course the habit of raising their hands to be called on, and I have responded out of habit by calling on them by name for their comments. This keeps the discussion directed toward me and interferes with my efforts to minimize my role as authoritative teacher. I shall try nodding instead of calling names, in order to keep my voice out of it, and I shall try to avoid a response of any kind in the early stages of an exchange which develops between the students directly. Second, my responses to student remarks have so far been exclusively responses to the remark immediately before me; I have given almost no attention to the matter of bringing out relationships between remarks. I hesitate here because of the increased possibility of imposing an interpretation and a pattern of my own; I must be extremely careful not to go beyond the descriptive. But if I can do it successfully, it will contribute both to the minimizing of focus upon me and to the strengthening of focus and unity within the class.

From Samuel Moon, "Teaching the Self" in *Improving College and University Teaching*

Verbal and Nonverbal Interaction Games

Take a medium sized ball or a bean bag. The ball represents speech. The way you use the ball indicates your mode of communication with another person. Keep the game nonverbal. The person who begins the game might represent "the teacher" by tossing the ball to one "student" at a time who tosses it back. Different people can assume the teacher role. Once the ball begins to fly, let it go. Take time at the end to make the exercise verbal again. Talk about what kind of interactions were symbolized by the ballgame.

Three people sit together in a row. Whoever is in the middle converses continuously with the person on his right and the person on his left, who have each selected two subjects to talk on. The middleman keeps the talk going and is involved in both conversations simultaneously.

Form groups of three in which two people converse without asking any questions. The third person is the observer. Switch roles.
****

Role play the start of a unit of study on "ecology" or some subject of general interest. One person plays the teacher, whose job it is to encourage and accept all student suggestions without using words of praise.

Tape or videotape a class session in action. Use the verbal interaction category system (page 178) that follows the games to analyze classroom talk. Is change needed?

****

Form two lines facing each other. The first persons in each line begin a conversation. At any point, the person behind a speaker can tap his shoulder. The speaker then goes to the end of the line and the conversation continues between the new speakers at the exact point it was interrupted.

Divide the class into three parts: the talkers, the medium talkers, and the nontalkers. Give each group a number. When their number is called, that group can talk and at no other time. How do the talkers feel being silenced? How do the nontalkers feel speaking up?

Form couples. One is the "talker" and one is the "listener." If you're the talker, talk about something personal in your life that's on your mind. If you're the listener, listen and then "put down" the "talker." Then listen and "give advice." Listen and then "talk about yourself" a lot. Listen and try to help the person express himself without your making judgments. Reverse. Which responses does the talker prefer?

From *Improving Teaching* by Edmund Amidon and Elizabeth Hunter

THE VERBAL INTERACTION CATEGORY SYSTEM (VICS)

TEACHER-INITIATED TALK

1. Gives information or opinion: presents content or own ideas, explains, orients, asks rhetorical questions. May be short statements or extended lecture.
2. Gives direction: tells pupil to take some specific action; gives orders; commands.
3. Asks narrow questions: asks drill questions, questions requiring one or two word replies or yes-or-no answers; questions to which the specific nature of the response can be predicted.
4. Asks broad question: asks relatively open-ended questions which call for unpredictable responses; questions which are thought-provoking. Apt to elicit a longer response than 3.

TEACHER RESPONSE

5. Accepts: (5a) Ideas: reflects, clarifies, encourages or praises ideas of pupils. Summarizes, or comments without rejection.
   (5b) Behavior: responds in ways which commend or encourage pupil behavior.
   (5c) Feeling: responds in ways which reflect or encourage expression of pupil feeling.

6. Rejects: (6a) Ideas: Criticizes, ignores or discourages pupil ideas.
   (6b) Behavior: discourages or criticizes pupil behavior. Designed to stop undesirable behavior. May be stated in question form, but differentiated from category 3 or 4, and from category 2, Gives direction, by tone of voice and resultant effect on pupils.
   (6c) Feeling: ignores, discourages or rejects pupil expression of feeling.

PUPIL RESPONSE

7. Responds (7a) Predictably: relatively to short replies, usually, Teacher: which follow category 3. May also follow category 2, i.e., "David, you may read next."
   (7b) Unpredictably: replies which usually follow category 4.

8. Responds to another pupil: replies occurring in conversation between pupils.

PUPIL-INITIATED TALK

9. Initiates talk to teacher: statements which pupils direct to teacher without solicitation from teacher.
10. Initiates talk to another pupil: statements which pupils direct to another pupil which are not solicited.

OTHER

11. Silence: Pauses or short periods of silence during a time of classroom conversation.
Z. Confusion: considerable noise which disrupts planned activities. This category may accompany other categories or may totally preclude the use of other categories.

If a class is dominated by a teacher giving directions, asking narrow questions, initiating all talk, rejecting student ideas, what kind of class is this? Read the following situation. Apply the VICS to it. Role play the situation and change it. Apply the VICS to your own class and others and to stories in this book.

Mr. Barrett read off the committee assignments to his seventh-grade class. "This time Jack will work with Jean's group."

From several spots around the room were heard, "Aw heck," "Ugh," and "Poor us!"

"I hear some sounds of complaint," said Mr. Barrett. "What's the problem? Come on—don't be afraid to speak up. We'll see what we can do about things."

"Nobody wants to work with Jack, Mr. Barrett. He's such a pest, and he tries to run everything and he always wants his own way."

"Yeah—he's so hard to get along with. If you don't agree with him he has a fit. He spoils everything he's in."

"Jack—do you have anything to say for yourself?" asked Mr. Barrett.

"Aw, they're always complaining. Anyway, I don't care if no one wants to work with me. I'll work by myself, and I'll bet I do a better job than any of the committees anyway," responded Jack.

"That's not a very healthy attitude, Jack. This is committee work, and you have to join with one of the committees," Mr. Barrett said. "You know, I understand why the other boys and girls feel the way they do about you. You do think your ideas are the best, but you need to learn that other people have ideas too, and that if you're going to get along in this world you've got to share with others. Now you join the committee I assigned you to, and I don't want any trouble from you. If you have any trouble there, Jean, you just let me know. We're all going to be watching you, Jack, so you'd better get along."

From Edmund Amidon and Elizabeth Hunter, *Improving Teaching*

The Conscientious Observer In Space

The spaces we control give us away.
From Herbert Kohl, *The Open Classroom*

We have now become aware of the possibility of arranging the entire human environment as a work of art, as a teaching machine designed to maximize perception and to make everyday learning a process of discovery. . . . Environments are not passive wrappings, but are, rather, active processes which are invisible. . . . The interplay between the old and the new environments creates many problems and confusions.
From Marshall McLuhan and Quentin Fiore, *The Medium Is the Massage*

Exploring Outer Space Games

Walk around the space, trying to experience it as if for the first time. Take your time. Touch, smell, taste everything you can. Quiet music can help. Find yourself a nest. Crawl in for awhile. Come out again.

Find a partner. Use a blindfold to cover your partner's eyes or have him keep his eyes closed. Lead him by the hand in, out, around, under, upon, between, behind rooms, halls, stairs, grass, sidewalks, etc. Introduce him to many new sensory experiences. Use no words. Establish a non-verbal way to signal "stairs ahead" or "danger." You are totally responsible for your partner. Take care of him. Educate him. Reverse roles. After the blind walks, share experiences. Tell each other what you resented and appreciated about the experiences.

"I learned more today about sitting in the back by sitting in the back than by hearing about it. I want to talk about it." Everytime you come to class sit in a different place or arrange yourselves in rows alphabetically by last names. What does your place in space mean to you?

Darken your room as much as you can. With flashlights and overhead projectors, play with your space in a new way.

Have an environmental happening. Bring materials to class. Use what's already there. Make something new that's part of you. Play music, eat, dance. Invite in friends to see and participate. Bring your children, if you have some, to join in. Take pictures before and after. What does the room say about the group when it's finished?

I want a rug to sit on !!

I WOULD LIKE A COUCH IN MY CLASS THEN IT WOULD BE MORE LIKE HOME.

I want a drinking fountain so I don't keep having to ask permission.

I want a tree in my class with big green leaves.

181

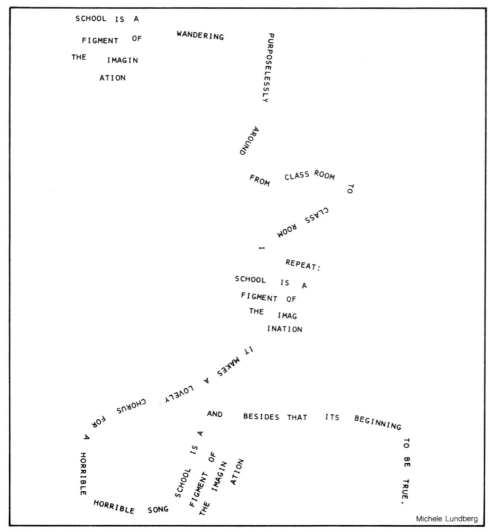

SCHOOL IS A FIGMENT OF THE IMAGINATION
WANDERING PURPOSELESSLY AROUND FROM CLASS ROOM TO CLASS ROOM
I REPEAT:
SCHOOL IS A FIGMENT OF THE IMAGINATION
IT MAKES A LOVELY CHORUS FOR A HORRIBLE SONG
AND BESIDES THAT ITS BEGINNING TO BE TRUE.
SCHOOL IS A FIGMENT OF THE IMAGINATION
HORRIBLE SONG

Michele Lundberg

How does the poem's arrangement in space reinforce its meaning? What does the spatial organization of the words suggest about the young poet's feeling of herself in the space called school? Try arranging some of your own thoughts in a new spatial way on a page. What happens? Try arranging yourself in space in a new way. What happens?

What do the painting of an Indo-Chinese class by Mai-Thu and the photograph of the chairs and desk on page 180 tell you about the teacher, the students, the curriculum, the culture? Reread or review your own description or drawing of a classroom you remember. Did you feel "at home" in that space called school? Sketch or describe what would be a comfortable classroom for yourself now as a student, tomorrow as a teacher. Sketch or describe a room in your house. Compare your spatial preferences with others. Do you prefer much openness with little furniture or the opposite of that? Do you like everything in its proper place or are you more comfortable with a bit of clutter? Do you emphasize space for togetherness or privacy or do you balance the two? What colors do you prefer? What shapes? What sizes? Place yourself in the room. Do you think any of your preferences reflect your cultural background? Your home life? To what extent do the spaces you inhabit reflect YOU? Do you "own" them or simply "rent" them?

From *The Open Classroom*
by Herbert Kohl

Teachers must learn to work in open and creative ways themselves if they want their classrooms to become less authoritarian. Recently I conducted a seminar for teachers which was designed to get the participants to do things rather than to talk about techniques of teaching. For example, instead of discussing the teaching of writing or music or painting, we wrote, made music, and painted.

During one session we all tried to think back to our own earliest experiences in school and to recreate them in writing or through drawing. Most of our memories went back to kindergarten or the first grade, and an unusual number of them were spatial. I remembered my first-grade classroom and how confined and boxlike it felt. The tables were placed in rows and their tops were hard and rectangular. I was afraid that I would move things from their proper places and walked cautiously whenever I left my seat. For the most part I tried to disappear into my chair, hide from the teacher, and let my imagination invest the room with wild and secret places.

Many of the other teachers had similar memories. Some remembered windows they were not allowed to look out of, books and papers that had to be treated reverently, chalkboards with rules and assignments posted on them, new briefcases that had to be kept neat and clean. The drawings were full of boxes representing rooms, papers, books, tables, buildings—our memories of school were predominantly closed and rectangular.

It is no accident that spatial memories are strong. The placement of objects in space is not arbitrary and rooms represent in physical form the spirit and souls of places and institutions. A teacher's room tells us something about who he is and a great deal about what he is doing.

Often we are not aware of the degree to which the spaces we control give us away, nor conscious of how much we could learn of ourselves by looking at the spaces we live in. It is important for teachers to look at the spatial dimensions of their classrooms, to step back so they may see how the organization of space represents the life lived within it. To illustrate this and give a picture of what differences exist from classroom to classroom I would like to consider some hypothetical classrooms, each with identical furniture and dimensions yet arranged by different teachers. I'll start by examining the spatial organization of these rooms on the first day of school, and then look back at them during the middle of the school year. In this way it may be possible to show the many seemingly minor yet crucial ways in which an open classroom differs from an authoritarian and closed one.

The rooms I have in mind can be found in most schools in the United States. They are rectangular in shape, not too large, and contain chalkboards, bulletin boards, cabinets, windows, and perhaps closets, arranged around the periphery of the rectangle. Occasionally there are a sink and drinking fountain and, in execptional cases, toilets built into the room. The interior has no partitions and is occupied by combinations of chairs, desks, desk chairs, and tables. The desks are rectangular and the tables rectangular or round. Sometimes the chairs and desks are bolted to the floor but there is a tendency to have movable furniture in newer buildings. The teacher's desk is distinguished from the pupils' desks by its size and the presence of abundant drawer space.[1]

There are some classrooms which also have bookcases, magazine racks, work benches, and easels. Also there are usually wastebaskets in the room.

These are the common elements—now let's turn to the way they are fitted into the classroom environments. The first teacher[2] I want to consider has had several years' experience; she is talented and popular with

---

[1] In colleges teachers are often given lecterns or their desks are placed on platforms or above the level of their students' chairs.

[2] These portraits are fictional versions of classrooms I've visited.

her pupils. In her room the authoritarian mode of teaching does not seem particularly oppressive. She is an attractive woman and spends time trying to make her room as pleasant as possible. This fits very well with her teaching style. She is quite friendly with her students in a maternal way and prides herself on being able to get them to perform well. She enjoys teaching gifted children the most, but will take her turn with the less bright classes. She is a bit of a cynic yet gets along with the staff. Her main fault (though it is not seen as such by her co-workers) is a deep intolerance of, and dislike for, defiant and "lazy" pupils.

This teacher works very hard getting her classroom in order before the first day of class. She has read the class record cards, knows how many girls and boys there are, who the troublemakers are likely to be. She arranges the desks, tables, and chairs accordingly. The wall with the chalkboard is designated the front of the room (many teachers don't realize that this needn't be the case), making the opposite wall the back of the room, and the two remaining walls the sides. This may seem a simple-minded thing to mention but it isn't. Why does a classroom have to have a front, a back, and two sides? The notion that there is a "front of the class" and the authoritarian mode of delivering

knowledge received from above to students who are below—both go together.

Having designated the front of the room, the teacher moves all the tables and desks into a position where they face the chalkboard. They are also arranged in evenly spaced rows. Chairs are placed accordingly, one to a desk, or to a designated place around a table. Extra chairs and tables are set aside until the teacher's desk is in place. The teacher I'm describing is sympathetic to the progressive movement in education. She doesn't believe that the teacher should put her desk in the front of the room, even though she accepts the notion of a "front" of the room. Consequently she moves her desk to the side, a bit apart from the students' desks but in a convenient position to survey them.

An extra table, round if possible, is placed in the back of the room. The wastebasket is placed next to the teacher's desk.

So much for the movable furniture. Next the teacher turns to the chalkboard. On the far right (or left) of the chalkboard in the front of the room the teacher prints neatly her name (prefaced by Miss), the class designation, room number, and several other things that may look like this:

Miss A. Levinton
Class 6-543 (hs)
Date
Attendance: B——G——
Assignment:

Homework:

After the chalkboard come the bulletin boards. The teacher has prepared ingenious and elegant displays to put up around the room. There are photographs, charts, signs, maps—things designed to illustrate and illuminate the curriculum for the year and make the classroom handsome though somewhat antiseptic. A small part of one bulletin board is set aside and neatly labeled "Students' Work."

The bookcase in the back of the room holds the books the teacher has accumulated, and the table in the back of the room is labeled "Library Corner." The cabinets and closets are full of neatly stacked books and papers and the teacher checks to see that their doors are all closed. Another closet, one with a lock, has been set aside as the teacher's closet. It has been stocked with a smock, some comfortable shoes, a coffee cup and saucer, and a bottle of instant coffee, etc. It also contains a metal box with the students' record cards.

The classroom is ready to receive its students. The teacher has made the room a familiar place for her to function in and, armed with rules and routines, is ready to face her new class and tell them exactly what will be expected of them in the coming year. The students are free to fit in or be thrown out.

A visitor to the class three months later would be struck by the similarities of the room on the first day and ninety days later. A few changes would be evident, however.

There would be neat papers on the bulletin board under the label "Students' Work," as well as a new but equally elegant bulletin board display. There would also be books and papers in the students' desks. But the wastebasket would still be next to the teacher's desk and the library would still be bare except for its label. All would be in order.

It is hard to distinguish between apparent chaos and creative disorder. The next classroom I will describe could present problems for an observer; he would have to attend as much to what is not done as to what is done. Interesting and natural patterns of classroom life can emerge through a collaboration of all the people involved; but this may take time and patience, and one has to have seen the process of development in order to understand the result.

When the second teacher I have in mind arrives before the start of school, the classroom is a mess. The chairs have been piled upon the tables and pushed into a corner. The teacher, a young man who has taught for several years, can't make up his mind what to do with the furniture. As he enters his room he feels disoriented. He can't tell the front of the room from the rear. It strikes him that there may be advantages in seeing the room as a neutral space without points of orientation. Perhaps his students would also be struck by the neutrality of the space and see for the first time that many things could be done with it.

Why not leave the room just as it is and see what happens when the students enter?

He had other plans, ones carefully nurtured over the summer. He would set up the tables in small groups and let the children sit where they chose. He would also turn the teacher's desk into a resource table which he would occupy at certain times and which could, he hoped, become the communications center of the classroom rather than the seat of power and authority. But the idea of leaving things as they are may be a better way to begin the year. Perhaps it might be possible to make organization of the class a collaborative venture between him and his students, and among the students themselves. Besides, he has come to realize that the things that work best in class for him are the unplanned ones, the ones that arise spontaneously because of a student's suggestion or a sudden perception. He trusts his intuitions and isn't too upset to abandon plans that had consumed time and energy.

The previous year he had run a reasonably open classroom. Still he had organized the room from front to back; and though the tables and chairs were movable, they faced in only one direction during the year. He had used the class record cards to tell him who his pupils were though he very frequently found them misleading and inaccurate. For half the year he'd used textbooks and finally got up the courage to drop them after one of his pupils turned in a devastating parody of one of the stories in the book.

He had worried that the principal of the school might object to this but he did not announce what he was doing and no one complained. During the remainder of the year he built a library of students' writing and books to replace the textbooks. He found one interesting set of readers and kept them because he liked group reading himself and wanted to have one book he could read together with his students and discuss with them. That was one of his pleasures in teaching.

He also managed to piece together a set of dictionaries and obtain a record player and a collection of records, a slide machine, a $15 tape recorder, tapes and film strips, and a miscellaneous collection of junk that filled the closets of the room leaving him no place to hang his coat. He took to hanging it in the wardrobe along with his students' coats.

The stuff he had collected the previous year was still in the closets and cabinets. He threw open all the doors in the room as he had planned. The blackboard and bulletin boards in the room had been untouched since June as he had requested. Except for the tables and chairs everything was as it was the last day of school the previous year.

The plan was quite simple. The first day of school would consist of a dismantling of the previous year's work, an examination of things in the classroom by the new students, and an exploration of what was available. He didn't want to impose a structure upon the class; at the same time he knew that it was crucial to have enough stuff in his room to suggest to his pupils the range of things they might do.

It is impossible to predict what his classroom would look like after three months. That would depend upon the students and the teacher, and also upon what happened to be engaging their attention at the moment. Things would most certainly be in a state of flux. Certain groupings of chairs and tables would be just forming, others would be in the process of disintegration. The bulletin boards would be full of the students' works, or of pictures they liked or the teacher liked. Some might look worn but sacred and bound to last out the year; others would be in the process of being assembled or dismantled. The stuff—the record player, tape recorder, books, etc.—would be distributed throughout the room and there is no telling where the wastebasket would be. Those who need it would use it—and would not have to come up to the teacher's desk in order to throw things out.

The teacher's desk might also be anywhere. It might not even be the teacher's any more, the teacher settling for a desk like the pupils' and abandoning his privileged piece of furniture to some other use.

In order to find out what this all meant, an observer would have to discover what the pupils were doing and what the teacher were doing at that particular moment in the year. The observer might not discover chaos, however, but a more complex and freer order than is usually found in classrooms in the United States, or in the society at large for that matter.

It may be useful to look at a third classroom. The room and its furniture are the same but it is in a high school where not one but four or five classes use it daily. It is the teacher's room in a more real sense than is possibly in the elementary school since the teacher is the only person there throughout the school day.

There is another problem—the teacher is a specialist. She has been hired to teach a specific subject and, by virtue of that fact, is restricted in her own freedom. Still within limits this teacher has managed to have an open class—or rather, four open classes, since she is required to teach four different English[3] classes a day. The students in her classes are grouped according to what the school considers to be ability, and whatever her personal opinion of tracking, she has to teach tracked classes. She has a "bright" class, a "slow" class, and two middle classes. There are several tables and many movable chairs with armrests in the room. There are also many makeshift bookcases filled with dozens of books, magazines, newspapers, collections of students' writing. The walls still have the previous year's accumulation of writing, drawings, cartoons on them. A section of wall is covered with newsprint and set aside for the students' graffiti (a possible form of writing).

The teacher's main problem is to make her room available to all four classes in the same way. There are temptations to simplify things, have a pet class and structure the room for them. The "bright" class is an easy one to choose since the students in it are usually cooperative.[4] The room can be ar-

---

[3]English is not the only subject that can be presented in an open classroom. I have seen history, science, math, and physical education classes based on nonauthoritarian principles. In each case the teachers introduce the students to the possibilities for learning in their subjects and then step back and let the students discover what they care to learn. A science lab or the equipment room of a gym are wonderful places to explore. In math there are many problems of measurement, timing, bargaining, gambling that can be presented. In history there are central themes such as war, exploitation, love, power that can be explored. It is surprising how naturally students respond to being presented with choices in any subject.

---

[4]This may be changing. Bright students in many schools I have visited recently are the leaders of student movements and feel social action is more important than academic success. This poses a great problem for authoritarian adminstrators since the threat of giving poor grades to rebels no longer holds much force. One administrator complained to me that when he threatened to fail some A-track students they told him to go ahead since they didn't care to succeed in his type of school. He felt disarmed—and he was. His only resort was to call in the police to control his students.

ranged for them and the other three classes that use the room would have to squeeze themselves into a space designed for the bright students.

Another way of dealing with the situation would be to neutralize the room—place the chairs and desks in columns and rows and force each class to sit segregated according to sex, and arrange in alphabetical order.

Yet chairs and tables can be moved about every period. It is possible, though a bit noisy, to let the students in each class decide their own placement. The hypothetical teacher I'm describing here has gotten used to noise and accommodated herself to a constantly changing space. She even finds advantages in having her students move the chairs each period. It brings the students together, calms them down, and enables them to experience a return to stability during a day in which they are forced to move from space to space every 45 or 50 minutes.

The first day of school in this classroom is hard to describe. Each class that visits the teacher starts in its own way. The students are forced to move the chairs about and find their own places. Four different arrangements of space exist within that room. The same is true three months later.

I know teachers who can manage four classes and four different arrangements of space a day. Yet few people can live with this institutionalized schizophrenia and no one should be made to function within it. The idea that a teacher can offer something to four or five groups of twenty-five to thirty-five young people each day at intervals of 50 minutes is absurd. Exceptional people can do creative things within the departmental structures as they exist today in high schools and junior high schools—but at what cost to themselves?

Teachers must fight for a sane existence for themselves as well as for their pupils. At the same time they must not turn their frustrations and sense of powerlessness upon their pupils and compound the miseries of school existence. In the sanest circumstances students are allies and not enemies.

During the first year of teaching there are as many problems with the surroundings in which one works as with oneself and with the students. Beginning to teach in a school is like moving into a furnished apartment. One has no familiarity with the furniture, the lighting, the resources, or the drawbacks of the room. For example, it is impossible to estimate beforehand the effect the position of doors and windows in the room will have upon the movement of students and consequently upon the life of the class. I remember my first classroom. It was in an old school and the windows were six feet from the floor. The students couldn't look out into the world and there was a sense of the room being sealed off from the outside. The next year I was in a newer school. My room had a wall of large windows facing on a busy street. The world was practically in the room. I couldn't keep from looking out myself since so much was happening on the street, and so window-watching became one of the activities that were possible in the class.

Doors are often more troublesome than windows. For example, during a school day there is a constant stream of messengers and monitors that enter the room. The farther away the door is from the center of activity the more time monitors and messengers spend in the room, and the more chance they have to distract one's students. On the other hand there is an advantage to the door being away from activity. Nosey teachers and administrators will see less when they sneak a look into the room.

Beginning teachers always worry about mastering school routines—taking attendance, collecting lunch money, appointing monitors, distributing and collecting books and papers, etc. Spatial malaise is as great a problem as all of these and underlies most of them. One doesn't know how to move throughout the room, how to use the light. All of this develops with familiarity and most of it without any conscious awareness of change. The second year is often easier than the first because the setting of one's encounter with young people is familiar and comfortable. One of the most important and helpful things a teacher can do is explore the space of his classroom with and without his pupils and make it as comfortable and familiar a place as possible.

What do these arrangements in space tell you about what is happening? Do you prefer one to the other? As a teacher, could you see yourself using all four arrangements? What other ones are possible? Sketch or cut out moveable pieces from colored paper. Play around with shapes in space. What's the difference between a painting and a room we live in? To what extent do you think seating arrangements affect what goes on between people? There are many ways of looking at our environment, at our spatial organizations. No one arrangement is correct. Space should reflect what we do in it and, at the same time, allow for new experiences, new discoveries.

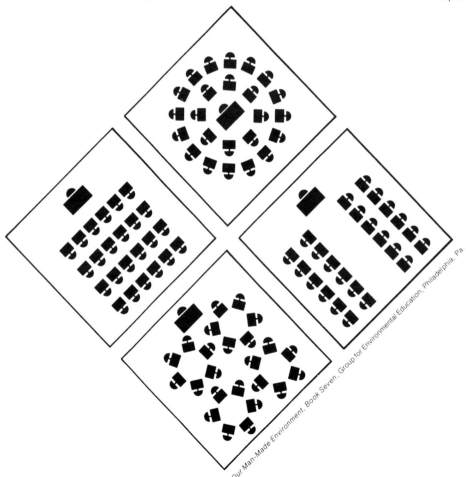

Our Man-Made Environment, Book Seven, Group for Environmental Education, Philadelphia, Pa.

From *The Hidden Dimension*
by Edward T. Hall

Several years ago, a talented and perceptive physician named Humphry Osmond was asked to direct a large health and research center in Saskatchewan. His hospital was one of the first in which the relationship between semifixed-feature space and behavior was clearly demonstrated. Osmond had noticed that some spaces, like railway waiting rooms, tend to keep people apart. These he called sociofugal spaces. Others, such as the booths in the old-fashioned drugstore or the tables at a French sidewalk cafe, tend to bring people together. These he called sociopetal. The hospital of which he was in charge was replete with sociofugal spaces and had very few which might be called sociopetal. Furthermore, the custodial staff and nurses tended to prefer the former to the latter because they were easier to maintain. Chairs in the halls, which would be found in little circles after visiting hours, would soon be lined up neatly, in military fashion, in rows along the walls. One situation which attracted Osmond's attention was the newly built "model" male geriatrics ward. Everything was new and shiny, neat and clean. There was enough space, and the colors were cheerful. The only trouble was that the longer the patients stayed in the ward, the less they seemed to talk to each other. Gradually, they were becoming like the furniture, permanently and silently glued to the walls at regular intervals between the beds. In addition, they all seemed depressed.

It should be noted that what is fixed-feature space in one culture may be semifixed in another, and vice versa. In Japan, for example, the walls are movable, opening and closing as the day's activities change. In the United States, people move from room to room or from one part of a room to another for each different activity, such as eating, sleeping, working, or socializing with relatives. In Japan, it is quite common for the person to remain in one spot while the activities change. The Chinese provide us with further opportunities to observe the diversity of human treatment of space, for they assign to the fixed-feature category certain items which Americans treat as semifixed. Apparently, a guest in a Chinese home *does not move his chair* except at the host's suggestion. To do so would be like going into someone else's home and moving a screen or even a partition. In this sense, the semifixed nature of furniture in American homes is merely a matter of degree and situation. Light chairs are more mobile than sofas or heavy tables. I have noted, however, that some Americans hesitate to adjust furniture in another person's house or office. Of the forty students in one of my classes, half manifested such hesitation.

As whose home did the students regard Mr. Hall's classroom? Who owns your space?

How much variety is there in your space? Is there private and public space? Is there open and closed space? Is there indoor and outdoor space? Is there space for everyone, space for some, space for a few, space just for you?

Which of these pictures illustrate sociofugal space? Which sociopetal?

How fixed or flexible is your space? If it is too fixed, how can you "flex" it? If it is too flexible, how can you fix it?

Privacy and safety are critical for learning of all kinds. It is certain that the highly anxious, frightened child who is the typical failure or troublemaker needs more rather than less privacy, more rather than less safety and insulation. It is essential that structures be created in the classroom, if they are but large cardboard cartons and paper block walls, that enable children to build safety and privacy into their social life at school.

From George von Hilsheimer, *How to Live with Your Special Child*

How soft or hard is your space?
How can you soften it? How can you harden it?

From "The Continuum"
by Anthony Barton

Sometimes it is useful to make a list of what the institution has, and what it has not. Think of a school which you know well and see how many items on the following list apply to it. Find a pencil and draw a smiling face beside each item which exists in the school. ☺

◯ A notice on the wall prohibiting something.

◯ A system of bells or speakers with which it is possible to interrupt the work of many people simultaneously.

◯ A classroom with a chalkboard, a set of chairs with built-in book racks, and a tidy floor.

◯ A bulletin board with a timetable pinned to it.

◯ A set of thirty or more identical books, or a row of thirty or more private lockers too small to fit a guitar.

◯ A computer terminal dispensing programmed instruction.

◯ A system whereby meals are prepared by those other than students and staff.

◯ An understanding that the school is run by the staff, who respect the wishes of the students.

○ A room which students enter only with the permission of a member of staff.

○ A library in which as many books as possible are numbered and catalogued.

○ A locked storeroom from which an appointed member of the staff dispenses stationery or other materials.

○ A janitor who sweeps the corridors regularly.

○ A cold wall which is hard to touch and is painted a pastel shade.

○ An asphalt playground.

○ A daily assembly.

○ Organized competitive games.

○ A telephone which students use only with the permission of a member of staff.

○ Large television sets used by whole classes to watch educational TV.

○ A stage with lighting, flats and curtains.

○ A carpeted resource center or library with audio-visual equipment in carrels with headphones for students to use quietly.

○ A swimming pool.

○ Supervised visits to places outside the school by large numbers of students.

○ A room which members of the staff use only with the permission of a student.

○ A garden or grounds with mown lawns and trim paths.

○ Still and movie cameras which students are told how to use.

○ A precision instrument, such as a telescope or a machine tool, which students use under supervision.

○ Still and movie cameras which students use without instruction.

○ A resource center or library in which students are free to use projectors and record players and to make a noise and a mess.

○ A copying machine free for the use of students and staff.

○ A hobbies room open to all and equipped with benches, power tools and materials.

○ A flexible area with an overhead grid carrying power and communications, which is used for informal drama, moviemaking, discussions and dances.

○ A number of mobile chairs, tables, cameras, spotlamps, mirrors and "hospital" screens.

○ An open storeroom from which people take what they need when they need it.

○ A warm wall painted a bold color, into which your fingers sink.

○ Unsupervised visits to places outside the school by small numbers of students.

○ A large surface (such as the walls and ceiling of an auditorium) on which people paint murals and slogans.

○ Unrestricted use of a telephone, *or* unrestricted use of all the audio-visual equipment in the school.

○ An informal cooking area where students fry eggs and brew cocoa when they feel like it.

○ An understanding that decisions affecting the community are made by students and staff together.

○ A room serving no particular purpose.

○ A school vehicle which students drive.

○ A bin filled with free learning materials.

○ A pile of junk, or a room which is *never* tidy.

○ Spontaneous noncompetitive games.

○ Trees which are climbed.

○ Space in which people run.

○ Water with which people play.

○ Mud in which people roll.

○ Long grass in which people lie.

○ Sky.

Consider the *number* of items that you checked. The more the better. If you checked less than half of the items, your school must lack facilities which are essential to the wellbeing of its inmates. Consider the *spread.* Are the items which you checked spread all over the place? They should be. If your checks are clustered thickly in one part of the continuum and spread thinly in another, then there is work to be done in the thin area. The missing faces are neglected children. After all, a school is a mixture of many different kinds of students and teachers. If it fails to spread itself evenly right across the continuum, it will surely harm some of its people, if only by ignoring them. Drawing faces on a continuum list is a quick way to discover some of the things that are missing. It can help you to decide which way to spread your budget and which gaps to fill in first. For example, I know of a school near Erie with a beautiful library filled with beautiful children's books on beautiful shelves, beautifully catalogued by a beautiful librarian. The place is so beautiful that the majority of the children avoid it like the plague. The smiling faces are clustered at the structured end of the continuum and none of the messy kids in the school are given a chance to express themselves.

HOW TO SOFTEN YOUR HARD SCHOOL

1. USE THE CORRIDORS. Sell the steel lockers for scrap and use the money to buy cushions. Scatter the cushions around the corridors and let the students lie around on the floor. Have the floor cleaned very seldom but leave brooms about.

2. TAKE ALL THE AV EQUIPMENT OUT OF THE STOREROOM AND PUT IT IN THE CORRIDORS. Let the students use it when they feel the need for it. Let them break projectors, tape recorders and viewers. Let them take machines home, steal tapes.

3. HIRE A XEROX MACHINE AND PUT IT IN THE CORRIDOR. Place no restrictions whatever upon its use. Find a kid willing to keep it running. Put a thermofax copier in the corridor too. With a mountain of paper and acetate.

4. OPEN UP THE LIBRARY. Take the doors off their hinges. Roll up the carpet and sell it. Let the students cut up the books with scissors. Provide scissors, paste, paper. With the money provided by the sale of the carpet, buy:

a. A bucket full of magazines.
b. A bucket full of comics.
c. A bucket full of newspapers.
d. Several incomprehensible thick medical tomes. Try McAinsh, Toronto.
e. A number of books in Chinese, Japanese, Sanskrit and other languages.
f. A barrowload of old books from the Old Favorites Bookstore, Toronto.
g. Photographs, maps, geological maps, plans, blueprints, research papers.
h. A bin of scrap film, clear leader, and old prints of movies.
i. A pile of large reproductions of great works of art, new and old.
j. Masses of records of all kinds. Raid the second floor at the A & A Record Store, Toronto.
k. A stack of mail-order catalogues, models kits, calendars, and so on.
l. Circular stands full of cheap paperbacks by journalists, hack novelists.

Let the children destroy and refashion material. Be farsighted. Allow a child to learn by breaking, if you judge that the learning is worth more than the thing broken. Very often it is.

5. ANNOUNCE THAT THE SCHOOL WILL BE OPEN ALL AROUND THE CLOCK ALL YEAR. Rip out any steel grills designed to slide across corridors. Unbar windows. Abandon all official paperwork, or give it to some student who would like to do it for you. Join in, start doing your own research in the library, on a pet topic, or build a model aeroplane. When the inspector calls, ask him to hold the fuselage while you glue on the wings. HAVE A BONFIRE of all personal files, I.Q. scores, examination results, attendance records and the like.

6. BUILD A ROUGH ANNEX ONTO THE SCHOOL with a corrugated iron roof, a wood stove, naked plumbing and bare, dangling lightbulbs. Supply paints and brushes for home-made murals. Forbid the janitor to enter the annex at anytime.

7. SELL THOSE BIG, HEAVY TELEVISION SETS and buy little Japanese ones for small groups and individuals. Get a VTR and let the kids record commercials, static, programs, anything. If you can afford it ($1400) buy a back-pack camera and recorder for instant TV.

8. INVITE THE WORLD IN. Lure real artists, engineers, laborers, nurses, scientists, technicians, typists into the school to work with the students. Many *parents* are qualified experts . . . put them to work inside the school.

9. LET THE STUDENTS OUT INTO THE WORLD. Let them travel as individuals or in very small groups to investigate insurance buildings, crawl down sewers, and watch courtrooms, washrooms, construction projects. Let them fly to Alaska, telephone long, long distance to talk to professors in Califor-

nia. PUT TELEPHONES IN THE CLASSROOMS.

10. INVITE FORD FOUNDATION, OISE, AND OTHERS TO VISIT. Show them your extraordinary school and ask for money, lots of money. And ask for computer terminals, teaching machines and other gimmicks. Keep asking.

If you are frightened to attempt such sweeping changes, try quietly rearranging existing facilities. The technological wonders of our North American society are founded upon the concept of repetition, a concept which envelops us in clocks, apartment blocks and newspapers. Repetition is not the only way to work wonders, and in certain areas of the school you may change the whole atmosphere if you *search out repetition and break it up.* If there is a room furnished with tubular chairs and another furnished with wooden chairs, mix them. If there are desks arranged in rows, heap them in the corner. If anything is screwed to the floor, unscrew it. Unplug the electric clocks. Let me hasten to add that this advice applies only to those who become aware that their schools are too structured. Many free schools need the reverse treatment, all their smiling faces are crammed into the unorganized end of the continuum. For free school people, here is a ten-point plan for tightening up.

HOW TO HARDEN YOUR SOFT SCHOOL

1. ESTABLISH A SYSTEM FOR SUPPLYING THE SCHOOL WITH MATERIALS. On several occasions I have walked into a free school and been bitterly disappointed by the lack of materials. No school dedicated to making a decent mess should open its doors before it has obtained two truck loads, say 5 tons, of information in the shape of string, glue, magnets, records, magazines, books, paints, testtubes, chemicals, transistors, advertisements, felt pens, catalogues, newspapers, rocks, fossils, microscopes, herbs, wire, acetate, sliderules, typewriters, tapes, film stock, stuffed owls, old pieces of machinery, cloth, thread, animals, bones, fishing flies, photographs, paintings, slides and films. Treat information like water from a tap.

2. PUT YOUR FINANCES UPON A SOUND FOOTING. It's romantic to be starving anarchists, but it's lousy for education.

3. ORGANIZE A FEW BOOKS. Wade into the sea of information, clear a few shelves, and arrange 30 reference books in alphabetical order. Stick numbers on their spines, stamp them NOT TO BE REMOVED and chain them to the shelf. While you are in the mood, padlock a few doors and windows.

4. MAKE A HARD ROOM. Set aside at least one room to represent the organized side of life. If you can afford it, build a laboratory with identical stools, gas taps, electrical outlets and small sinks for washing retorts. Have a ten-week course in the laboratory for which interested students have to sign in advance and attend at regular times. If you have no science teacher, immediately appoint a meticulous chemist.

5. STOP CHOOSING NEW STUDENTS to fit the community. The next person whom you choose should be unlike anyone else you've ever had before.

6. ESTABLISH A SCHOOL UNIFORM. Hair must reach the shoulders. All clothes must be so outrageously comfortable that they appear to be a uniform worn by abnormal children and their teachers. Mom pops a piece of TV chicken into her mouth and shudders. If there were no electric bells, detentions and examinations, our kids might look like *that.*

7. BUILD A BARN and write the Seven Commandments on the wall. Create a solid enough alternative to the public educational system, and the pendulum will swing your way . . . but many people are not swingers. Try to be fair to everyone and you may find yourself working towards the continuum.

8. ENJOY A HARD RITUAL EVERY MORNING. Knit a flag and sing a song.

9. RULE AND DIVIDE. Post rules for using the telephone, create a shortage of paper, and generally gum up communications. Watch people develop stiff backs, stiff collars and stiff upper lips.

10. DIVIDE AND RULE. To really harden the school, create a lavatory for children only, a staff room for adults only, and a sewing room for girls only. Have tense discussions about sex and the generation gap.

Children, like zoologists, sense the *safety* of diversity. A species which avoids the rut of repetition retains a certain flexibility which is valuable for survival in a changing world. As a group, the children want to extend the range of environments and experiences in school life. They are suggesting that we use our imagination and spread both ways at once, towards more structure and towards more freedom. They are asking us to build for the continuum.

How much can space change? That depends partly on you and what you're willing to do. Your environment affects you. Can you affect it? Why not try? Here's what was done by one third-grade class with a little help from their friends.

From Merle Burnick, *Trash Can Do It*, Farallones Designs/Institute Publication

The architects were students from Sim Vander Ryn's class at U.C. Berkeley. They were coming to our class, bringing us the possibility of changing the room, if we wanted to change it.

We sat on the floor, most of us under the age of nine—Shirley, Pat, David, Ross and the rest of us, and then it came. "School is like a prison." "Everybody sits in one place." "You can't go outside when you want to." "It's not like home." "There's a fence all around." "The room's dull." "There's nothing soft. Everything's hard, our desks, our chairs, the floor."

Five hours a day in a place that's like a prison? A place that's supposed to free the mind to think starts by confining the body.

The ideas on how we could change the room came fast. Shirley said we should paper the walls with flowered wallpaper. John said if that was done, he was moving out. Fiona said the kids could each take a part of the walls and decorate it the way they wanted to. Patrick said the room would be a mess and he didn't want a hippie pad. Karen wanted her own place. Carlos wanted a swimming pool, if not in the room at least in the school. They wanted a place to go besides their desks. The boys called the idea a fort. The girls called it a house. The kids drew pictures of a new room with colors and places to go.

The kids remembered the Tuesdays because those were the days when the architects came. They remembered Rick who brought a red wall on cannisters, with a roll of paper on the bottom that could climb the wall and make it an art board.

One Tuesday, the architects came with thick, heavy cardboard shaped in hexagons, squares and triangles—to make a room within our room. We got together all the paint we could find and painted the shapes. Then we taped them together. One was a huge geodesic dome. The other one was a smaller dome. The girls claimed the small one; the boys claimed the large one.

For the large dome, we needed several people to raise the sides and roof. It was a thing of beauty, a huge beehive with different surfaces and planes supporting each other. There were about eight of us holding the sides, while others taped them together. Then, before anyone realized what was happening, one boy crawled underneath the dome, then another and another and another and another, and then the sides began to heave and the roof began to cave and finally the powers pushing up on the outside gave in to the forces on the inside.

The need to build became the need to destroy. The boys were joyous in their abandon—cardboard ripping at the seams, bodies falling through the air smashing down the sides, while war noises came from behind the stockpile. A voice from underneath said, "This is just like Saturday." The process took two minutes, maybe. I was in a state of sad shock.

Then something absolutely amazing happened. There was quiet, then buzzing around around the ruins. Then as quickly and contagiously as the destructive process began, the boys began to build—in their own image—a two-room suite. Replacing the geodesic dome was an A-shaped structure attached to a square room. It was constructed entirrely from the ruins. It was the boys' fort—a place to go, away from the desks, another world without leaving the room. The boys' fort lovingly lasted a month and then collapsed, not from destruction but from use. The girls' house outlasted the boys' by a few weeks.

By now we were ready for something more permanent, a place to go that wouldn't fall down in a month. We decided what we would need to build a quiet corner in the room. For days the kids brought in empty egg and milk cartons, tin cans and newspapers. Kris and Jenny from Sim's class came to tie and dye cloth with the kids. Bill came with pieces of rug. About two weeks later we began to build.

The quiet corner started with box benches, padded with an unusual assortment of rug patterns sewn together, extending over the benches and covering the floor. The area, about six feet square, now looked like an empty wading pool. At each corner there was a huge tube that stood six feet high and about one foot in diameter. A wood frame was nailed to the top of these poles so that panels could be hung from them.

The kids rolled newspapers and tied them together, forming panels that looked like xylophones. Others strung egg cartons, using yarn to attach them or taped milk cartons together to make milk carton towers. Then the kids hung these panels along with the tie and dye cloths, and the quiet corner had sides. A large batik cloth was stretched to make the roof.

On the day the quiet corner came, the barrels also came—big barrels, big enough to hold a good-sized gorilla. Arched openings were cut in each barrel so that the kids could crawl in for the ultimate privacy. People have come in the room and commented on how small the class is, until I point to the barrels.

The quiet corner and study barrels freed the kids from their desks. They moved around the room discovering and claiming other spaces in the room. Norman had his own study space. It was between the sink and the bookshelf—just big enough for his book and his body. Willie and Jon went under the tables. With the extra tie and dye cloths, the kids hung dividers under the table.

A few people discovered the hall as a place to study rather than a place to go when you didn't behave in the class. Others came down from their desks to a rug sample on the floor beside them. Then came the time to build forts and clubs, improvisations with corrugated paper or cardboard, involving two or three desks and the area found between them. These forts and clubs moved like molecules—gathering another member or letting one go. Their shape and movement was governed by the ever-changing social order of the class.

As the room began to dance, I had the sensation I was addressing a merry-go-round. I didn't know who was up and who was down. When I looked to the west for someone, I found him in the east. I heard myself ask, "Where's Karen? Where's Willie? Where's Fiona?" The kids would answer, "She's under the table. He's in the barrel. She's in the quiet corner." As for David, he escaped me completely because he found places I never knew existed in the room. Would you think of looking for a boy among the coats in the coatrack?

If this story sounds anything like Alice in Wonderland, it was that kind of trip. What I learned from all of this—was that I was going to be teaching in a different style. By freeing the space in the room and encouraging movement, we had taken the first step in removing the prison atmosphere.

Who owned the space in the first place? I didn't realize it, but I did. I was the owner of the space, the governor of the air, who determined who would breathe in what place, where the children could keep their bodies, and consequently limiting what they could express by determining when and to whom they could say it. Freeing the space in the room released new energy in the room. It was harder to get the kids together to respond to the same thing at the same time. When I owned the space, things were much easier.

This situation called for the Super-Striped Charger—a nine by twelve rug that everyone could sit on. All group lessons are held on the rug. We usually meet there three or four times a day to explain a concept or assignment, to share experiences, to discuss things or watch a play.

The natural grouping of the kids leads to natural teaching situations. I gave up my space and with it I gave up my right to be the only teacher in the room. If someone knows how to borrow with two place numbers, does a teacher have to tell him how to borrow with three-place numbers, or can he be his own teacher and discover through the underused teaching aid called thinking, how to do it himself. I have seen a smile like no other smile, when a self-teacher asks me, "Is this right?" and I say, "Yes it is."

The kids teach each other, often better than I can. For instance, a girl had trouble with multiplication. I asked if there was anyone in the class who thought he could teach her. Several hands went up. One by one they went up to the board to show her how to multiply. One by one she rejected them because she couldn't understand. They could do it, but they couldn't teach it. Then she called on Ross. In clear terms, he explained it. She understood and Ross took her outside

the room and worked with her until lunchtime.

Then there are things in the room that are teachers: dictionaries, encyclopedias, books of all varieties, counting beans and marbles, chalkboards.

Most important there are people, the kids themselves, me and anyone else who walks into the room. If you're coming, you're it.

Another aspect of calming the merry-go-round, but also keeping it running—is me. Yes, part of the space in the room is mine. I have the freedom to express myself too—to set priorities and affect the tone of the room. I am learning from my teachers in the room and from the living we do every day.

Perhaps the most creative act we did came during the last part of the school year. We succeeded against all odds in getting the present desks, the heavy, awkward pieces of furniture with chairs soldered to the front, out of the room.

The way it happened was that Kris from Sim's class designed a small desk resembling a mail box. She brought it into the room about the time we built the quiet corner. Of course, only one person could have the desk—and that choice was hard enough. But it spurred on some of the other kids to devising their own types of desks. For instance, Karen brought her small rocker from home and placed it in front of a box where she stored her things and wrote on the top surface. John put a rug on the floor in front of an orange crate and made this into his desk. Dana chose the piano bench for hers,

since we had no piano to go with it. These improvisations began to spring up all over the room.

When Kris walked in one day and said she was ready to make her mailbox desks on a large scale, we were ready to help. The desks were constructed out of tubing used for concrete molds and plywood. The concrete molds were donated, but we needed about $50 for the plywood. We had a bake sale and made $38.00. We scrounged up the rest.

"When are the desks coming? When can we paint them? When are they coming?" Everyday for two weeks we thought about the desks. The plywood sides came first. The kids sanded the sides and the carrying holes so they wouldn't get splinters. Then we sent the sides back so they could be glued to the tubing. When Jenny and Kris brought them back a few days later, we carried them from the back of a pick-up truck to the room, where each person chose one that was his size.

The kids painted the tubing with tempera. Jon had "GIZMO" painted on the front. Alan wrote "DUNE BUGGY" on his, and Robert wrote "RIGHT ON" on his. Karen made hers into a horse. On mine, I made a collage. Later that week we took the desks outside and enameled the plywood in bright colors.

If you can picture a mailbox that stands about one and a half feet high, with a roll top and a board that pulls out for a writing surface, that's what the desks look like. The kids sit on the floor, usually on a pillow or a rug sample.

In the process of making new desks, we learned such things as what "portable" meant, what a jig saw was, how sandpaper can change the texture of a surface, the impermanence of tempera and the permanence of enamel, the business of raising money, making publicity, selling cakes and counting money. We became more conscious of how the room looked, that the new desks had a unique form—one that was pleasing to the eye as well as being a useful tool.

What's coming next? I don't know. But it has been a full year, one of living, stretching, growing, loving and learning.

Here's a college student's feelings about an environmental happening. He made the room his own. He began to make the school his own. Can you?.

In the beginning there was a classroom. What kind of room? A traditional, usual, ordinary classroom with chairs, tables and desks. Everyone sitting in a square waiting for the teacher to come and speak with undullable wisdom.

But
   then
"I've got the scotch tape; will that help?" "Nope, put staples in it." "All the tacks are gone, use string." "Here's a poster. Put it up." "Can I have a doughnut?"
   Now
     I
John Kress own 1/300,000,000,000 of this school. One three billionth of Alameda is mine and mine alone and I'm not going to sell it no matter the price.
   I
     did
       it
         all
           by
             myself
along with thirty other students. I did it by putting up my mobile way over there in the corner, my pictures that mean something to me. Some people brought nothing so they helped the rest of us put things up or they

made a quick search and found something, a doughnut, or a soda pop can.
   But
     all
       the
         people
were not completely there. Our happening was supposed to represent a new beginning but the beginning is in people with their minds still wandering around in old places. It takes time to change ways and ideas but
   I
     was
       willing
         to
           do
            it.

John Kress

Are you willing?

An Elementary School Classroom in a Slum

Far far from gusty waves, these children's
  faces.
Like rootless weeds, the hair torn round their
  pallor.
The tall girl with her weighed-down head.
  The paper-
Seeming boy, with rat's eyes. The stunted,
  unlucky heir
Of twisted bones, reciting a father's gnarled
  disease,
His lesson from his desk. At back of the
  dim class
One unnoted, sweet and young. His eyes live
  in a dream
Of squirrel's game, in tree room, other than
  this.

On sour cream walls, donations. Shake-
  speare's head,
Cloudless at dawn, civilized dome riding all
  cities.
Belled, flowery, Tyrolese valley. Open-hand-
  ed map
Awarding the world its world. And yet, for
  these
Children, these windows, not this world, are
  world,
Where all their future's pointed with a fog,
A narrow street sealed in with a lead sky,
Far far from rivers, capes, and stars of words.

Surely, Shakespeare is wicked, the map a
  bad example

With ships and sun and love tempting them
  to steal—
For lives that slyly turn in their cramped
  holes
From fog to endless night? On their slag
  heap, these children
Wear skins peeped through by bones and
  spectacles of steel
With mended glass, like bottle bits on stones.
All of their time and space are foggy slum.
So blot their maps with slums as big as doom.

  Unless, governor, teacher, inspector, visi-
  tor,
This map becomes their window and these
  windows
That shut upon their lives like catacombs
Break O break open till they break the town
And show the children to green fields, and
  make their world
Run azure on gold sands, and let their
  tongues
Run naked into books, the white and green
  leaves open
History theirs whose language is the sun.

Stephen Spender

Visit a classroom in which you are not a student. Try to see and describe it with fresh
eyes; use images that will bring the environment and people to life as does Spender when
he speaks of "sour cream walls," or "the
stunted, unlucky heir of twisted bones." What
is Spender's recommendation for school reform? Do you agree? How would you relate
this poem to John Malcolm Brinnin's "Views
of the Favorite Colleges"? What would you
regard as a relevant education for children
of the inner cities? A suitable environment?
How would you break open the classroom?

Herbert Kohl asks, "Why does a classroom
have to have a front, a back and two sides?"
Why does a classroom have to be a room?
Why does a school have to be a certain building? Can't a classroom be any place? Can't
a school be anywhere? Where have you
learned some of the important things of your
life? Can you imagine being a teacher, a student in a "school without walls." Explore your
environment. Visit a park, a playground, a
restaurant, a bar, an expensive neighborhood, a poor one. What are the people learning? Who is the real teacher? How does the
environment. Visit a park, a playground, a
to each other. Talk to the people. How do
they feel? What do they want to change. Listen. A classroom is anywhere. A school is
any place.

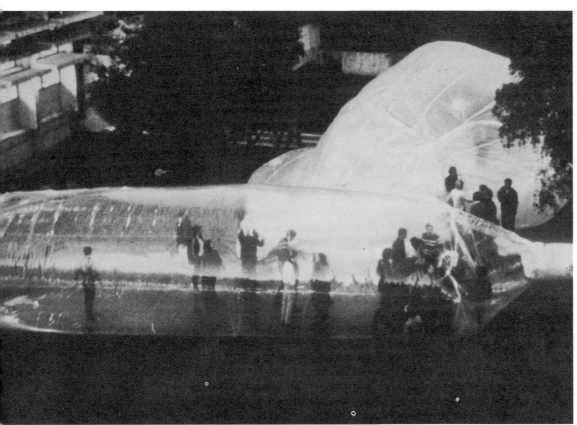

Family Circle Magazine, August 1970.

Mini-Schools: A Prescription for the Reading Problem by Paul Goodman

What follows is a statement I recently made when asked to testify on teaching reading, before the borough president of Manhattan:

A chief obstacle to children's learning to read is the present school setting in which they have to pick it up. For any learning to be skillful and lasting, it must be or become self-motivated, second nature; for this, the schooling is too impersonal, standardized, and academic. If we tried to teach children to speak, by academic methods in a school-like environment, many would fail and most would stammer.

Although the analogy between learning to speak and learning to read is not exact, it is instructive to pursue it, since speaking is much harder. Learning to speak is a stupendous intellectual achievement. It involves learning to use signs, acquiring a vocabulary, and also mastering an extraordinary kind of algebra—syntax—with almost infinite variables in a large number of sentence forms. We do not know scientifically how infants learn to speak, but almost all succeed equally well, no matter what their class or culture. Every child picks up a dialect, whether "correct" or "incorrect," that is adequate to express the thoughts and needs of his milieu.

We can describe some of the indispensable conditions for learning to speak.

1. The child is constantly exposed to speech related to interesting behavior in which he often shares. ("Now where's your coat? Now we're going to the supermarket, etc.")

2. The speakers are persons important to the child, who often single him out to speak to him or about him.

3. The child plays with the sounds, freely imitates what he hears, and tries to approximate it without interference or correction. He is rewarded by attention and other useful results when he succeeds.

4. Later, the child consolidates by his own act what he has learned. From age three to five he acquires style, accent, and fluency by speaking with his peers, adopting their uniform but also asserting his own tone, rhythm, and mannerisms. He speaks peer speech but is uniquely recognizable as speaking in his own way.

Suppose, by contrast, that we tried to teach speaking academically in a school-like setting:

1. Speaking would be a curricular subject abstracted from the web of activity and reserved for special hours punctuated by bells.

2. It would be a tool subject rather than a way of being in the world.

3. It would not spring from his needs in immediate situations but would be taught according to the teacher's idea of his future advantage, importantly aiming at his getting a job sixteen years later.

4. Therefore the child would have to be "motivated," the exercises would have to be "fun," etc.

5. The lessons would be arranged in a graded series from simple to complex, for instance on a false theory that monosyllables precede polysyllables, or words precede sentences, or sentences precede words.

6. The teacher's relation to the infant would be further depersonalized by the need to speak or listen to only what fits two dozen other children as well.

7. Being continually called on, corrected, tested, and evaluated to meet a standard in a group, some children would become stutterers; others would devise a phony system of apparently speaking in order to get by, although the speech meant nothing; others would balk at being processed and would purposely become "stupid."

8. Since there is a predetermined range of what can be spoken and how it must be spoken, everybody's speech would be pedantic and standard, without truth to the child's own experience or feeling.

Turn now to teaching reading. These eight disastrous defects are not an unfair caricature of what we do. Reading is treated as abstract, irrelevant to actual needs, instrumental, extrinsically motivated, impersonal, pedantic, not expressive of truth or art. The teaching often produces awkwardness, faking, or balking. Let me also make four further points specific to learning reading:

1. Most people who have learned to read and write fluently have done so on their own, with their own material, whether library books, newspapers, comic books, or street signs. They may have picked up the ABCs in school, but they acquired skill, preserved what they had learned, on their own. This self-learning is an important point, since it is not at the mechanical level of the ABCs that reading retardation drastically occurs, but in the subsequent years when the good readers are going it alone

2. On neurological grounds, an emotionally normal child in middle-class urban and suburban surroundings, constantly exposed to written code, should spontaneously learn to read by age nine just as he learned to speak by age two or three. (This is the conclusion of Walla Nauta of the National Institute of Mental Health.) It is impossible for such a child *not* to pick up the code unless he is systematically interrupted and discouraged, for instance by trying to teach him.

But of course our problem has to do with children in the culture of poverty, which does not have the ordinary middle-class need for literacy and the premium put on it. Such children are not exposed to reading and writing in important relations with their parents and peers; the code does not constantly occur in every kind of sequence of behavior. Thus there is an essential need for the right kind of schooling, to point to the written words and read them aloud, in use.

3. Historically, in all modern countries, school methods of lessons, copying, and textbooks, have been used, apparently successfully, to teach children to read. But this evidence is deceptive. A high level and continuing competence were required of very few—e.g., in 1900 in the United States only 6 percent graduated from high school. Little effort was made with children of the working class, and none at all with those in the culture of proverty. It is inherently unlikely that the same institutional procedures could apply with such a change of scale and population. Where a dramatic effort has been made to teach adults to read, as in Cuba, the method has been "each one teach one," informally.

4. Also, with the present expansion of higher education. teachers of freshman English uniformly complain that the majority of middle-class students cannot really read and write, though they have put on a performance that got them through high school. As John Holt has carefully described, their real life need was not reading or writing but getting by. (This is analogous to the large group among Puerto Rican children in New York who apparently speak English well, but who in fact cannot say anything that they need or mean, that is not really simply parroted.)

I trust that the aim of the borough president's hearings is how to learn reading as truth and art and not just to fake and get by. Further, since poor children do not have the continual incentives and subtle pressures of middle-class life, it is much harder for them to learn even just to fake and get by. And even if they do get by, it will not pay off for them in the end, since they do not have money and connections. To make good, they must really be competent.

The question is, is it possible and feasible to teach reading somewhat in the way children learn to speak, by intrinsic interest, with personal attention, and relating to the whole environment of activity? Pedagogically it is possible and feasible. There are known methods and available teachers, and I will suggest an appropriate school setting. Economically it is feasible, since methods, staff, and setting do not cost more than the $850 per child that we now spend in the public schools. (This was demonstrated for two years by the First Street School on the Lower East Side, and it is in line with the budget of Erik Mann's new school for Negro children in Newark which uses similar principles.) Politically, however, my present proposal is impossible and unfeasible, since it threatens both vested interests and popular prejudices, as will be evident.

For ages six to eleven, I propose a system of tiny schools, radically decentralized. As one who for twenty years has urged democratic decentralization in many fields, including the schools, I am of course interested in the Bundy recommendation to cut up the New York system into sixty fairly autonomous districts. This would restore some relevance of the culture (and the staff) of the school to the culture of the community. But however valuable politically, it is an administrative arrangement; it does not get down to the actual pedagogical operation. And it certainly is not child-centered; both poor and middle-class communities have their own ways of not paying attention to children, according to their own prejudices and distant expectations. By "tiny school," therefore, I here mean twenty-eight children . . . with four teachers (one grownup to seven children), and each tiny school to be largely adminstered by its own staff and parents, with considerable say also for the children, as in Summerhill. The four teachers are:

A teacher regularly licensed and salaried. Since the present average class size is twenty-eight, these are available.

A graduate from the senior class of a New York college, perhaps just embarking on graduate study. Salary $2000. There is no lack of candidates to do something interesting and useful in a free setting.

A literate housewife and mother, who can also prepare lunch. Salary $4000. No lack of candidates.

A literate, willing, and intelligent high-school graduate. Salary $2000. No lack of candidates.

Such a staff can easily be racially and ethnically mixed. And it is also the case, as demonstrated by the First Street School, that in such a small setting, with individual attention paid to the children, it is easy to get racially and ethnically mixed classes: there is less middle-class withdrawal when the parents do not fear that their children will be swamped and retarded. (We have failed to achieve "integration" by trying to impose it from above, but it can be achieved from below, in schools entirely locally controlled, if we can show parents that it is for their children's best future.)

For setting, the tiny school would occupy two, three, or four rooms in existing school buildings, church basements, settlement houses otherwise empty during school hours, rooms set aside in housing projects, storefronts. The setting is especially indifferent since a major part of activity occurs outside the school place. The setting should be able to be transformed into a clubhouse, decorated and equipped according to the group's own decision. There might be one school on every street, but it is also advisable to locate many in racial and ethnic border areas, to increase intermixture. For purposes of assembly, health services, and some games, ten tiny schools could use the present public school facilities.

The cost saving in such a setup is the almost total elimination of top-down administration and the kind of special services that are required precisely because of excessive size and rigidity. The chief uses of central administration would be licensing, funding, choosing sites, and some inspection. There would be no principals and assistants, secretaries and assistants. Curriculum, texts, equipment would be determined as needed—and despite the present putative economies of scale, they would be cheaper; much less would be pointless or wasted. Record-keeping would be at a minimum. There is no need for truant officers when the teacher-and-seven can call at the absentee's home and inquire. There is little need for remedial personnel since the staff and parents are always in contact, and the whole enterprise can be regarded as remedial. Organizational studies of large top-down directed enterprises show that the total cost is invariably at least 300 percent above the cost of the immediate function, in this case the interaction of teachers and children. I would put this 300 percent into increasing the number of adults and diversifying the possibilities of instruction. Further, in the conditions of New York real estate, there is great advantage in ceasing to build four-million-dollar school buildings, and rather fitting tiny schools into available niches.

Pedagogically, this model is appropriate for natural learning of reading:

1. It allows exposure to the activities of

the city. A teacher-and-seven can spend half the time on the streets, visiting a business office, in a playground, at a museum, watching television, chatting with the corner druggist, riding the buses and subways, visiting rich and poor neighborhoods and, if possible, homes. All these experiences can be saturated with speaking, reading, and writing. For instance, a group might choose to spend several weeks at the Museum of Natural History, and the problem would be to relabel the exhibits for their own level of comprehension.

2. It allows flexibility to approach each child according to his own style and interests, for instance in choice of reading matter. Given so many contexts, the teacher can easily strike when the iron is hot, whether reading the destination of a bus or the label on a can of soup. When some children catch on quickly and forge ahead on their own, the teacher need not waste their time and can concentrate on those who are more confused. The setting does not prejudge as to formal or informal techniques, phonics, Montessori, rote drill, Moore's typewriter, labeling the furniture, Herbert Kohl's creative writing, or any other method.

3. For instance, as a writer I like Sylvia Ashton-Warner's way of teaching little Maoris. Each day she tries to catch the most passionate concern of each child and to give him a card with that key word: usually these are words of fear, anger, hunger, loneliness, or sexual desire. Soon a child has a large ineradicable but very peculiar reading list,

not at all like Dick and Jane. He then easily progresses to read and write anything. From the beginning, in this method, reading and writing are gut-meaningful, they convey truth and feeling. This method could be used in our tiny school.

4. The ragged administration by children, staff, and parents is pedagogically a virtue, since this too, which is real, can be saturated with reading and writing, writing down the arguments, the rules, the penalties. Socially and politically, of course, it has the advantage of engaging the parents and giving them power.

I am assuming that for the first five school years, there is no merit in the standard curriculum. For a small child everything in the environment is educative, if he attends to it with guidance. Normal children can learn the first eight years' curriculum in four months anyway, at age twelve.

Further, I see little merit, for teaching this age, in the usual teacher-training. Any literate and well-intentioned grown up or late teenager knows enough to teach a small child a lot. Teaching small children is a difficult art, but we do not know how to train the improvisational genius it requires, and the untrained seem to have it equally: compare one mother with another, or one big sister or brother with another. Since at this age one teaches the child, not the subject, the relevant art is psychotherapy, and the most useful course for a teachers' college is probably group therapy. The chief criterion for

selection is the one I have mentioned: liking to be attentive to children. Given this setting, many young people would be introduced to teaching and would continue with it as a profession; whereas in the New York system the annual turnover approaches 20 percent, after years of wasted training.

As I have said, however, there are fatal political and administrative objections to this proposal. First, the public school administration does not intend to go largely out of business. Given its mentality, it must see any radical decentralization as impossible to administer and dangerous, for everything cannot be controlled. Some child is bound to break a leg and the insurance companies will not cover; some teenager is bound to be indiscreet and the *Daily News* will explode in headlines.

The United Federation of Teachers will find the proposal to be anathema because it devalues professional perquisites and floods the schools with the unlicensed. Being mainly broken to the public school harness, most experienced teachers consider free and inventive teaching to be impossible.

Most fatally, poor parents, who aspire for their children, tend to regard unrigidly structured education as downgrading, not taking the children seriously, and also as vaguely immoral. In the present black power temper of Harlem, also, the possible easy intermixing is itself not desired. (Incidentally, I am rather sympathetic to black separatism as a means of consolidating the power of black communities. But children, as Kant said, must be educated for the future better society which cannot be separated.)

In spite of these fatal objections, I recommend that, instead of building the next new school building, we try out this scheme with 1200 children.

After this statement had been circulated, the following statement appeared in the Chelsea Clinton News, *Nov. 30, 1967:*

Paul Goodman's analysis and proposal are an extremely important contribution to educational thinking. I shall submit the article to headquarters with recommendation that the proposal should be tried out. I am convinced that it has great merit.

Dr. Elliott Shapiro

(Dr. Shapiro is assistant superintendent of School District 3, which includes Chelsea and Clinton.)

Dr. Shapiro informs us that some versions of these schools do now exist. The schools are not quite so "mini" as he had hoped, but they are somewhat similar to Mr. Goodman's proposal.

How many students attended your own elementary school? Would you have liked to have gone to a mini-school? Would you like to teach in one? What advantages or disadvantages do you see?

The Ideal School

The ideal school for me would be
Made of glass and suspended in a tree.
You swing on a grapevine
   from door to door
And classes would never be a bore.
Parachuting from a tree
   would be the main activity.
The tree in which the
   school would stand
Would hold the great
   big loyal school band.

Wynn-Anne Cole

The Conscientious Observer In Time

Sitting in my history class
listening to my teacher
talking, talking to her sleepy students
I feel brainwashed!
Looking at the clock, it's grooving one-twenty. . . .

IOIOIOIOIOIOIOIOIOIOIOIOIOI

You have been examining sound and space in school. Take a look at time. In your own class or one that you are observing, notice how time is organized. Clock 30–50 minutes at five-minute intervals. What does the use of time tell about the teacher? The students? The system? The culture? CLock one of your own days or weeks.

LAND OF CLOCKS

Do you think these teachers are killing or wasting time? Would you use school time this way? Why?

From George Dennison, *The Lives of Children*

Perhaps the single most important thing we offered the children at First Street was hours and hours of *un*supervised play. By unsupervised I mean that we teachers took no part at all, but stood to one side and held sweaters. We were not referees, or courts of last resort. Indeed, on several occasions with the older boys, I *averted* violence simply by stepping out of the gymnasium! We provided some measure of safety in the event of injury, and we kept people out. It was a luxury these children had rarely experienced.

I would like to return to this subject later, and say in some detail why it is and how it is that children, left to their own devices, have a positively curative effect on one another. This is the kind of statement that many professionals look upon askance and identify as Romantic, as much as to say that the sphere of the world rides upon the tortoise of their own careers. Many teachers and parents, however, will recognize in this assertion one of the loveliest and most meaningful of the facts of life. Would growth be possible—indeed, would there be a world at all—if the intake of the young were restricted to those things deliberately offered them by adults? Consider, too, how shocking it would be if for two minutes we adults could reexperience the powers of mind—the concentration, the memory, the energy for detail—to say nothing of the physical elan—we possessed at the age of ten.

From Frederich Buechner, *The Hungering Dark*

Late one winter afternoon as I was walking to a class that I had to teach, I noticed the beginnings of what promised to be one of the great local sunsets. There was just the right kind of clouds and the sky was starting to burn and the bare trees were black as soot against it. When I got to the classroom, the lights were all on, of course, and the students were chattering, and I was just about to start things off when I thought of the sunset going on out there in the winter dusk, and on impulse, without warning, I snapped off the classroom lights. I am not sure that I ever had a happier impulse. The room faced west so as soon as it went dark, everything disappeared except what we could see through the windows, and there it was—the entire sky on fire by then, like the end of the world or the beginning of the world. You might think that somebody would have said something. Teachers do not usually plunge their students into that kind of darkness, and you might have expected a wisecrack or two or at least the creaking of chairs as people turned around to see if the old bird had finally lost his mind. But the astonishing thing was that the silence was as complete as you can get it in a room full of people, and we all sat there unmoving for as long as it took the extraordinary spectacle to fade slowly away.

For over twenty minutes nobody spoke a word. Nobody *did* anything. We just sat there in the near-dark and watched one day of our lives come to an end, and it is no immodesty to say that it was a great class because my only contribution was to snap off the lights and then hold my tongue. And I am not being sentimental about sunsets when I say that it was a great class because in a way the sunset was the least of it. What was great was the unbusy-ness of it. It was taking unlabeled, unallotted time just to look with maybe more than our eyes at what was wonderfully there to be looked at without any obligation to think any constructive thoughts about it or turn it to any useful purpose later, without any weapon at hand in the dark to kill the time it took. It was the sense too that we were not just ourselves individually looking out at the winter sky but that we were in some way also each other looking out at it. We were bound together there simply by the fact of our being human, by our splendid insignificance in face of what was going on out there through the window, and by our curious significance in face of what was going on in there in that classroom. The way this world works, people are very apt to use the words they speak not so much as a way of revealing but, rather, as a way of concealing who they really are and what they really think, and that is why more than a few moments of silence with people we

do not know well are apt to make us so tense and uneasy. Stripped of our verbal camouflage, we feel unarmed against the world and vulnerable, so we start babbling about anything just to keep the silence at bay. But if we can bear to let it be, silence, of course, can be communion at a very deep level indeed, and that half hour of silence was precisely that, and perhaps that was the greatest part of it all.

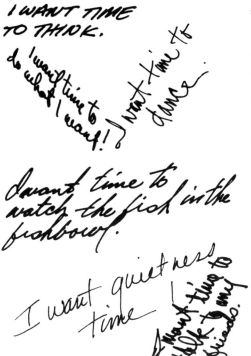

How fixed or flexible is our time?

Should children begin public school at five and remain there until 17? Should classes start at 8:30 A.M. and end at 3:00 P.M.? Why do we go to school from September to June and never on Sunday? Is the fifty minute hour practical? Should all college courses last a full quarter or semester? Should some last longer? Can time for change be built in to schools? Ten minutes a day? Two days a week? What do you do with time outside of school? What does "free" time mean to you'

How we use time and what it means to us is part of our cultural inheritance and tends, therefore, to remain invisible and unexplored. As westerners we are usually in a hurry to get somewhere and often keep our sights focused ahead on the future, sometimes missing the meaning of the present. Eric Berne in *Games People Play* uses an anecdote to illustrate different cultural meanings of time:

A Chinese man started to get into the local subway train, when his Caucasian companion pointed out that they could save twenty minutes by taking an express, which they did. When they got off at Central Park, the Chinese man sat down on a bench, much to his friend's surprise. "Well," explained the former, "since we saved twenty minutes, we can afford to sit here that long and enjoy our surroundings."

The need I see is for The Educated Perception. I am tired of psychoanalysis. I want psychosynthesis, for we are in an age in which we are in danger of going analytical all the way—on both verbal and nonverbal levels—and thus destroying the human being. Oh, how we need education that creates the ability to perceive; the ability to wake up each morning and see the world the good Lord created as it is on each particular morning. Much as I hate war, I am even more afraid of the poverty of the imagination. The Educated Perception will give each one of us more of life—and more of compassion. For compassion is the greatest gift we can give each other through all the tomorrows.

From Peter Drucker, "How to Be an Employee"

To believe in the "experientially well-calibrated mind" of Fritz Redl or the "educated perception" of Peter Drucker is to believe in looking to see, listening to hear, touching to feel. Why should a teacher be a trained observer of human behavior and human life space? Why must a teacher beware the impoverished imagination? Should a teacher practice awareness as a pianist practices scales? Is awareness enough? Is compassion enough? Are you observing or helping in a class now? Are you teaching? What follows is a kind of handy frame of reference for observing a class in action. What can you add?

1. *Space*

What is the size of the room? Shape? Colors? Textures? Smells? Lighting? Ventilation? What kinds of furniture? Fixed or flexible use of space? Arrangement? What dominates—sociofugal or sociopetal arrangements? Draw a diagram of the room. Are there wall decorations? Bulletin boards? Blackboards? Art work? Equipment? Is it student or teacher decoration? What is the over-all use of space? Organized? Disorganized? Imaginative? Dynamic? Static? Open? Closed? Is the feeling of space in this room reflected in the rest of the school? Remember what Herbert Kohl said in *The Open Classroom*? "A teacher's room tells us something about who he is and a great deal about what he is doing."

2. *Time*

How is time organized? How long were you the observer there? Is the use of time fixed or flexible? (Math for 20 minutes, spelling for 15.) Whose needs are primarily reflected in competition predominate? What verbal and nonverbal clues do you have of students' interests, commitments, values? What do they seem to be learning? Is what they are learning what the teacher thinks he is teaching? Are the students learning facts, skills, habits, aesthetic appreciation, self-awareness, attitudes? Is there evidence of creativity, enthusiasm? Are the students all doing the same thing? Do certain students stand out from the group? Why?

3. *The Teacher*

What is the teaching style? Authoritarian? Democratic? Permissive? What is the physical appearance? Dress? Voice? Manner? Special traits? Is the teacher a good visual aid? Attitude toward self and students? Where in space is the teacher most of the time? Diagram his typical relationship to the class. (In front of the class, moving around, etc.) Is there evidence of planning? A lesson plan? Does it take precedence over students' needs? How much are textbooks used? Workbooks? Other materials? Is the teacher responding to individual or group needs? Both? Is he using group techniques such as those of Kelley, Glasser, Holt, Moreno, and Dennison? Is there evidence of spontaneity? Creativity? How much of the real person shows through? How are feelings dealt with? What evidence is there of the use of discipline to solve problems? How is he addressed by students? First name? Last name? Nickname? Check the Verbal Interaction Category System. What categories predominate? Does the teacher dominate the talk? Students? Or do they share?

4. *Students*

How many are there? What is the age, sex, race, grade level, socio-economic level? How are they dressed? How are they addressed by the teacher? What is their involvement in the class? Interaction with each other? The teacher? Do they seem with the teacher or against him? Is there much game playing? If so, give examples.

5. *The Schooldom or Larger Realm*

In what kind of community is the school situated? Does it seem part of or apart from the community in which it stands? Is the school closed off, fenced, boarded up or open? How many buildings comprise the school? How are they arranged? How is space used? How are inside and outside related? Is there recess time? Observe the children playing. How much equipment is there for physical activities? How much space in which to run? Is the inside of the school attractive? Can students move freely or are passes required in the halls? Do bells ring? Are there indoor facilities for music, art, dance, sports, etc? Is there a library? Is there adequate audiovisual equipment? Are all spaces fixed or flexible? Are all walls solid and immovable? Talk to some students. How do they like their school? What seems to be the student's attitude toward school? What seems to be the school's attitude toward the students?

6. *Summary*

How do you feel as observer or aide in this class in this school? Are you interested, comfortable, tense, lost, angry? Would you recommend this class to a friend? Would you model yourself after the style of the teacher? What, if anything, would you change in human interaction, use of space or time? Does the class or school need more ''softness'' or ''hardness'' in your estimation? What additional questions would you like to ask the principal, the teacher, or the students, the community? Would you enroll your child there? Would you teach there? Would you have liked to have been a student there?

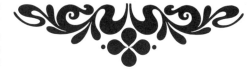

Here are the titles of some books you may want to read if you are interested in improving your conscientitious observing:

Amidon, Edmond, and Hunter, Elizabeth. *Improving Teaching: The Analysis of Classroom Verbal Interaction*. New York: Holt, Rinehart and Winston, 1966.

Birdwhistell, Roy L. *Kinesics and Context*. Philadelphia: University of Pennsylvania Press, 1970.

Gyorgy Kepes, ed. *Education of Vision*. New York: George Braziller, 1965.

Fantini, Mario D., and Young, Milton A. *Designing Education for Tomorrow's Cities*. New York: Holt, Rinehart and Winston, 1970.

Farallones Family Scrapbook. Farallones Designs Publisher, Distributed by Book People, Berkeley, California, 1971.

Fast, Julius. *Body Language*. N.Y.: M. Evans & Co., 1970.

Hall, Edward T. *The Hidden Dimension*. Garden City, N.Y.: Doubleday & Co., 1969.

___. *The Silent Language*. Garden City, N.Y.: Doubleday & Co., 1959.

Illich, Ivan. *Deschooling Society*. New York: Harper & Row, 1970.

Kelley, Earl C. *Education for What Is Real*. New York: Harper & Row, 1947.

Our Man-made Environment, Book Seven. Philadelphia, Pennsylvania, Group for Environmental Education, Inc., 1970.

Paramenter, Ross. *The Awakened Eye*. Middletown, Conn.: Wesleyan University Press, 1968.

Ruesch, Jurgen, and Kees, Weldon. *Nonverbal Communication: Notes on the Visual Perception of Human Relations*. Berkeley and Los Angeles: University of California Press, 1956.

Sommer, R. *Personal Space*. Englewood Cliffs, N.J.: Prentice-Hall, 1969.

"LEARNING IS THE DISCOVERY THAT SOMETHING IS POSSIBLE"
-FRITZ PERLS

Epilogue: Commencement

Legend has it that Rabbi Schneur Zalman, one of the great Hasidic rabbis of the late eighteenth and early nineteenth centuries, was imprisoned in St. Petersburg on false charges. While awaiting trial, he was visited by the chief of police, a thoughtful man. Struck by the quiet majesty of the rabbi's appearance and demeanor, the official engaged him in conversation, asking a number of questions that had puzzled him in reading the Scriptures. Their discussion turned to the story of the Garden of Eden. Why was it, the official asked, that a God who was all-knowing had to call out when Adam was hiding and ask him, "Where art thou?"

"You do not understand the meaning of the question," the rabbi answered. "This is a question God asks of every man in every generation. After all your wanderings, after all your efforts, after all your years, O man, where art thou?"

It is a question asked of societies as well as of individuals. One is almost afraid to ask it of this society at this moment in time; the crisis in the classroom is but one aspect of the larger crisis of American society as a whole, a crisis whose resolution is problematical at best. It does no good, however, to throw up our hands at the enormity of the task; we must take hold of it where we can, for the time for failure is long since passed. We will not be able to create and maintain a humane society unless we create and maintain classrooms that are humane. But if we succeed in that endeavor—if we accomplish the remaking of American education—we will have gone a long way toward that larger task, toward the creation of a society in which we can answer the question "Where art thou?" with pride rather than with dread.

From Charles E. Silberman, *Crisis in the Classroom*

The San Francisco Weather Report

Gee, You're so Beautiful That It's
   Starting to Rain
Oh, Marcia,
I Want your long blonde beauty
to be taught in high school,
so kids will learn that God
lives like music in the skin
and sounds like a sunshine harpsichord.
I want high school report cards
  to look like this:
Playing with Gentle Glass Things
    A
Computer Magic
    A
Writing Letters to Those You Love
    A
Finding out about Fish
    A
Marcia's Long Blonde Beauty
    A+!

Richard Brautigan

Where are you today?

Close your eyes. Choose three people in this class to evaluate you. Who are they? What grade do they give you? Do you agree with them? Whose evaluation is most important

Make up your own report card.

Tell where you are. Then ask someone else where he is. Pass it around.

Where do you want to go?

Create a school of tomorrow. Who would go to it? What would they learn? Who would teach? What would they teach? Where would the learning take place? How would you use space and time? What other questions can you ask? What kind of answers can you find?

Write your future autobiography. Imagine yourself as you think you will be in 10 or 20 years. How will you look? Where will you be living? What will you be doing? What will you want?

Concluding activities can take on a ritual-like quality and often allow people to realize dramatically how far they have traveled as individuals and as a group. You may have ideas of your own for closing. Here are some of ours.

✳✳✳✳✳✳✳✳✳✳✳✳✳✳✳✳✳✳✳✳✳✳✳✳

Bring in something you can part with.
Then find something in the school
(paper clip, piece of wood, etc.).
Together make an
assemblage of these materials.

§§§§§§§§§§§§§§§§§§§§§§§§§§§§§§§§§

What have you learned?
Write one idea on a slip
of paper. Drop it in a box.
One by one, come up,
pick a slip, read it, and
comment.
Guess who said it.

◖◖◖◖◖◖◖◖◖◖◖◖◖◖◖◖◖◖◖◖◖◖◖◖◖

Put on the board
a question you've discovered.
What's worth knowing?
What's worth teaching?

|◇|◇|◇|◇|◇|◇|◇|◇|◇|◇|◇|◇|◇|◇|◇|◇|◇|◇|◇|◇|

End with the same
game you
started with.

Carl Rogers delivered the following commencement address at Sonoma State College in California on June 7, 1969.

The Person of Tomorrow
by Carl R. Rogers

I am fascinated these days by what I am convinced is a most significant phenomenon. I am seeing a New Man emerging. I belive this New Man is the person of tomorrow. I want to talk about him.

I have seen him emerging, partially formed, from encounter groups, sensitivity training, so-called T-groups. I realize that for many years I saw facets of him emerging in the deep relationship of individual psychotherapy. I see him showing his face in the rapidly growing trend toward a humanistic and human psychology. I see him in the new type of student emerging on our campuses, and in campus unrest all over the world—Paris, Czechoslovakia, Japan, Columbia, Berkeley, San Francisco State, Harvard and many other places. He is not all lovable, he is sometimes frightening, but he is emerging. I see him in the surge toward individualism and self-respect in our black population in and out of the ghettos, and in the racial unrest which runs like a fever through all our cities. I see elements of him in the philosophy of the "drop-outs" in our generation—the hippies, the "flower people." I see him, strangely enough, in the younger members of industrial management today. I catch what to my older eyes is a confusing glimpse of him in the musicians, the poets, the writers, the composers of this generation—I'll mention the Beatles, and you can add the others. I have a feeling that the mass media—especially television—have helped him to emerge, though on this I am not very clear. But I have named, I think, a number of the areas and trends which perhaps have caused the emergence, and certainly permit us to see, the qualities of this New Man.

Though I am excited and full of anticipation about this person of tomorrow, there are aspects of the situation which are very sobering. I believe the New Man has characteristics which run strongly counter to the orthodoxies, dogmas, forms, and creeds of the major western religions—Catholicism, Protestantism, Judaism. He does not fit at all into traditional industrial management and organization. He contradicts, in his person, almost every element of traditional schools, colleges, universities. He certainly is not suited to become a part of bureaucratic government. He doesn't fit well into the military. Since our culture has developed all these orthodoxies and forms of present-day life, we have to ask ourselves seriously if this New Man is simply a deviant misfit, or whether he is something more hopeful.

There is another reason for thinking deeply and soberly about him. He is almost the antithesis of the Puritan culture, with its strict beliefs and controls, which founded our country. He is very different from the person admired by the industrial revolution, with that person's ambition and productivity. He is deeply opposite to the Communist culture, with its controls on thought and behavior in the interest of the state. He in no way resembles the medieval man—the man of faith and force, of monasteries and Crusades. He would not be congenial with the man produced by the Roman Empire—the practical, disciplined man. He is also very alien to today's culture in the United States, which emphasizes computerized technology, and the man in uniform—whether military, police, or government inspector.

If, then, he is new in so many ways, if he deviates so deeply from almost all of the gradually developed norms of the past and even the present, is he just a sport in the evolutionary line, soon to die out or be discarded? Personally I do not believe so. I believe he is a viable creature. I have the conviction that he is the person of tomorrow, and that perhaps he has a better chance of survival than we do. But this is only my own opinion.

I have talked about him at some length, but I have made no attempt to describe his attitudes, his characteristics, his convictions. I should like to do this very briefly. I would like to say that I know of no one individual to whom all of the following statements would apply. I am also keenly aware that I am describing a minority, probably a small minority, of our present-day population, but I am convinced that it is a growing minority. What follows is a groping, uncertain characterization of what I see as the New Man. Some of his qualities are probably temporary ones, as he struggles to break free from the cocoon of his culture. I shall try to indicate these. Some, I believe, represent the process person he is becoming. Here then are some of his characteristics as I see them.

He has no use for sham, facade, or pretense, whether in interpersonal relationships, in education, in politics, in religion. He values authenticity. He will not put up with double talk. He hates statements such as these: "Cigarette smoking is a romantic, exciting pleasurable, satisfying thing—(and of course it kills many through lung cancer)." Or, "We are following a noble pathway in protecting South Vietnam and living up to our commitments and treaties—(but in doing so we kill thousands of men, women and children, many of them completely innocent, others whose only crime is that they have a goal for their country different than ours)." He hates this kind of thing with a passion. He regards the current culture as almost completely hypocritical. I believe that this hatred for phonyness is perhaps the deepest mark of the New Man.

He is opposed to all highly structured, inflexible, institutions. He wants organizations to be fluid, changing, adaptive, and *human*. It will be clear from what follows how deep is his dislike for bureaucracy, rigidity, form for form's sake. He simply will not buy these qualities.

He finds educational institutions mostly irrelevant and futile so far as he is concerned. His unrest—in college and high school —arises out of a hundred specific issues, but none of these issues would be important if his school were truly meaningful for him. He sees traditional education as it is—the most rigid, outdated, incompetent institution in our culture.

He wants *his* learning to involve feelings, to involve the *living* of learnings, the *application* of relevant knowledge, a *meaning* in the here and now. Out of these elements he sometimes likes to become involved in a searching for new approximations to the truth, but the pursuit of knowledge purely for its own sake is not characteristic.

Religious institutions are perceived as definitely irrelevant and frequently damaging to human progress. This attitude toward religious institutions does not mean at all that he has no concern for life's mysteries or for the search for ethical and moral values. It seems, in fact, that this person of tomorrow is deeply concerned with living in a moral and ethical way, but the morals are new and shifting, the ethics are relative to the situation, and the one thing that is not tolerated is a discrepancy between verbal standards and the actual living of values.

He is seeking new forms of community, of closeness, of intimacy, of shared purpose. He is seeking new forms of communication in such a community—verbal and nonverbal, feelingful as well as intellectual. He recognizes that he will be living his transient life mostly in temporary relationships and that he must be able to establish closeness quickly. He must also be able to leave these close relationships behind, without excessive conflict or mourning.

He has a distrust of marriage as an institution. A man-woman relationship has deep value for him only when it is a mutually enhancing, growing, flowing relationship. He has little regard for marriage as a ceremony, or for vows of permanence, which prove to be highly impermanent.

He is a searching person, without any neat answers. The only thing he is certain of is that he is uncertain. Sometimes he feels a nostalgic sadness in his uncertain world. He is sharply aware of the fact that he is only a speck of life on a small blue and white planet in an enormous universe. Is there a purpose in this universe? Or only the purpose he creates? He does not know the answer but he is willing to live with this anxious uncertainty.

There is a rhythm in his life between flow and stability, between changingness and structure, between anxiety and temporary security. Stability is only a brief period for the consolidation of learning before moving on to more change. He always exists in this rhythm of process.

He is an open person, open to himself, close to his own feelings. He is also open to and sensitive to the thoughts and feeling of others and to the objective realities of his world. He is a highly aware person.

He is able to communicate with himself much more freely than any previous man. The barriers of repression which shut off so much of man from himself are definitely lower than in preceding generations. Not only is he able to communicate with himself, he is also often able to express his feelings and thoughts to others, whether they are negative and confronting in nature, or positive and loving.

His likes and dislikes, his joys and his sorrows are passionate and are passionately expressed. He is vitally alive.

He is a spontaneous person, willing to risk newness, often willing to risk saying or doing the wild, the far-out thing. His adventuresomeness has an almost Elizabethan quality—*everything* is possible, *anything* can be tried.

Currently he likes to be "turned on"—by many kinds of experiences and by drugs. This dependence on drugs for a consciousness-expanding experience is often being left behind as he discovers that he prefers to be "turned on" by deep and fresh and vital interpersonal experiences, or by meditation.

Currently he often decides to obey those laws which he regards as just and to disobey those which he regards as unjust, taking the consequences of his actions. This is a new phenomenon. We have had a few Thoreaus but we have never had hundreds of people, young and old alike, willing to obey some laws and disobey others on the basis of their own personal moral judgment.

He is active—sometimes violently, intolerantly, and self-righteously active—in the causes in which he believes. Hence he arouses the most extreme and repressive antipathies in those who are frightened by change.

He can see no reason why educational organizations, urban areas, ghetto conditions, racial discrimination, unjust wars, should be allowed to remain unchanged. He has a sustained idealism which is linked to his activism. He does not hope that things will be changed in 50 years; he intends to change them *now.*

He has a trust in his own experience and a profound *distrust* of all external authority. Neither pope nor judge nor scholar can convince him of anything which is not borne out by his own experience.

He has a belief in his own potential and in his own direction. This belief extends to his own dreams of the future and his intuitions of the present.

He can cooperate with others with great effectiveness in the pursuit of a goal which he is convinced is valid and meaningful. He never cooperates simply in order to conform or to be a "good fellow."

He has a disregard for material things and material rewards. While he has been accustomed to an affluent life and readily uses all kinds of material things, taking them for granted, he is quite unwilling to accept material rewards or material things if they mean that he must compromise his integrity in order to do so.

He likes to be close to elemental nature; to the sea, the sun, the snow; flowers, animals, and birds; to life, and growth, and death. He rides the waves on his surfboard; he sails the sea in a small craft; he lives with gorillas or lions; he soars down the mountain on his skies.

These are some of the qualities which I see in the New Man, in the man who is emerging as the person of tomorrow. He does not fit at all well into the world of the present. He will have a rough time trying to live in his own way. Yet, if he can retain the qualities I have listed so briefly, if he can create a culture which would nourish and nurture those qualities, then it may be that he holds a great deal of promise for all of us and for our future. In a world marked by incredibly rapid technological change, and by overwhelming psychological sham and pretense, we desperately need both his ability to live as a fluid process, and his uncompromising integrity.

Perhaps some of you in this audience will have resonated to my description because you see in yourself some of these same qualities emerging in you. To the extent that you are becoming this person of tomorrow and endeavoring to sharpen and refine his qualities in a constructive fashion, I wish you well. May you find many enduring satisfactions as you struggle to bring into being, within yourself and in your relationships with others, the best of this New Man.

EPILOGUE

Dear Reader,

I cannot write an epilogue. There is no conclusion to education, there is only a process, and the process has no conclusion.

A process of emerging education.
An experimental approach to learning.
The integration of the "I" and the "educator."
The "I" as the creator, I, creating an environment for discovery.
The when, where, and how of learning.
Cooperative living . . . The child and the adult.
I and Thou.
The poetry of self.
My own rhythm.
Resting.
Flowing.
The heat of energy awakening the dormant "I."
I am flowing, I am dancing. I am singing, I am crying.
Together and apart.
The flow of in and out contracting and expanding.
One generation flowing into the other.
Getting through the impasse, transcending the status quo.

From Janet Lederman, *Anger and the Rocking Chair*

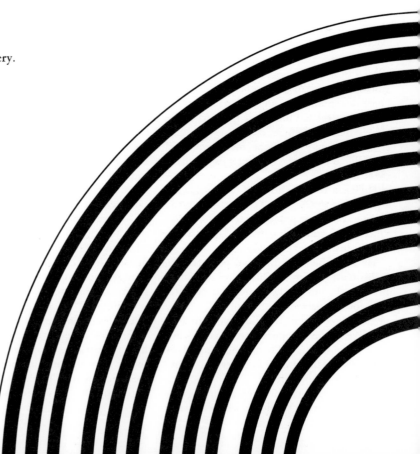

Mr. X on page 51 is *Socrates*.
"Miss Tilly" on page 141 likes words with double consonants.
The resolution to the class conflict on page 158 follows:

By the next day, the underground was organized. The kids came in to class and scattered themselves around the room. When the victims walked in, they couldn't find seats together. Delightful! I'd never even thought of the divide-and-conquer tactic.

It was a tense class. Everyone seemed waiting for a chance to make his move. At the first bitchy remark of the day, Haughty Mae stood up and put one hand on her hip and said in a very slurry, dramatic way, "Pardon me, but the teacher is trying to teach." She sat down like a queen. It was probably the first time in her life she'd fought without fists. She seemed as pleased with herself as I was.

It was a long hour, but by the end it was obvious that the balance of power had changed. By the end of the week the girls had begun to do some work. A week later, one of them smiled at me. I smiled back, and the day after she was perched on my desk showing me snapshots of her boyfriend. Frankie walked in on the scene, and gave me a very grownup-type smile. He'd won, and he wasn't even gloating.

From Sunny Decker, *An Empty Spoon*

How do you feel about the group's solution to its problem? Can you think of alternative methods Sunny Decker and her class might have used to deal with "the victims"?

The Tangram is a seven piece Chinese puzzle. All pieces can be made from a square: two small, one medium-sized and two large triangles, plus a square and a lozenge shaped piece. Make your own pieces and see how many recognizable shapes you can create from different arrangements of the parts.

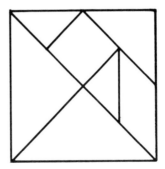

People, Places, and Things

Find out what's going on out there. Send a self-addressed, stamped envelope, get on the mailing list, ask for information.

Alternatives Foundation, 1526 Gravenstein Hwy. No., Sebastopol, Calif. 97452. Directories of free schools, personal growth, social change.

Ant Farm, 247 Gate 5 Rd., Sausalito, Calif. 94965. Changing environments.

Apprenticeship Service Program, L. Haas, R.D. 403A, Upper Black Eddy, Pa. 18972.

Association for Humanistic Psychology, 584 Page St., San Francisco, Calif. 94117. School list, growth centers.

Borton, T., and Alschuler, A., Harvard Graduate School of Education, Cambridge, Mass. A bibliography on Affective Education, psychological education, the Eupsychian Network, Curriculum of Concerns, personological education, Synectics, Personal Learning, etc.

Catalog for Learning Things, The Workshop For Learning Things, 55 Chapel St., Newton, Mass. 02160.

Catalog of Free Teaching Materials, G. Salisbury, P.O. Box 1075, Ventura, Calif. 93001.

Center for Educational Reform, 2115 S Street N. W., Washington, D.C. 20008.

Center for the Study of Development and Social Change, 1430 Massachusetts Ave., Cambridge, Mass. 02138. Copy of Paolo Freire monograph on education, etc.

Children's Music Center, 5373 West Pico Blvd., Los Angeles, Calif. 90019.

Centro Intercultural de Documentacion, Order from CIDOC, APDO 479, Cuernavaca, Mexico. Free catalog.

Committee for Freedom of Choice in Education, Box 3223, Inglewood, Calif. "The Case Against Public Education," article.

Community Resource Center, 21–41 East 117 Street and Third Avenue, New York, N.Y. 10035.

Council for Parks and Playgrounds, 15 Gramercy Park, New York, N.Y. 10003. List of playground equipment.

Craft Catalogue and Idea Book, Lewiscraft, 284–286 King St. West, Toronto 2B, Ontario, Canada.

Creative Playthings, 5757 West Century Blvd., Los Angeles, Calif. 90045.

Cuisenaire Company of America, Inc., 9 Elm Avenue, Mt. Vernon, N.Y. 10550.

Center for Volunteer Service Assn, CVSA, Room 830, 475 Riverside Dr., New York, N.Y. 10027. Catalog of voluntary service projects and placements with 150 worldwide agencies.

Domebook One and Two. Pacific Domes, Box 219, Bolinas, Calif. 94924. Art of domebuilding.

Dover Publications, 180 Varick Street, New York, N.Y. 10014. Catalog of original reprints.

Education Development Center, EDC Resources Center, 42 Hawthorne Street, Roxbury, Mass. 02119.

Edmund Scientific Catalog, 3 Bridge St., Newton, Mass. 02195.

Education Innovation, Productive Thinking Program, Box 9248, Berkeley, Calif. 94719. Comic strip detective stories and problems to solve.

El Centro Commercial, Box 1074, San Antonio, Tex. Spanish list. Catalogo 1966 free.

Esalen Institute, 1776 Union St., San Francisco, Calif. 94123; also Big Sur, Calif. 93920. Growth center.

Freestone Publishing Company, 440 Bohemian Wy, Freestone, Calif. 95472. *Rasberry Exercises* I and II. How to start your own school and how to get on with it.

Group for Environmental Education, 1214 Arch St., Philadelphia, Pa. 19107.

Guide to Alternative Service, National Interreligious Service Board for Conscientious Objectors, 1550 Washington Bldg., Fifteenth St. and New York Avenue N.W., Washington, D.C. 20005.

How To Get A Job Overseas, Arc Books, Inc., 219 Park Ave. South, New York, N.Y. 10003.

Humanitas Systems, Green Valley School, Box 606, Orange City, Fla. 32763. Free catalog, electronic gear, math primer.

Integrative Materials Exchange, Center for Integrative Education, 12 Church St., New Rochelle, N.Y. 10805. Bibliography.

League for Industrial Democracy, 112 E. 19 Street, New York, N.Y. 10003. Anthology, "Urban School Crisis."

Learning Directory, A Comprehensive Guide to Teaching Materials, over 200,000 items. Westinghouse Learning Corp., 100 Park Ave., New York, N.Y. 10017.

Lichtman, J., 53 Stanley Rd., South Orange, N.J. 07079. List of free universities and experimental colleges, also issue #62, *New Schools Exchange Newsletter*.

Lucis Trust Library, 866 United Nations Plaza, Suite 556–567, New York, N.Y. 10017. Magical books.

Maslow, Abraham, "Eupsychian (Utopian) Network," names and addresses, Appendix, in *Toward A Psychology of Being*. (New York: Van Nostrand, 1968.)

Media Learning Design, Box 239, Rt. 2, Hobenwald, Tenn. 38462.

National Information Centre for Educational Media, University of Southern California, Los Angeles, Calif. 90007. Clearing house for films, tapes, etc.

National Training Laboratories Institute for Behavioral Science, 1201 16th St. N.W., Washington, D.C.

Neal, J. A. Reference Guide for Travelers. (R. R. Bowker: New York, 1969.) At your local library.

New Life Environmental Designs Institute, 5701 Marshall Foch, New Orleans, La. 70124.

New Nation Seed Fund, Box 4026, Philadelphia, Pa. 19118. Send 25¢, 50¢, $1 "to help alternative schools get started and existing ones to stay alive." George Dennison, Paul Goodman, Nat Hentoff, John Holt, Jonathan Kozol.

New Schools Manual, New Directions Community School, 445 Tenth St., Richmond, Calif. 94801.

Nichols, M., P. O. Box 2945, Stanford, Calif. 94305, Multicultural educational materials bibliography.

Ontario Institute for Studies in Education, 252 Bloor St. West, Toronto 5, Ontario, Canada.

Parks Council, 80 Central Park West, New York, N.Y. List of manufacturers of playground equipment. Write to individual firms for free samples, etc.

Pentagon, Washington, D.C., Chief of Naval Operations. Ships' logs, aerial photographs, weather balloons, etc.

Portola Institute, Inc., 1115 Merrill St., Menlo Park, Calif. 94025. Innovative educational projects. Portola Institute, *The Last Whole Earth Catalog, Access to Tools* (New York: Random House, 1971).

Postman, N., and Weingartner, C. *Soft Revolution*. Resource section. "Getting It Together Also Means Keeping It Together" (New York: Delacorte Press, 1971).

Puppetry Store, Ashville, O. 43103. Catalog.

Radical Education Project, Box 625, Ann Arbor, Mich. 48107.

Robin's Distributing Company, 6 North 13th St., Philadelphia, Pa. 19107. Free catalog, black reading list.

San Francisco Switchboard, 1830 Fell St., San Francisco, Calif. 94117.

School Services Publications, Pinck Leodas Assoc., Inc., 2000 Massachusetts Ave., Cambridge, Mass. 02140. Catalog and mailing list.

School Works, 33 Union Sq.W., New York, N.Y. 10003. *Some Notes On Making Places For Small People.*

Schools for the Future, 821 Broadway, New York, N.Y.

Selective Educational Equipment, 3 Bridge St., Newton, Mass. 02195. Catalog.

700 Science Experiments For Everyone, Doubleday & Co., Inc. 501 Franklin Ave., Garden City, N.Y. 11531.

Smithsonian Short-Lived Phenomena Center, 60 Garden St., Cambridge, Mass. 02138. Event cards written by scientists reporting plagues, earthquakes, and squirrel migrations as they happen.

SPANNER, Three by Five . . . And Beyond, Box 2602, Stanford, Calif. 94305. Resource pool experimental education.

Spoken Arts, Inc., 310 North Ave., New Rochelle, N.Y. 10801.

Student Information Center, 3210 Grace St. N.W. Washington, D.C. 20007.

Superintendent of Documents, U.S. Government Printing Office, Washington, D.C. 20402. Mailing list.

Synectics, A Way of Increasing Creativity, Problem-Solving Ability, Discovery, and Consciousness by Using Metaphorical Thinking, Synectics Education System, 121 Brattle St., Cambridge, Mass. 02138.

Teacher Dropout Center, Box 521, Amherst, Mass. 01002. Information on jobs and school list.

Teacher Organizing Project, New University Project, New University Conference, 852 West Belmont, Rm. #2, Chicago, Ill. 60657. Pamphlet, "Classes and Schools: A Radical Definition For Teachers."

The Sun, Farrallones Designs Institute, 731 Virginia St., Berkeley, Calif. Changing the environment.

The Thirties Box, Media Group, Department of Computer Applications, OISE, 102 Bloor St. West, Toronto 5, Ontario, Canada.

Travelers' Directory, Editor, Kacalanos, P. 51-02 39th Ave., Woodside, N.Y. 11377.

Vocations for Social Change, Canyon, Calif. 94516. Job listings in fields like peace, community organizing, and education.

Washington Area Free School Clearinghouse, 1609 19th St. N.W., No. 1, Washington, D.C. 20009.

Whole Earth Access Co., 2466 Shattuck Ave., Berkeley, Calif. 94704.

Whole Earth Cooperative, 845 E. Johnson, Madison, Wisc.

Whole Earth Truck Store, 558 Santa Cruz Ave., Menlo Park, Calif. 94025.

World Game Center, University of Southern Illinois, Carbondale, Ill.

Woulf, C. The Free Learner, 4615 Canyon Rd., El Sobrante, Calif. 94803. Survey of experimental schools, San Francisco Bay Area.

Zome Primer, Baer, S. Zomeworks Corp., P.O. Box 712, Albuquerque, N.M. 87103. Playground climbers, etc.

Periodicals

Ask for a free single copy.

About Education, 8th Floor, 219 Broad St., Philadelphia, Pa.

Anarchy Magazine, Freedom Press, 84A White Chapel, High Street, London, England, UK.

Behavior Today, Human Science Newsletter, Box 2993, Boulder, Colo. 80302.

Berkeley Tribe, P.O. Box 9043, Berkeley, Calif.

Big Rock Candy Mountain, Portola Institute, 1115 Merrill St., Menlo Park, Calif. 94025. This catalog takes over where Whole Earth left off.

Change, 59 E. 54th St., New York, N.Y. 10022.

Colloquy, United Church Press, 391 Steel Way, Lancaster, Pa.

Dialogist, King's College, Wilkes-Barre, Pa. 19702.

Earth, Earth Publishing Corp., The Agriculture Building, The Embarcadero at Mission, San Francisco, Calif. 94105.

Earth Read Out/SW, Box 1048, Las Vegas, N.M.

Eco-Log, Students Organized for Survival and the World, Cornell College, Mt. Vernon, Ia.

Expand, Voice of the Children, 200 Gold St., Brooklyn, N.Y. 11201.

Explorations, P.O. Box 1254, Berkeley, Calif. 94701.

Free People's Exchange Newsletter, Arrakis, R.F.D. 1, Jeffersonville, N.Y. 12748.

Free School Press, Box 22, Saturna Island, B.C., Canada.

Friends of the Earth, 451 Pacific, San Francisco, Calif. 94133.

Good Times, 2377 Bush St., San Francisco, Calif.

Grade Teacher, 23 Leroy Ave., Darien, Conn. 06820.

Green Revolution, Rt. 1, Box 129, Freeland, Md. 21053.

Harvard Educational Review, Longfellow Hall, Appian Wy, Cambridge, Mass. 02138.

Idea Exchange, Education Associates, Inc., Upward Bound, 171 Mass Ave., Washington, D.C.

Inequality in Education, Center for Law and Education, Harvard University, 38 Kirkland St., Cambridge, Mass.

Insights, New School of Behavioral Studies in Education, University of North Dakota, Grand Forks, N.D. 58201.

Integrated Education, 343 S. Dearborn St., Chicago, Ill. 60604.

Kaiser Aluminum News, Kaiser Corp., Kaiser Center 866, Oakland, Calif. 94604.

Libertarian Teacher, 36 Devonshire Rd., Mill Hill, London, NW 7, England, UK.

Los Angeles Free Press, 7813 Beverly Blvd., Los Angeles, Calif.

Manas, P.O. Box 32112, El Sereno Station, Los Angeles, Calif.

Media and Methods, 134 North 13 St.', Philadelphia, Pa. 19107.

Mother Earth News, P.O. Box 38, Madison, O.

Motivation Quarterly, Center for Study of Motivation and Human Abilities, College of Education, Ohio State University, Columbus, O.

Motive, Box 871, Nashville, Tenn. 37202.

Natural Life Styles, 53 Main St., New Paltz, N.Y. 12561.

New Directions in Teaching, a nonjournal committed to the improvement of undergraduate teaching, Department of Education, Bowling Green State University, Bowling Green, O. 43402.

New England Free Press, 691 Tremont St., Boston, Mass. 02118.

New Republic, 1244 19th St. N.W., Washington, D.C.

New School of Education Journal, 4304 Tolman Hall, University of California, Berkeley, Calif. 94720.

New Schools Exchange, 301 E. Canon Perdido, Santa Barbara, Calif. 93101. Free school directory and "people seeking places, places seeking people."

New York Review of Books, 250 W. 57 St., New York, N.Y. 10019.

No More Teachers' Dirty Looks, Bay Area Radical Teachers Organizing Committee, 1445 Stockton St., San Francisco, Calif. 94133.

Observations from the Treadmill, Yanow, M., 357 Hidden River Rd., Narbeth, Pa. 19072.

Outside the Net, Box 184, Lansing, Mich. 48901.

Psychology Today, P.O. Box 60407, Terminal Annex, Los Angeles, Calif. 90060.

Radicals in the Professions, Newsletter of Radical Education Project, Box 625, Ann Arbor, Mich.

Realist, 595 Broadway, New York, N.Y. 10012.

Red Pencil and Red Pencil Bulletin, Ewen, P., 131 Magazine St., Cambridge, Mass. 02139.

Rolling Stone, 746 Brannon St., San Francisco, Calif. 94103.

Saturday Review, 380 Madison Ave., New York, N.Y. 10017.

Summerhill Society Bulletin, 339 Lafayette Street, New York, N.Y. 10012, or 1778 S. Holt, Los Angeles, Calif. 90035.

Synergy. At the main branch of your public library.

Teacher Paper, 3932 SE Main, Portland, Ore. 97214.

This Magazine Is about Schools, 56 Esplanade St. E., Suite 301, Toronto 215, Ontario, Canada.

Village Voice, 80 University Place, New York, N.Y.

Wilderness Camping, Box 1186, Scotia, N.Y. 12302.

Films

Make your own. Order "clear leader" 16-mm. film on which to draw, scratch, or stamp. Tape your own sound. Check your college film catalogs for complete listings of films.

American Documentary Films, 379 Bay St., San Francisco, Calif. 94113 or American Documentary Co., ADC, 336 W. 84th New York, N.Y.

Audio Film Center, 34 MacQuesten Pkwy So., Mt. Vernon, N.Y. 10550.

Brandon Films, 221 W. 57th St., New York, N.Y. 10019.

Churchill Films, 622 North Robertson St., Los Angeles, Calif.

Contemporary Films, McGraw-Hill Publishing Co., Princeton Rd., Hightstown, N.J. 08520.

Education Development Center EDC, 55 Chapel St., Newton, Mass.

Educator's Guide to Free Films, Educators Progress Service, Randolph, Wisc. 53956.

Film Exchange, 2031 Pine St., Philadelphia, Pa. 19103.

Films, Inc., 4420 Oakton Street, Skokie, Ill. 60076.

Janus Films, 24 W. 58 St., New York, N.Y. 10019.

National Film Board of Canada, 1 Lombard St., Toronto, Ontario, Canada.

Newsreel Documentary Films, 162 North Clinton St., Rm 204, Chicago, Ill. 60606; 322 7th Avenue, New York, N.Y. 10001; 1234 Market St., Rm. 104, San Francisco, Calif. 94102.

Polymorph Films, 331 Newbury St., Boston, Mass.

Universal 16, 221 Park Ave. So., New York, N.Y. 10003.

United Artists UA/16 729 Seventh Ave., New York, N.Y. 10036.

Students' Writings

Baron, V., ed. *Here I Am*. New York: Bantam Books, 1970.

Stembridge, J. *I Play Flute*, Flute Publications, Box 109, Tougaloo, Miss. 1966.

Kids Magazine, Box 30, Cambridge, Mass. 02139.

Joseph, S., ed. *The Me Nobody Knows: Avon, 1969.*

Kohl, H. and Cruz, V. *Stuff*, New York: World Publishing, 1970.

Lewis, R., ed. *Journeys*. New York: Simon & Schuster, 1969; *Miracles*. New York: Simon & Schuster, 1966; *There Are Two Lives*. New York: Simon & Schuster, 1970; *The Wind and the Rain*. New York: Simon & Schuster, 1968.

Operation Rainbow, Fall 1970, The Fourth Street i, c/o Brigade in Action, 136 Ave. C, New York, N.Y. 10009.

Teachers and Writers Collaborative Newsletter, Pratt Center for Community Improvement, 244 Vanderbilt Ave., Brooklyn, N.Y. 11205.

The School That I'd Like, Baltimore, Maryland, Penguin, 1969.

Jordan, J. and Bush, T., eds. *Voice of the Children*. New York: Holt, Rinehart and Winston, 1970.

What's Happening: An Independent Student Voice, Inc., Box 113, Teachers College, Columbia University, New York, N.Y. 10027.

Books

Perhaps you'd rather browse in a bookstore or library or read some of the books excerpted in this anthology or find some favorites in this list.

Agee, J., and Walkers, E. *Let Us Now Praise Famous Men*, New York: Ballantine, 1960.

Allport, G. *Pattern and Growth in Personality*. New York: Holt, Rinehart and Winston, 1961.

Axline, V. *Dibs in Search of Self*, New York: Ballantine, 1966.

Barron, F. *Creativity and Psychological Health*, New York: Van Nostrand, 1963.

Barzun, Jacques, *Teacher in America*, Boston: Little, Brown, 1944.

Bateson, G. *Dialogue on Education*, Indianapolis: Bobbs-Merrill, 1967.

Bazeley, E. T. *Homer Lane and the Little Commonwealth*, New York: Schocken Books, 1928.

Becker, E. *Beyond Alienation*. New York: George Braziller, 1967.

Beck, J. *How to Raise a Brighter Child*. New York: Simon & Schuster, 1967.

Berg, I. *Education and Jobs: The Great Training Robbery*. New York: Praeger, 1970.

Berman, S. *Underground Guide to the College of Your Choice*. New York: New American Library, 1971.

Bettelheim, B. *The Informed Heart*. New York: Free Press, 1960.

———. *Love Is Not Enough*. New York: Free Press, 1968.

———. *Children of the Dream*. New York: Macmillan, 1969.

Bigge, M. *Learning Theories for Teachers*. New York: Harper & Row, 1964.

Birmingham, J., ed. *Our Time Is Now, Notes from the High School Underground*. New York: Praeger, 1970.

Bois, J.S. *The Art of Awareness*. Dubuque, Iowa: Wm. C. Brown, 1966.

Borton, T. *Reach, Touch, and Teach: Student Concerns and Process Education*. New York: McGraw-Hill, 1970.

Boulding, K. *The Meaning of the Twentieth Century*. New York: Harper & Row, 1964.

Boyd, W. *The Emile of Jean Jacques Rousseau*. New York: Teachers College, Columbia University, 1956.

Bronfenbrenner, U. *Two Worlds of Childhood: U.S. & U.S.S.R.* New York: Basic Books, 1970.

Brown, G.I. *Human Teaching for Human Learning*. New York: Viking, 1970.

Bruner, J. *The Process of Education*. Cambridge, Mass.: Harvard University Press, 1960.

———. *Toward a Theory of Instruction*. Cambridge, Mass.: Harvard University Press, 1966.

Brunton, P. *In Quest of the Overself*. New York: Dutton, 1938.

Buber, M. *On Knowing*. New York: Atheneum, 1962.

Bucke, R. *Cosmic Consciousness*. New York: Dutton, 1923.

Bugental, J. *The Search for Authenticity*. New York: Holt, Rinehart and Winston, 1965.

Bushnell, D.D., and Allen, D.W., eds. *The Computer in American Education*. New York: John Wiley & Sons, 1967.

Carpenter, E.S., and McLuhan, M., eds. *Explorations in Communications*, Beacon Press, Boston, 1960.

Castaneda, C. *A Separate Reality, Further Conversations with Don Juan*. New York: Simon & Schuster, 1971.

Channon, G. *Homework! Required Reading for Teachers and Parents*. New York: Outerbridge & Dienstfrey, 1970.

Clark, K. *Dark Ghetto*. New York: Harper & Row, 1965.

Coleman, M. *Adolescents and the Schools*. New York: Basic Books, 1965.

Combs, A. *Perceiving, Behaving, Becoming: A New Focus for Education*. Washington, D.C.: Association for Supervision and Curriculum Development Yearbook, 1962.

Conant, J. *The Education of American Teachers*. New York: McGraw-Hill, 1963.

Cook, A., and Mack, H. *Schools Are for Children*, New York: Praeger, 1971.

Cremin, L. *The Transformation of the School*. New York: Knopf, 1961.

Cullum, A. *Push Back the Desks*. New York: Four Winds Press, 1967.

Dawson, H. *On the Outskirts of Hope*. New York: McGraw-Hill, 1968.

Dewey, J. *Experience and Education*. New York: Macmillan, 1938.

———. *Democracy and Education*. New York: Free Press, 1966.

Divoky, Diane. *How Old Will You Be in 1984?* New York: Avon, 1969.

Dunstan, M.J., and Garlan, P. *Worlds in the Making*. Englewood Cliffs, N.J.: Prentice-Hall, 1970.

Eble, K.E. *A Perfect Education*. New York: Collier, 1966.

Eddy, E. *Walk the White Line*. New York: Doubleday Anchor, 1967.

Engleman, S., and Engleman, T. *Give Your Child a Superior Mind*. New York: Simon & Schuster, 1966.

Erikson, E. *Childhood and Society*. New York: Norton, 1950.

———. *Identity: Youth and Crisis*. New York: Norton, 1968.

Fabun, D. *Children of Change*. Beverly Hills, Calif.: Glencoe Press, 1969.

———. *Dynamics of Change*. Englewood Cliffs, N.J.: Prentice-Hall, 1970.

Fader, D., and McNeil, E. *Hooked on Books, Program and Proof*. Berkeley, Calif.: Medallion Books, 1968.

Fadiman, J. *The Proper Study of Man*. New York: Macmillan Co., 1971.

Farber, J. *The Student as Nigger*. New York: Pocket Books, 1970.

Freire, Paolo. *The Pedagogy of the Oppressed*. New York: Herder and Herder, 1970.

Freud, S. *The Interpretation of Dreams*. New York: Modern Library, 1938.

Friedenberg, E. *The Vanishing Adolescent*. New York: Dell, 1959.

———. *Coming of Age in America*. New York: Vintage, 1965.

———. *Dignity of Youth and Other Atavisms*. Boston: Beacon, 1965.

Fromm, E. *The Art of Loving*. New York: Bantam, 1956.

———. *Man for Himself*. New York: Rinehart, 1947.

———. *The Sane Society*. New York: Rinehart, 1955.

———. *The Heart of Man*. New York: Harper & Row, 1964.

———. *The Revolution of Hope*. New York: Harper & Row, 1968.

Fuchs, E. *Teachers Talk*. New York: Doubleday Anchor, 1969.

Fuller, B. *Education Automation*. Carbondale, Ill.: Southern Illinois University Press, 1962.

Gagne, R.M. *The Conditions of Learning*. New York: Holt, Rinehart and Winston, 1965.

Gardner, J. *Excellence*. New York: Harper & Row, 1961.

———. *Self-Renewal*. New York: Harper & Row, 1963.

Gattegno, C. *Toward a Visual Culture*. New York: Outerbridge & Dienstfrey, 1969.

———. *What We Owe Children*, New York: Outerbridge & Dienstfrey, 1970.

Gibran, K. *The Prophet*. New York: Knopf, 1923.

Gibson, J.M., and Hall, J.C. *Damn Reading: A Case against Literacy*. New York: Vintage, 1969.

Ginnot, H.G., *Between Parent and Child*. New York: Macmillan, 1965.

———. *Between Parent and Teenager*. New York: Avon, 1969.

Glines, D.E. *Implementing Different and Better Schools*. Mankato, Minn.: Campus Publishing.

Goodman, M. *Movement Toward a New America*. New York: Knopf/Pilgrim Press, 1970.

Goodman, P. *Growing Up Absurd*. New York: Vintage, 1960.

———. *Compulsory Mis-Education*. New York: Vintage, 1962.

———. *The New Reformation, Notes of a Neolithic Conservative*. New York: Random House, 1970.

Gordon, A.K. *Games for Growth*. Science Research Associates, 1970.

Green, H. *I Never Promised You a Rose Garden*. New York: Signet, 1964.

Green, R.L., ed. *Racial Crisis in American Education*. Chicago: Follett Ed. Corp., 1969.

Grier, W., and Cobbs, P. *Black Rage*. New York: Bantam, 1968.

Gross, R. *The Teacher and the Taught*. New York: Dell, 1963.

Gross, R., and Gross B. *Radical School Reform*. New York: Simon & Schuster, 1970.

Gunther, B. *Sensory Awakening and Relaxation*. Big Sur, Calif.: Esalen Publications, 1967.

Hamberg, J. *Where It's At: A Research Guide for Community Organizing.* Radical Education Project, Box 625, Ann Arbor, Mich. 48107.

Hart, L. *The Classroom Disaster.* Columbia University, New York, Teachers College Press, 1969.

Hayakawa, S.H. *Language in Action.* New York: Harcourt, 1942.

Hentoff, N. *Our Children Are Dying.* New York: Viking, 1966.

Hickerson, N. *Education for Alienation.* Englewood Cliffs, N.J.: Prentice-Hall, 1966.

Highet, G. *The Art of Teaching.* New York: Knopf, 1950.

Holmes, G. *The Idiot Teacher.* London, England: Faber and Faber, 1952.

Holt, J. *The Underachieving School.* New York: Pitman, 1969.

———. *What Do I Do Monday?* New York: Dutton, 1970.

Hopkins, L.B. *Let Them Be Themselves: Language Arts Enrichment for Disadvantaged Children in Elementary Schools.* New York: Citation Press, 1969.

Horney, K. *Self-Analysis.* New York: Norton, 1942.

Hutchins, R. *The Learning Society.* New York: New American Library, 1969.

Huxley, A. *The Perennial Philosophy.* New York: Harper & Row, 1944.

Illich, Ivan. *Deschooling Society.* New York: Harper & Row, 1971.

———. *Celebration of Awareness: A Call for Institutional Revolution.* New York: Doubleday, 1970.

Jackson, P.W. *Life in Classrooms.* New York: Holt, Rinehart and Winston, 1968.

James, W. *Talks to Teachers.* New York: Henry Holt & Co., 1904.

Janov, A. *The Primal Scream.* New York: Dell, 1970.

Jerome, J. *Culture Out of Anarchy.* New York: Herder and Herder, 1970.

Tersild, A. *In Search of Self,* New York: Teachers College, Columbia Press, 1952.

———. *When Teachers Face Themselves.* New York: Teachers College, Columbia University Press, 1955.

Johnson, H. *The Other Side of Main Street.* New York: Columbia University Press, 1943.

Jones, R. *Fantasy and Feeling in Education.* New York: New York University Press, 1968.

Jourard, S.M. *Personal Adjustment.* New York: Macmillan, 1963.

———. *The Transparent Self.* New York: Van Nostrand, 1964.

Jung, C. *Modern Man in Search of a Soul.* New York: Harcourt, 1933.

———. *Memories, Dreams, Reflections.* New York: Vintage, 1963.

Kelley, E.C. *In Defense of Youth.* Englewood Cliffs, N.J.: Prentice-Hall, 1962.

———. *Education and the Nature of Man.* New York: Harper & Row, 1952.

Kenniston, K. *The Uncommitted Alienated Youth in American Society.* New York: Harcourt, 1965.

Kilpatrick, W.H. *Education for a Changing Civilization.* New York: Macmillan Co., 1930.

———. *Education and the Social Crisis.* New York: Liveright, 1932.

Koch, K. *Wishes, Lies, and Dreams.* New York: Chelsea House, 1970.

Krishnamurti. *Education and the Significance of Life.* New York: Harper & Row, 1953.

———. *The First and Last Freedom.* New York: Harper & Row, 1954.

Kunen, J.S. *The Strawberry Statement.* New York: Random House, 1969.

Laing, R.D. *The Divided Self.* Baltimore, Maryland: Penguin, 1965.

———. *The Politics of Experience.* New York: Ballantine, 1967.

———. *Knots.* New York: Pantheon, 1970.

Laliberte, N. and Kehl, R. *100 Ways to Have Fun with an Alligator and 100 Other Involving Art Projects.* Blauvelt, N.Y.: Art Education, Inc., 1969.

Lao Tsu. *The Way of Life.* New York: Mentor, 1955.

Laubach, Frank, and Laubach, Robert. *Toward World Literacy.* Syracuse, N.Y.: Syracuse University Press, 1960.

Lauter, P., and Howe, F. *The Conspiracy of the Young.* New York: World, 1970.

Leonard, G. *Education and Ecstasy.* New York: Dell, 1968.

Lewis, C.S. *Surprised by Joy.* New York: Harcourt, 1956.

Libarle, M. and Seligson, T., eds. *The High School Revolutionaries.* New York: Random House, 1970.

Lieberman, M. *Future of Public Education.* Chicago: University of Chicago Press, 1960.

Lingo, T.D. *Syllabus of Survival.* Adventure trails Survival School, Laughing Coyote Mountain, Black Hawk, Colo. 80422.

Lurie, E. *How to Change the Schools: A Parents' Action Handbook on How to Fight the System.* New York: Random House, 1970.

MacKinnon, F. *The Politics of Education.* Toronto: University of Toronto Press, 1962.

Macrorie, K. *Uptaught.* New York: Hayden, 1970.

Makarenko, A.S. *A Collective Family.* New York: Doubleday Anchor, 1967.

Marcuse. H. *Eros and Civilization.* Boston: Beacon, 1955.

Marin, P. *The Free People.* New York: Outerbridge and Diensfrey, 1969.

Marin, P., and Cohen, A. *Understanding Drug Abuse.* New York: Harper & Row, 1971.

Maslow, Abraham H. *Motivation and Psychology.* New York: Harper & Row, 1954.

———. *Toward a Psychology of Being.* New York: Van Nostrand Co., 1968.

May, R. *Man's Search for Himself.* New York: Signet, 1967.

———. *Love and Will.* New York: Norton, 1969.

Mayer, M. *The Schools.* New York: Harper & Row, 1961.

McLuhan, M. *Understanding Media: The Extensions of Man.* New York: McGraw-Hill, 1965.

——. *The Medium Is the Massage*, New York: Random House, 1967.

McNeil, D. *Moving Through Here*. New York: Knopf, 1970.

Missildine, W.H. *Your Inner Child of the Past*. New York: Simon & Schuster, 1963.

Montagu, A. *The Direction of Human Development*. New York: Harper & Row, 1955.

——. *Man in Process*. New York: World, 1961.

Montessori, M. *Dr. Montessori's Own Handbook*. New York: Schocken, 1965.

Moulds, G.H. *Thinking Straighter*. Dubuque, Iowa: W.C. Brown, 1965.

Moustakas, C. *The Self*. New York: Harper & Row, 1965.

——. *The Teacher and the Child*. New York: McGraw-Hill, 1956.

——. *Creativity and Conformity*. New York: Van Nostrand, 1967.

——. *The Authentic Teacher*. Cambridge, Mass.: Doyle, 1966.

Mumford, L. *The Transformations of Man*. New York: Harper & Row, 1956.

Neill, A.S. *Summerhill*. New York: Hart, 1960.

——. *Freedom Not License*. New York: Hart, 1966.

——. *Last Man Alive*. New York: Hart, 1969.

Nyberg, D. *Tough and Tender Learning*. Palo Alto, Calif.: National Press Books, 1971.

O'Brien, B. *Operators and Things*. New York: Ace, 1958.

Oettinger, A.G. *Run, Computer, Run*. Cambridge, Mass.: Harvard University Press, 1970.

O'Gorman, N. *The Storefront*. New York: Harper & Row, 1970.

O'Hara. *Over 2,000 Free Publications*. New York: New American Library.

O'Neill, W.F. *Selected Educational Heresies*. Glenview, Ill.: Scott, Foresman, 1969.

Otto, H., ed. *Explorations in Human Potentialities*. Springfield, Ill.: C.C Thomas, 1966.

Otto, H., and Mann, J., eds. *Ways of Growth*. New York: Viking, 1968.

Overstreet, H.A. *The Mature Mind*. New York: Norton, 1949.

Owens, C.M. *Discovery of the Self*. North Quincy, Mass.: Christopher, 1963.

Passow, A.H. *Education in Depressed Areas*. New York; Columbia University Press, 1963.

Patterson, R. *26 Ways of Looking at a Black Man and Other Poems*. New York: Award Books, 1969.

Perls, F. *Gestalt Therapy Verbatim*. Walnut Creek, Calif.: Real People Press, 1969.

——. *In and Out of the Garbage Pail*. Walnut Creek, Calif. Real People Press, 1969.

Peterson, H. *Great Teachers*. Newark, N.J.: Rugters University Press, 1946,

Piaget, J. *The Language and Thought of the Child*. New York: Humanities Press, 1959.

——. *Play, Dreams, and Imitation of Childhood*. New York: Norton, 1962.

——. *The Origins of Intelligence in Children*. New York: Norton, 1963.

Pines, M. *Revolution in Learning*. New York: Harper & Row, 1970.

Platt, J. *The Step to Man*. New York: Wiley, 1966.

Postman, Neil, and Weingartner, Charles. *The Soft Revolution, A Student Handbook for Turning Schools Around*. New York: Delacorte Press, 1971.

Pratt, Caroline. *I Learn From Children*. New York: Simon & Schuster, 1948.

Putney, Gail. *The Adjusted American*. New York: Harper & Row, 1964.

Read, H. *Education through Art*. New York: Pantheon Books, 1945.

——. *The Redemption of the Robot*. New York: Simon & Schuster, 1969.

Redl, Fritz, and Wineman, David. *Children Who Hate*. New York: Free Press, 1951.

Reik, T. *Of Love and Lust*. New York: Farrar, Straus, 1957.

Reissman, F. *The Culturally Deprived Child*. New York: Harper & Row, 1962.

Renfield, R. *If Teachers Were Free*. New York: Acropolis Books, 1969.

Repo S., ed. *This Book Is About Schools*. New York: Random House, 1970.

Richards, M.C. *Centering*. Middletown, Conn.: Wesleyan University Press, 1962.

Richmond, W.K. *The Teaching Revolution*. London, England: Methuen, 1967.

Riesman, D. *The Lonely Crowd*. New York: Doubleday Anchor, 1953.

Rogers, C. *On Becoming a Person*. Boston: Houghton Mifflin, 1961.

——. *Freedom to Learn*. Columbus, Ohio: Merrill, 1969.

Rogers, C., and Stevens, B. *Person to Person: The Problem of Being Human*. Walnut Creek, Calif.: Real People Press, 1967.

Rossi, P.H., and Biddle, B.J., eds. *The New Media and Education*. New York: Anchor, 1967.

Roszak, T.H., ed. *The Dissenting Academy*. New York: Vintage, 1967.

Rousseau, Jean Jacques. *Emile*. New York: Everyman's Library, Dutton, 1932.

Sarason, S. *Culture of the School and the Problem of Change*. Boston: Allyn and Bacon, 1971.

Satir, V. *Conjoint Family Therapy*. Palo Alto, Calif.: Science & Behavior Press, 1967.

Schoolboys of Barbiana, Letter to a Teacher. New York: Random House, 1970.

Sexton, P. *Education and Income*. New York: Viking, 1961.

——. *The Feminized Male*. New York: Viking, 1969.

Shostak, A.B. *Blue-collar World*. Englewood Cliffs, N.J.: Prentice-Hall, 1964.

Silberman, C. *Crisis in the Classroom*. New York: Random House, 1970.

Sinnott, E.W. *Matter, Mind, and Matter*. New York: Harper & Row, 1957.

Skinner, E.F. *Walden Two*. New York: Macmillan, 1948.

Snitzer, H. *Living at Summerhill*. New York: Collier, 1967.

Spiro, M.E. *Children of the Kibbutz*. New York: Schocken Books, 1967.

Sprott, W.J. *Human Groups*. Baltimore, Maryland: Penguin, 1958.

Standing, E.M. *The Montessori Method, A Revolution in Education*. New York: Schocken, 1966.

Stein, M. and Miller, L. *Blueprint for Counter Education: Curriculum, Handbook, Wall Decoration, Shooting Script*. New York: Doubleday, 1970.

Stephens, J.M. *The Process of Schooling*. New York: Holt, Rinehart and Winston, 1967.

Strouse, J. *Up Against the Law: The Legal Rights of People under 21*. New York: New American Library, 1970.

Sullivan, N. *Now Is the Time, Integration in the Berkeley Schools*. Bloomington, Ind.: Indiana University Press, 1970.

Tanner, R. *I Know a Place*. City Schools Curriculum, 60 Commercial Wharf, Boston, Mass. 02110.

Taylor, H. *The World as Teacher*. New York: Doubleday, 1968.

Teilhard de Chardin, P. *The Future of Man*. New York: Harper & Row, 1964.

Tillich, P. *The Courage to Be*. New Haven, Conn.: Yale University, 1952.

Tolstoy, L. *On Education*. Universit. Phoenix, 1967.

Torrence, E.P., and Myers, R.E. *Creative Learning and Teaching*. New York: Dodd, Mead and Co., 1970.

Tussman, J. *Experiment at Berkeley*. Oxford, England: Oxford University Press, n.d.

Urofsky, M., ed. *Why Teachers Strike*. New York: Anchor Books, 1970.

Vermont Department of Education. *Vermont Designs for Education*. Montpelier, Ver., 1969.

von Hilsheimer, G. *How to Live With Your Special Child*. Washington, D.C.: Acropolis, 1970.

Walmsley, J. *Neill and Summerhill*. Baltimore, Maryland: Penguin, 1969.

Warburg, S.S. *I Like You*. New York: Houghton Mifflin, 1965.

Wasserman, M. *The School Fix, NYC, USA*. New York: Outerbridge & Dienstfrey, 1970.

Watts, A.W. *The Book (on the Taboo Against Knowing Who You Are)*. New York: Collier, 1966.

——. *Nature, Man, and Woman*. New York: Pantheon, 1958.

——. *This Is It*. New York: Pantheon, 1960.

Weinstein, G. and Fantini, M. *The Disadvantaged*. New York: Harper & Row, 1968.

—— and ——. *Toward Humanistic Education*. New York: Praeger, 1970.

White, M. *Mirrors, Messages, Manifestations*. Aperture, Inc., 276 Park Ave. So., New York, N.Y., 1969.

Whitehead, A.N. *Aims of Education*. New York: Mentor, 1949.

Wright, N., ed. *What Black Educators Are Saying*. New York: Hawthorne, 1970.

ACKNOWLEDGMENTS

The Warm-up

xix   Arnold Arnold, *Pictures and Stories from Forgotten Children's Books*, with the permission of Dover Publications.

xxii   John Barton, *Egomania*, American Dialog, Summer, 1966.

xxiii   Arthur W. Combs, "What Can Man Become?" in *California Journal for Supervision and Curriculum Development* 4 (1961): 15–28. California Association for Supervision and Curriculum Development. Reprinted by permission of the author.

Chapter One

opp. 1   © Jules Feiffer, 1967. Reprinted with the permission of the artist.

1   William Saroyan, "The First Day of School," from *Little Children* (London: Faber & Faber Ltd., 1955). Reprinted with the permission of the author. Laurence Pollinger Ltd., and Harcourt Brace Jovanovich.

4   Jean Geoffroy, *The Infant School*, courtesy of the Birmingham Art Gallery, Birmingham, England.

5   William Steig, from *Agony in the Kindergarten*, reprinted with the permission of the artist.

6   Irene Paull, "To Die Among Strangers." Reprinted with the permission of the author and *Jewish Currents* New York, N.Y., which owns and retains the copyright.

12   Joyce A. Richardson, "Upon Hearing that My Son Sits All Day Under the Table at Nursery School." Copyright © 1969 by The Writer, Inc.

12   George Bernard Shaw, from *Pygmalion* from *Complete Plays* (N.Y.: Dodd and Co.; 1962.) Reprinted with the permission of The Society of Authors on behalf of the Bernard Shaw Estate.

12   From Chapter 12, from *Pygmalion in the Classroom* by Robert Posenthal and Lenore Jacobson. Copyright © 1968 by Holt, Rinehart and Winston, Inc.

12   Hughes Mearnes, "Johnny." From *Creative Power* by Hughes Mearnes. Dover Publications, Inc. New York, 1958. Reprinted through the permission of the publisher.

13   From "Woman as Nigger" by Naomi Weisstein, *Psychology Today* Magazine, October, 1969. Copyright © Communications/Research/Machines, Inc.

13   Reprinted with permission of The Macmillan Company from *When We Deal with Children* by Fritz Redl. Copyright © by The Free Press, a Division of The Macmillian Company.

13   Dan Lamblin, "Evaluation." Reprinted with the permission of the author.

14   Arnold Arnold, *Pictures and Stories from Forgotten Children's Books*, with the permission of Dover Publications.

15   Sybil Marshall, An Experiment in Education (New York: Cambridge University Press, 1966). Reprinted with permission of the publisher.

18   Charles M. Schulz, © 1967 United Features Syndicate, Inc. Reprinted by permission.

22   Madeline Gleason, "They Say to the Child" from *Poems* (San Francisco: Grabhorn Press, 1944). Reprinted with the permission of the publisher.

23   James Thurber, "University Days." From *Vintage Thurber* by James Thurber, copyright © 1963 (Hamish Hamilton, London.)

27   From *Human Teaching for Human Learning* by George Isaac Brown. Copyright © 1971 by George Brown. All rights reserved. Reprinted by permission of The Viking Press, Inc.

28   Brian McGuire, "On Achieving the Highest Grade Point Average," *The Daily Californian*, May 21, 1968. Reprinted with the permission of the publisher.

29   Calvin Ketter, "My Personal Experience," by permission of the author.

30   Robert Coles, from *Teacher and the Children of Poverty*, Potomac Institute, 1970. Reprinted by permission of the author.

30   Arthur W. Combs, "A Perceptual View of the Adequate Personality" from *Perceiving, Behaving, Becoming* ASCD 1962 Yearbook, ASCD Publications. Reprinted by permission of the author.

31   "Girl Graduate's Stunning Speech," *San Francisco Chronicle*, June 11, 1971. Reprinted by permission of the publisher.

Chapter Two

33   Abraham H. Maslow, "Some Education Implications of the Humanistic Psychologies, *Harvard Educational Review* 38 (Fall 1968): 685–96. Copyright © 1968 by President and Fellows of Harvard College. Reprinted by permission of the publishers.

36   From *The Story of My Life* by Hellen Keller copyright 1902, 1903, 1905 by Helen Keller. Reprinted by permission of Doubleday & Company Inc.

40   Terry Borton, from "Reach Touch and Teach," Copyright © 1969 Saturday Review, Inc. Reprinted by permission of the author and the publisher.

44   From *Toward Humanistic Education*, Gerald Weinstein and Mario D. Fantini, eds. © 1970 by The Ford Foundation. Published by Praeger Publishers, Inc. New York. Reprinted with permission.

46   Dan Lamblin, "Hey, Teacher," reprinted by permission of the author.

47   From George Leonard, *Education and Ecstasy*. Reprinted by permission of the publisher, Delcorte Press.

Chapter Three

48   Bond of Union, original lithograph by M. C. Escher. Photo courtesy of the Vorpal Gallery, San Francisco.

50   John Gauss, "Teacher Evaluation," *Phi Delta Kappan*, Jan. 1962. Reprinted by permission of the *Kappan*.

52   Charles Dickens, "M'Choakumchild's Schoolroom."

53   Arnold Arnold, *Pictures and Stories from Forgotten Children's Books* with the permission of Dover Publications.

56   Herman Hesse, from *Beneath the Wheel*. Copyright © 1970. Reprinted by permission of Farrar, Straus & Giroux, Inc.

57   Russell Hill, "This Is an English Test." Reprinted by permission of the author.

58   Kris Sagen, "The Kid Pinger," "The Bud," Berkeley Unified Schools, Vol. 2 No. 6, Feb. 1969. Reprinted by permission of the publisher.

59   William Stimson, "Instructor's Rebellion," *The Easterner*, April 1969. Reprinted by permission of the author.

60, 61   Reprinted by permission of The World Publishing Company from *36 Children* by Herbert Kohl. Copyright © 1967 by Herbert Kohl. Also by permission of A.M. Hrath & Company on behalf of the author and Victor Gollanczm Ltd; and by permission of the Robert Lescher Literary Agency.

60   Arnold Arnold, Pictures and *Stories from Forgotten Children's Books*, with the permission of Dover Publications.

61   Reprinted by permission of the publishers from Jerome S. Brunner, *Toward a Theory of Instruction*. Cambridge, Mass.: The Belknap Press of Harvard University Press, Copyright, 1966, by the President and Fellows of Harvard College.

62   Charles M. Schulz, © 1962 United Features Syndicate, Inc. Reprinted by permission.

63   From pp. 1–7 in *An Empty Spoon* Sunny Decker. Copyright © 1969 by Sunny Decker. Reprinted by permission of Harper & Row, Publishers, Inc.

68   Jay Neugeboren, "Luther" Reprinted with the permission of Farrar, Strauss & Giroux, Inc. from *Corky's Brother* by Jay Neugeboren, copyright © 1966, 1969 by Jay Neugeboren. Also reprinted with the permission of Victor Gollancz, Inc.

77   Reprinted with the permission of The Macmillan Company from *To Make a Difference* by Larry Cuban. Copyright © 1970 by The Free Press, a Division of The Macmillan Company.

Chapter Four

81   From *Teaching as a Subversive Activity* by Neil Postman and Charles Weingartner. Copyright © 1969 by Neil Postman and Charles Weingartner. Reprinted by permission of the publisher, Delacorte Press.

83   Jack R. Frymier, from "Stimulation and the Need to Know." Reprinted by permission of *Motivation Quarterly*, January 1971, Vol. 1, No. 2.

85   "British Infant Schools—American Style" by Beatrice and Ronald Gross. *Saturday Review*, 1970. Copyright © 1970 by Saturday Review Inc. Reprinted by permission of the publisher.

91   Barbara Shiel, "Class Journal," from Carl R. Rogers, *Freedom to Learn*, Charles E. Merrill Publishing Co., 1969. Reprinted by permission of the publisher.

95   Bonnie Barrett Stretch, "The Rise of the Free School," Saturday Review, June 20, 1970. Copyright © 1970 by Saturday Review, Inc. Reprinted by permission of the publisher.

105   From *Students Without Teachers* by Harold Taylor. Copyright © 1969 by McGraw-Hill Inc. Used with permission of McGraw-Hill Book Company.

105   Bruce McGregor "A Teacher" from *Miracles*, ed. Richard Lewis. Copyright © 1966 by Richard Lewis. Reprinted by permission of Simon & Schuster, Inc. and Penguin Books, Ltd.

106   From "The Zaddik" by Sheldon B. Kopp, *Psychology Today* Magazine, October 1969. Copyright © Communications/Research/Machines, Inc. Reprinted by permission of the publisher.

106   H. R. Wolf, "Teaching and Human Development: Truth's Body," *New Directions in Teaching* Vol. 2, No. 1, Summer-Fall, 1969. Reprinted by permission of the author and publisher.

107   Arthur W. Combs, "Signs of Creative Teaching" from *Perceiving, Behaving, Becoming*, ASKD 1962 Yearbook, ASCD Publications. Reprinted by permission of the author.

107   Theodore W. Hipple, "Teaching in a Vacuum." Reprinted from the February-March issue of *Education*. Copyright, 1969, by the Bobbs-Merrill Company, Inc. Reprinted by permission of the author and publisher.

109   John Dewey, *The Child and the Curriculum*. Reprinted by permission of the author and the University of Chicago Press.

110   Scott Hope, "Relations Stop Nowhere," Spring, 1970, *New Directions in Teaching*. Reprinted by permission of the author and publisher, and Daedalus.

110   Edna St. Vincent Millay, "The Cairn," from *Collected Poems* Harper & Row. Copyright © 1923, 1951 by Edna St. Vincent Millay and Norma Millay Ellis.

110   Donald McNassor from the *Northbay Paceline*, November 1967 Reprinted by permission of the author.

111   Sylvia Ashton-Warner. From *Myself*. Copyright © 1967 by Sylvia Aston-Warner. Reprinted by permission of Simon & Schuster and Martin Secker & Warburg Limited, Publishers.

112   From "A Teacher Affects Eternity" in *The Education of Henry Adams* by Henry Brooks Adams. Artist Williams Baziotes. Courtesy of the Container Corporation of America.

113   Frederick S. Perls, "The Gestalt Prayer" from *Gestalt Therapy Verbatim*, Real People Press, 1969. Reprinted by permission of the publisher.

Chapter Five

120   *The Listening Chamber* by René Magritte. Courtesy of William N. Copley, Photograph by N. Robin, New York.

121   Reprinted with permission of The Macmillan Company from *When We Deal with Children* by Fritz Redl. Copyright © by The Free Press, a Division of The Macmillan Company.

123   *The Country School* by Winslow Homer, Courtesy of the City Art Museum of Saint Louis.

126   *Chalk-In, Family Circle* Magazine 1970. Reprinted by permission of the publisher.

127   Arthur W. Combs, *Perceiving, Behaving, Becoming*, ASCD 1962 Yearbook ASCD Publications. Reprinted by permission of the author.

Chapter Six

129   James Marshall, "Conflicting Educational Interests," *Teaching and Learning*, Ethical Culture Schools of New York City. Reprinted by permission of the publisher.

130   William Steig, from *Agony in the Kindergarten*, reprinted with the permission of the artist.

131   David N. Aspy, "Readiness for Democracy and Teacher Training," *New Directions in Teaching*, Spring, 1970. Reprinted by permission of the author.

134   Arnold Arnold, *Pictures and Stories from Forgotten Children's Books* with the permission of Dover Publications.

135   Jerome S. Bruner, from "The Skill of Relevance or the Relevance of Skill," *Saturday Review*, April 18, 1970. Copyright 1970 Saturday Review, Inc. Reprinted by permission of the publisher.

136, 143   From pp. 36–46 in *The Workshop Way of Learning* by Earl C. Kelley. Copyright 1951 by Harper & Row, Publishers, Inc. Reprinted by the permission of the publishers.

143   H. R. Wolf, "Teaching and Human Development: Truth's Body," *New Directions in Teaching*, Vol. 2, No. 1, Summer–Fall, 1969. Reprinted by permission of the author and publisher.

144   Rachel M. Lauer, "General Semantics and the Future of Education," Vol. XXIV, No. 4, December 1967. Reprinted by permission of the International Society for General Semantics.

145   From *Culture Against Man* by Jules Henry. Copyright © 1963 by Random House, Inc. Reprinted by permission.

144   Arnold Arnold, *Pictures and Stories from Forgotten Children's Books* with the permission of Dover Publications.

145   Viola Soplin, *Improvisation for the Theater* (Evanston, Ill., Northwestern University Press, 1963). Reprinted by permission of the publisher.

147   Jerome S. Bruner, "The Skill of Relevance or the Relevance of Skill," *Saturday Review*, April 18, 1970. Copyright 1970, Saturday Review, Inc. Reprinted by permission of the publisher.

148   William Glasser, from *Schools Without Failure* (New York: Harper & Row, 1969). Reprinted by permission.

150   John Malcolm Brinnin, "Views of the Favorite Colleges" (New York: Alfred A. Knopf, Inc. 1924). Reprinted by permission of the author.

151   John Updike, "Tomorrow and Tomorrow and So Forth." Copyright © 1955 by John Updike. Originally appeared in *The New Yorker*. Reprinted from *The Same Door* by John Updike by permission of Andre Deutsch Ltd. and Alfred A. Knopf, Inc.

Chapter Seven

157   Fannie R. Staftel and George Shaftel, *Role—Playing for Social Values: Decision-Making in the Social Studies.* © 1967. Reprinted by permission of Prentice Hall, Inc., Englewood Cliffs, New Jersey.

158   From *An Empty Spoon* by Sunny Decker, Copyright © 1969 by Sunny Decker. Reprinted by permission of Harper & Row, Publishers, Inc.

158   Reprinted with permission of The Macmillan Company from *Between Man and Man* by Martin Buber, Copyright © Martin Buber, 1965. Also reprinted with the permission of Routledge & Kegan Paul Ltd.

159   J. L. Moreno, *Psychodrama*, Vol. 1 (Beacon, N.Y.: Beacon House, Inc. 1964). Reprinted by permission of the publisher.

159   William Glasser, from *Schools Without Failure* (New York: Harper & Row, 1969). Reprinted by permission.

161   Reprinted with permission of The Macmillan Company from *Living at Summerhill* by Herb Snitzer. Copyright © 1964 by Herb Snitzer.

163   Fannie R. Shaftel and George Shaftel, *Role-Playing for Social Values: Decision-Making in the Social Studies.* © 1967 Reprinted by permission of Prentice-Hall, Inc., Englewood Cliffs, New Jersey.

165   From p. 77 *The Culturally Deprived Child* by Frank Riessman (Harper & Row, 1962). Reprinted by permission.

165   Elwood Murray, "Sociodrama and Psychodrama in the College Basic Communication Class," in *Psychodrama and Sociodrama in American Education* (Beacon, N.Y.: Beacon House, Inc. 1964) Reprinted by permission of the publisher.

165   From the book *To Sir, with Love* by E.R. Braithwaite. © 1959 by E. R. Braithwaite. Published by Prentice-Hall, Inc. Englewood Cliffs, New Jersey, and Bodley Head, London. Reprinted by permission of Prentice-Hall and David Higham Associates, author's agents.

Chapter Eight

173   Reprinted with permission of The Macmillan Company from *When We Deal with Children* by Fritz Redl. Copyright © by The Free Press, a Division of The Macmillan Company.

175   From the book *How Children Learn* by John Holt. Copyright 1964 by Pitman Publishing Corporation. Reprinted by permission of the Pitman Publishing Corporation.

177   Samuel Moon, "Teaching the Self," from *Improving College and University Teaching*, Autumn, 1966. Copyright Oregan State University Press. Reprinted by permission of the publisher.

178, 179   From *Improving Teaching: The Analysis of Classroom Verbal Interaction*, by Edmund Amidon and Elizabeth Hunter. Copyright © 1966 by Holt, Rinehart and Winston, Inc. Reprinted by permission of the publisher.

180   From *The Medium is the Massage* by Marshall McLuhan and Quentin Fiore. Copyright © 1967 by Marshall McLuhan, Quentin Fiore, and Jerome Agel. By permission of Bantam Books, Inc. and Penguin Books Ltd.

180   Herbert Kohl, from *The Open Classroom*. Reprinted with permission from *The New York Review of Books*. Copyright © 1969 by Herbert Kohl.

180   Arnold Arnold, *Pictures and Stories from Forgotten Children's Books* with the permission of Dover Publications.

180   Mai-Thu, *The Class*. Courtesy of Graphics Arts Unlimited, Inc., New York, N.Y.

182   Michele Lundberg, from *36 Children* by Herbert Kohl. Reprinted by permission of The World Publishing Company and A. M. Hrath Publishing Company on behalf of the author and Victor Gollanczm Ltd; and by permission of the Robert Lescher Literary Agency.

183   Herbert Kohl, from *The Open Classroom*. Reprinted with permission from *The New York Review of Books* Copyright © 1969 Herbert Kohl.

188   Drawings of Alternative Classroom Seating Arrangements from *Our Man-Made Environment*, Book Seven. Reprinted by permission of The Group for Environmental Education, Inc.

189   From *The Hidden Dimension* by Edward T. Hall. Copyright © 1966 by Edward T. Hall Reprinted by permission of Doubleday & Company, Inc.

192   Reprinted with permission from *How to Live with Your Special Child* by George von Hilsheimer ($7.50) published by Acropolis Books Ltd., Washington, C.C. 20009.

193   Anthony Barton, from "The Continuum Checklist, How to Soften Your Hard School and How to Harden Your Soft School," *The Newsletter*, March 1970. Reprinted by permission of the author.

198   Merle Burnick, from *Trash Can Do It*. Farallones Designs/Institute Publications, Berkeley, Calif. Reprinted by permission of the author.

202   Stephen Spender, "An Elementary School Classroom in a Slum." Reprinted by permission of Faber and Faber Ltd. and Random House from *Collected Poems 1928–1953*.

204   Paul Goodman, "Mini-Schools: A Prescription for the Reading Problem." Reprinted by permission of the author.

208   Wynn-Anne Cole, "The Ideal School." Copyright *Media and Methods*, April, 1969. Used with permission.

210   George Dennison, from *The Lives of Children* (New York: Random House, 1969). Reprinted by permission of the publisher.

210   Frederick Beuchner, from *The Hungering Dark*. ⓒ 1969 The Seabury Press. Reprinted by permission of the publisher.

212   Peter Drucker, from "How to Be an Employee," *Fortune* Magazine. Reprinted by permission; ⓒ 1952.

215   Charles E. Silberman. Crisis in the classroom. Copyright ⓒ 1970 by Charles E. Silberman. Reprinted by permission of William Morris Agency, Inc., on behalf of author, and Random House, Inc.

216   Charles M. Schultz, ⓒ 1970 United Features Syndicate, Inc. Reprinted by permission.

216   From *The Pill Versus the Springhill Mine Disaster* by Richard Brautigan. A Seymour Lawrence Book/Delacorte Press. Reprinted by permission of the publisher.

218   Carl R. Rogers, "The Person of Tomorrow." Reprinted by permission of the author.

222   From *Anger and the Rocking Chair* by Janel Lederman. Copyright ⓒ 1969 by Janet Lederman. Used with permission of McGraw-Hill Book Company and The Sterling Lord Agency.

223   From Sunny Decker, *An Empty Spoon*, copyright ⓒ 1969 by Sunny Decker. Reprinted by permission of Harper & Row, Publishers.